CRASH IN COURSE

MANAGING PEOPLE

CRASH COURSE IN

MANAGING PEOPLE

Brian Clegg
Paul Birch

KOGAN PAGE

First Indian Edition 2009

Kogan Page India Private Limited
4737/23 Ansari Road,
Daryaganj
New Delhi 110 002

This edition is for sale in the Indian subcontinent only. Not for export elsewhere.

ISBN-10: 81-7554-431-7
ISBN-13: 978-81-7554-431-4

Published by Vinod Vasishtha for Kogan Page India Private Limited,
4737/23, Ansari Road, Daryaganj, New Delhi 110 002.

Printed and bound by Anand Sons, Delhi - 110 092.

Contents

Introduction

When you begin to look at the nature of management a number of things become obvious. First is the importance of communication – two-way flows of information are at the heart of management – and second is the need to distinguish between two very different management styles.

These two styles are usually referred to as leadership and management. Although this course is titled *Crash Course in Managing People*, in fact it concentrates on leadership. Alongside pure leadership, you will see themes developing around motivation, coaching and interviewing. Other parts of the course concentrate on developing you as an individual.

Much of the original material for the course came from four books for the Kogan Page *Instants* series, *Instant Leadership*, *Instant Motivation*, *Instant Coaching* and *Instant Interviewing*, apparently wide-ranging topics, yet when we pulled them together it became obvious just how much they combined and interlinked to make up the essential management toolkit.

The tried and trusted techniques from the *Instants* books form a unified course that will enable you to develop your management skills without taking up too much of your valuable time.

The book comprises two main sections. In the 'getting the basics' chapter we lay the foundation of understanding on which the exercises and techniques are built. It is very important to have this understanding before engaging in an activity like managing people – without understanding why you are undertaking the exercises you will find it difficult to use the techniques effectively. This chapter is short and can be read in a couple of hours.

The second section contains a programme of exercises and techniques – exercises to develop your personal skills and techniques you can bring into play when working with others. The programme is split into units, designed to be manageable in your spare time in a week, though if you want to take the crash course to its extreme, each unit can be fitted in within a day. Each unit also introduces one or two recommended books. Wider reading is an essential when working on management skills, and though it is not necessary to read all (or even any) of these specific books, they have been selected to enhance the impact of the course.

At the back of the book you will find a review section to pull together what you have learned, including a collected reading list (in case you decide not to go with the books at the time of working through the programme) and tables that support the techniques or can be used to pick and choose individual techniques for a specific requirement. You will also find Web links for further reading and to help with the exercises.

Be prepared to learn, but also be prepared to enjoy yourself – management involves many challenges, but provided that you like people and want to work with them you are bound to find the challenge stimulating.

1 Getting the basics

MANAGING PEOPLE?

What's it all about?

This is a course in handling people – the people you work with, the people who work for you, or people you have no direct business link with, but whom you still need to influence. Underlying much of the course is communication – because that's almost interchangeable with handling people, unless you intend to physically manipulate them. But this is a very special case of communicating in order to get something done.

In putting the course together, based on the exercises we developed for our series of *Instant* books, we have identified four strands of action involved in the process of managing people. Each will be discussed separately in this chapter, but when it comes to the course itself, you will find that they inevitably blur together. The four strands are leadership, motivation, coaching and interviewing.

LEADERSHIP

Management or leadership?

To many, the words 'leadership' and 'management' can be used interchangeably. In fact we have done so in the title of this course. As 'a crash course in managing people' it's a Trojan horse. Because leadership and management are different, and it's leadership that this course will be majoring on. The differences between the two help to define the essence of leadership.

It is a broad generalization, but often managers are concerned with tasks and leaders are concerned with people. This is not to say that leaders ignore the task. Indeed, one thing that characterizes a great leader is that they achieve. The difference is that the leader realizes that the achievement of the task is through the goodwill and support of others, while the manager may not. (Perversely, job titles often fail to recognize this distinction – many 'team leaders' are acting as managers, while many people who are actually leaders have the job title 'manager'. Arguably, job titles are a waste of space.)

The goodwill and support generated by the leader results from seeing people as individual human beings, not as another resource to be deployed in support of the task. The role of a manager is often to organize resources to get something done. People become just one more of these interchangeable resources. The role of a leader is to cause others to follow a path he or she has laid down, or to make real a vision created in order to achieve a task. Often the task is seen as subordinate to the vision. For instance, the overall task of an organization might be to generate profit, but a good leader will see profit as a by-product that flows from whatever aspect of their vision differentiates their company from the competition.

This is not to say that leadership is purely a business phenomenon. Most of us can think of an inspiring leader we have met in our lives who had nothing whatever to do with business. It might be a politician, it might be an officer in the armed forces, it might be a Scout or Guide leader, it might even have been a teacher or head teacher. Similarly, management is not a purely business phenomenon. Again, we can think of examples of people filling the management niche in non-business organizations. In such cases it should be easier to find an inspiring vision that is not money driven, supporting true leadership. Unfortunately this is often not the case.

Given that there is a difference between leadership and management, why is it leadership we advocate? Leaders achieve more than managers. Managers get done what could have been done anyway. Leaders achieve things that could not have been done without them. They do this by releasing a hidden business power – the power of employees who have been assisted and motivated to achieve. Leaders succeed in times of change and uncertainty, managers in times of stability. Which seems a more appropriate role to you in the current business climate?

The second reason for being a leader is that there is a glass ceiling for managers. Managing can only get you so far in any organization. You will not be able to move beyond a position that allows you to rely on the skill of your boss or the support of the organization. Or, perhaps if the Peter Principle holds true you will be able to rise one level above this, into a position of incompetence, and no further.

The third reason for preferring leadership is the fulfilment gained from the job you do. Being a leader is significantly more fulfilling than being a manager. Of course it can also be significantly tougher and significantly more frustrating.

The final reason has nothing to do with your wants, needs and desires. A led organization is significantly happier and livelier than a managed organization. This is reflected in the results but that's not really the issue. The reason for mentioning it here is that it becomes a much, much better place for your employees to work.

However, always remember there is a necessary place for management. Management, being about organizing resources, is essential to business success. The difficulty for you as a leader is that it is essential in you as well as your organization. You need to be able to straddle a wide divide and to be both a leader and a manager. You need to be able to inspire with broad vision and yet still focus on small details. You need to be able to let go of control completely and yet still be in charge. You need to be able to trust yourself absolutely and yet trust your people too (even when, or especially when, they disagree with you).

Hey, look, nobody said it was going to be easy.

It's fundamental

The leadership mantle is not one that you don and remove like a fashionable coat or even a badge of office. It is a way of life. In some ways it becomes your life. As you work through the exercises in the course you will find that some are about what you do at work and the ways that you do it, but many touch on the very essence of you and the way that you live your life.

Leadership is all-consuming. It takes over your thinking and most importantly your actions. Leadership is about giving a point to the working lives of others. You cannot even hope to do that unless you see a point to your own working life. And that means that you must live your life in a way that is an expression of that point. Your values as a leader, your actions as a leader, your very thoughts as a leader will permeate your organization. It is rather like Ghandi's comment, you must 'be the change you wish to create'.

Finding the time

As you work through the course and look at the mass of things required of you, one of the first things that will strike you is that you don't have time for any of this. You are far too busy already and this stuff will only make things worse.

Ask yourself what you are busy with. There are exercises later that will help sort the wheat from the chaff but I can say with confidence now that 67.3 per cent of your current activity is a waste of time. I can say that with such confidence because I made up that statistic and it felt right enough for me to be confident about it. Actually, you probably already know some of the areas of your activity that waste time. I'm not talking about the time you spend drinking coffee or chatting. I'm talking about the real work that you do that makes no difference whatsoever to the success or failure of the enterprise.

For everything that you write, for everything that you respond to, particularly for every meeting you attend, ask yourself, 'What difference does this make to the company's results?' If the activity is not delivering something that does this then it should be dispensed with post haste.

Some of the things you do will be done for the benefit of internal politics. 'I have to go to that meeting; it would be career suicide not to.' Is this really true? Are there other, less time-consuming (and more honest) ways that you can demonstrate your value? If not then you may well be a hopeless case and it may be that you'll waste your time attempting this course. If so, thanks for buying it or borrowing it. Enjoy the read and we'll just hope that this can make some difference along the way.

Piggy in the middle

Some leaders are at the top of the organization. We have all at some time or another aspired to this role – being unfettered and able to do whatever we want. In reality there are no leadership roles that are unaccountable. There is always someone to answer to.

For most of us this is obvious. We have a boss. Our boss has a boss. Even the top person in an organization has many stakeholders to whom he or she is responsible. Our leadership role is a small cog in an enormous machine. This puts you as a leader in the position of piggy in the middle. Unless you have a true leader as a boss then you will need to cope with being managed in one way whilst leading in a totally different way. This is one of the hardest tricks of all to pull off. When you are being dumped on and micro-managed and told to do it this way, it is awfully difficult to lift your head and look up away from the detail. It is awfully difficult to see the big picture. It is awfully difficult to be inspired and inspiring. Awfully difficult but far from impossible.

From now on, every time your boss is giving you a hard time or managing the detail of what you are trying to do, lift your head and focus on your vision. Think about why you get up in the morning; what inspires you to carry on leading in the way that you do. Just because others are down in the gutter doesn't mean that you can't be looking at the stars.

Trust

Now we're getting to the heart of what leadership is about. I believe that there are two fundamental fears that hit every leader at some time or another. The first is the fear of being wrong and the second is the fear of letting go.

Being wrong is often not a big deal for most of us. We sometimes have a really important project to work on, or a decision that is make or break for our career, but they are rare. Even when they happen we often have support mechanisms around us that allow us to lay off the risk and share it with others. When you are a leader, a true leader rather than a cog in the machine, you are truly alone. You have no one to turn to but yourself. This is when trust of yourself is really tested. To what degree are you sure you are right? If you aren't absolutely sure, to what degree are you prepared to go with your intuition?

Some people find trusting themselves easy. They are often regarded as arrogant by others, usually with good cause. But then, leaders need a dose of arrogance just to allow them to function. If you are not good at trusting yourself you need to develop mechanisms that make it easier. One will be a track record of success. Another will be a support mechanism that allows you to check out ideas before launching them. The most fundamental is just doing it. Don't worry, go with the intuition and do it. After all, the worst that will happen is that you destroy the company and your career.

The other fear at the heart of leadership is the fear of letting go. This is another trust issue. There is still an element of trusting yourself here, but mainly it is about trusting those you are leading. Make no mistake, for better or worse, if you want to be a leader you have to trust those you lead. No options. No get-out clauses. No caveats. You have to trust them. If you don't you can manage them, but you will never lead. If you do invest in trust, you may just find that they can work miracles that you never knew they had in them. In fact, I guarantee that some of them will.

Think about it. The people that work for you have active lives outside the office. Many of them lead groups of their own, scout troops, youth clubs, football teams, amateur dramatics. Many of them achieve things in their private lives that would astound you. At work they keep quiet about these because most of us are excellent at separating our private from our work lives.

When you manage to overcome the fear of letting go and you really start to trust people you will find that they move above and beyond your highest expectations. Oh, to be sure at first they will mistrust *you*. If this is a change of behaviour then they will be looking for a catch. They'll be expecting you to pull in the reins at any moment. Eventually they will realize that you really mean this and their testing will take the form of pushing harder and harder at any limits you have imposed. The more you trust, the more they'll take. The more they take, the more they'll achieve. The more they achieve, the more you achieve. Leaders of the world let go. You have nothing to lose but their chains.

MOTIVATION

Leadership = motivation?

According to one dictionary, motivation is the stimulation of action towards a goal, whether that stimulus is conscious or unconscious. Although motivation is a necessary part of leadership, we have pulled it out as a separate strand because it has such a significant role to play. Once you have begun to operate in leadership mode you will realize that your approach to motivation has to be outward looking rather than inward looking – about those you are to motivate, rather than about you. Broadly, motivation differs depending on whether you are motivating an individual, a team or a large group of people. There are common themes, but the approach will vary.

Once we take an external view of motivation, it becomes obvious that it's a term that can mean very different things depending on exactly where you sit. According to another dictionary it's about giving someone a motive or an incentive or, rather more darkly, about inducing something. If I am motivating someone else, it's easy to see that it is positive. When was there ever anything wrong with an incentive? If I am on the receiving end of motivation, there is a danger of feeling manipulated – not so much given an incentive as forced into a particular behavioural pattern by sleight of hand. And because we are dealing with human behaviour this is a particularly sensitive issue.

Part of the skill of motivation is ensuring that there is a win-win outcome. You should feel that you are achieving your goals by motivating others – if you have staff, for example, you might hope to get better quality work out of them by motivating them. Those who are being motivated should either not notice it all (and thus be pleased with their own success) or consider it a positive support, increasing their job satisfaction. Because of the fine line between support and manipulation, motivation isn't a skill that can be codified as a set of rules. Instead, it is based on guiding principles and practical experience at putting those principles into action.

The target of your effort could be anyone – anyone can be motivated, and you can be the one to do it. In fact the potential for motivation starts with yourself. Self-motivation is very important – but though there are some overlaps with motivating others, they fit more with the self-development skills covered in the sister book to this, *Crash Course in Personal Development*.

If we confine ourselves to looking outwards, motivation is an extremely powerful tool, reaching far beyond the traditional image of motivating your staff at work. You can motivate your family when a holiday is flagging. You can motivate an individual to greater efforts, or a team to pull together. You can motivate a whole company to buy into the board's dreams and aspirations – or you can motivate a huge, diverse group like 'your customers' to buy more of your product. Advertising and marketing fall outside the scope of this course, but there is a strong overlap between some of the mechanisms of motivation and best practice in these disciplines.

The cynical view of motivation is that it is a matter of subtle manipulation. That motivation is just a way of getting other people to do what you want them to do, ideally without them realizing that this is your aim. This is the view of motivation of a manager I once knew who thought that staff were more productive if they *thought* you cared about them and so maintained that it was very important to fool them into thinking you cared. Insincere, faked motivation will deliver to a point, for a while – but then it will founder.

To have a deep, lasting effect, motivation has to be something more – something of benefit to all involved. Yes, those doing the motivation want to get something out of it, but not just more efficiency or better quality output – and certainly not a set of robots who respond automatically to the party line. They want those who are being motivated to get real satisfaction out of what they are doing. Like it or not, truly effective motivation can't just give lip service to the feelings and desires of those being motivated, it has to have real concern for the recipients as people.

This can make motivation sound painfully woolly and touchy-feely. In taking this course you are looking for a practical business tool, not a social worker's charter. Don't worry – practical business applications are what it's all about, but it is always necessary to bear in mind that motivation is about people, not numbers or data or machinery. The human element will always be present. Hopefully, for most people involved in leading or managing staff this won't be a problem – isn't it part of why you wanted to be a manager in the first place? Part, in fact, of your own motivation.

One to one

One of the hardest motivational challenges is dealing with an individual. You may be coaching an under-performer or helping someone with low self-esteem. You may be dealing with a very talented individual who is under-using those talents. Whatever the need for motivation, the starting point has to be that you are dealing with an individual. I've intentionally used that word a lot in this paragraph. That's because in most companies, there's a lot of historical baggage to overcome. Let's spend a moment looking at it.

Those who have seen re-runs of the sixties cult TV show *The Prisoner* will recall the recurrent cry of Patrick McGoohan's central character Number Six – 'I am not a number'. This reduction of the individual to a faceless component was not just a feature of fantasy TV shows, but the devastatingly costly outcome of one of the biggest mistakes humanity has ever made. (If this all sounds too philosophical for you, skip the next couple of paragraphs, but remember we are dealing with people, and people issues are at the core of motivation.)

Until very recent times, as we have seen when talking about leadership, those in charge have been happy to regard the rest of humanity as a set of interchangeable pawns. The general attitude to war, to slavery, to much of the class system prevalent until very recently (and still common in some parts of the world) makes this very obvious. Despite the entirely contrary Judaeo/Christian/Muslim ethics that form the basis of Western society, the ruling classes have managed to ignore the individuality of the rest.

When mechanization transformed business, there was no reason to challenge this picture. In fact the new world of production lines and mass manufacturing seemed to require the picture of the worker as just another cog in the great machine. Films from the period when mechanization was sweeping business, like Fritz Lang's still powerful *Metropolis*, portray the workers quite literally as parts of the machine. Of course no one thinks like that any more, do they? Yet the legacy of that past is still with us.

Consciously or unconsciously, most companies still do a lot to make sure that their employees realize that they are cogs in the machine. They issue them with staff numbers and job descriptions and organization charts and scores that show the relative value of their jobs. When looking at pay rises they give ratings, perhaps normalized to make sure there's a fair distribution, and make sure that different managers aren't dealing with their staff differently – after all, if they aren't careful they might treat the staff as individuals.

But that's an unfair picture, isn't it? All these things are done for very sensible reasons: because the computer needs a number, or the system will only work if we have a uniform system of ratings. Yet most of these sensible reasons are derived from a senseless value structure that comes back to thinking of people as interchangeable components. All too often still, senior managers think of an organization, then fit people into it (we've got *x* analysts, *y* admin staff and *z* managers) rather than building the organization round the people. Why? Not because it delivers the best results; it doesn't. It's because of that historical baggage and because it's easier to do.

Now, though, we live in a world where doing what is easiest isn't always good enough. We need to get the best out of people, which means treating them as individuals, not as components. It's trite, but it's true – everyone really *is* different, and so getting the best out of them means treating everyone differently. If that presents a problem for the systems, tough. If you want to survive you are going to have to change the systems. Ideally you also want to do it because you want people to actually enjoy their work – but even if you don't, the pragmatic truth is that you need to deal with each person differently. They *are* individuals.

Taking the message of the previous section, we've immediately got a problem when looking at motivating an individual. If everyone is different, and we can't treat them as interchangeable components any more, how is it possible to make any progress? Thankfully, while it is true that it is essential when motivating to consider the very personal needs of the individual, it is also possible to define a set of practices that will work across the population provided that you are prepared to establish just which elements an individual needs and the particular way of meeting those needs that fits best.

One approach to tailored motivation is the Maslow hierarchy, developed by Abraham Maslow. This provides a five-tier view of the factors that motivate people. Maslow's theory was that once one tier is satisfied it ceases to be a motivator and we move up to the next tier. The five stages are basic physiological needs, safety from fear, social needs, appreciation and pecking order, and realizing your potential. While Maslow's sequence seems much too structured for reality, these five elements all contribute to an individual's need for motivation, and at any one time an individual is likely to be more in need of certain elements – being in tune with this requirement can help a lot.

The need to choose an appropriate approach to motivation of an individual implies having a relationship with them. You need to know the individual to best be able to motivate them. This doesn't mean you have to be drinking buddies or soul mates – just that knowing them as a person is essential to tailoring the motivation to fit. Inevitably, then, motivation is particularly difficult when you have just moved into a new job. You don't know the people around you; there is suspicion from all sides. If you are at an early stage in a job, building these relationships – with your staff, your peers, your superiors – is an essential step towards making individual motivation possible.

This is why you will sometimes see social activities as part of the exercises – not just because the social activity can be a motivation in itself, but also because it gives you an opportunity to build a relationship and open the door to more focused individual motivation. As that relationship builds, you can see which type of motivation is best suited at the moment (needs aren't static, they will change over time).

Avoiding demotivation

Motivating a person is not just about enhancing the positive – often it is about removing the negative. Whatever the positive needs of the individual, there are dangers of demotivation from sources that are common to everyone. A number of common factors that are often regarded as motivational actually aren't. Instead they are elements which will demotivate if absent. A classic example is a good level of pay. Despite the gut reaction, paying people above the odds does not motivate them to do better – this is borne out by study after study. However, not paying people enough is a powerful demotivator. Pay isn't a motivational factor, it's a demotivation suppressor. These tranquillizers of the negative are sometimes referred to as hygiene factors, a term devised by psychologist Frederick Herzberg, but we find this term worryingly medical in tone and try to avoid it.

The frightening thing, once you start to look at which factors actually motivate and which just suppress demotivation, is that almost all the traditional ways that companies use to reward their staff are not motivational. Options like salary and perks, working conditions, job security and seniority all fall into the tranquillizer class. Much more motivational are actually achieving something (an outcome many bureaucracies seem devised to avoid), recognition, having true responsibility (not the same thing at all as seniority), having somewhere to go – the realistic potential to go further, and doing something interesting. Is it any wonder that motivation is a problem in many businesses? We've got our priorities skewed. Not upside down, because we still need to tranquillize the demotivators before we can get on with the positive, but certainly skewed the wrong way.

Team spirit

If the business world still hasn't really got a handle on the individual, it can hardly be said to have ignored the team. Teams have been fundamental to the business approach of the last 20 years of the 20th century and don't show any signs of disappearing in the 21st. You only have to compare the implied praise or criticism in the comments 'she's a real team player' and 'he's a bit of a loner' – we all know that teams are good. Yet knowing that something is good is not the same thing as understanding it, or being able to make it work. Pulling a team together to succeed is a complex activity. You are dealing with a group of individuals, with individual needs, yet it's not possible to take such a specific line as it is in a one-to-one. Having a broad understanding of how the individuals in the team will work together is essential. Most important of all is making the aims of the team something each member strives for, bringing synergy to their individual efforts.

If a team is to gain the benefits of synergy it needs to be able to interact smoothly. This is often illustrated by using the image of well-oiled cogs in a machine, or a sporting team – but neither presents the ideal image. A business team is much more like a living organism. It needs the basics of survival, which are similar to a machine – the fuel of appropriate tasks and the internal communications to make teamwork possible – but it also needs growth and fun. Growth, not in the sense of growing a team larger and larger (the empire builder does not make a good team leader), but constantly growing in capabilities – a learning team. Fun, because a team thrives on positive interaction, which implies a fun atmosphere.

Part of making a team work together well is about providing all those essentials. Appropriate tasks – setting a team tasks which are achievable but stretching. Internal communications – if a team can't be physically co-located it needs superb communications support across the whole spectrum. Growth – regular courses and reading, always pushing the boundaries of the team's capabilities. And fun – opportunities for social interaction and a working environment where fun isn't frowned on.

It also helps to have an understanding of team roles. Different individuals, with different psychological profiles, will take on different roles in the team and will interact with other members of the team in different ways. This isn't the place to go into profiles in any depth, but the use of a recognized test like Myers–Briggs or the Insights Colour Wheel can provide a valuable understanding of how a team will work together, and can give team members assistance in making it work.

An important step towards understanding teams and making them work is having clear goals. This doesn't have to involve a formal system of cascading mission and goals and objectives and tasks – it can be as simple as a regularly revised list of bullet points tacked up on the wall. The important thing about team goals is that they are visible, understood and bought into. Failure in any of these requirements can demotivate and reduce the team's effectiveness.

Buy-in is an essential from a motivational viewpoint. If individuals in the team don't support the goals, they will undermine the motivation of the whole team. It's worth making sure that individuals aren't just giving lip service to the goals but actually believe that they are worthwhile. One way to increase buy-in is to make sure that the team members have an input to the goals. They should not expect to say 'this goal is rubbish', but they should have a sympathetic hearing if they say 'why don't we change this goal like this, it will improve it?' Part of the process of confirming buy-in should be testing understanding. You can't be fully behind goals you don't understand. Misunderstanding can lead to friction between team members, a powerful blockage to motivation. It is only a shared understanding between team members that will bring the goals alive.

Where are you standing?

There's a world of difference between the phrases 'you are a team' and 'we are a team'. Teams are almost impossible to motivate from the outside. Most of the motivation has to come from within. Demotivation, on the other hand, can come in very easily from the outside – it's a one-way osmotic barrier. That's not to say that motivating factors can't be initiated from the outside. If your director gives your team an award, it will have a motivating effect, but most of the motivation will come from the reaction within the team. This means that any recognition for a team ought to have a team flavour to it. If an individual gets a glowing write-up in the in-house magazine it will have a big impact. For a team it will be less effective. However, if the team goes out for a meal on the boss, even though the visibility level of the recognition is much lower, it will have a big impact, because it is a team event and gives the team a chance to build on the morale boost.

If you want to bring a team on, it is important that the team regards you as 'one of us' not 'one of them'. Unfortunately, this isn't as simple as just stating the fact. When a large company's chief executive tells the staff that 'we're all one big team' he might be trying to achieve this sense of joint purpose and buy-in, but it simply doesn't work. Teams form by interpersonal interaction, not by organizational structure. You have to earn your position in the team before you will be 'one of us' – and that goes for everyone, even the chief executive. This doesn't mean you have to do one of the 'ordinary' jobs on the team, but that the team members have to consider your contribution relevant and meaningful.

Large scale

Whatever reason a large group of people has for getting together – a conference, an in-house training day, a company forum – there is likely to be a mix of attitudes from the enthusiastic to the cynical. Without the right motivation, a huge investment in time is likely to be wasted. But getting such a group motivated takes a broader-brush approach than a team – it's less personal, more oriented to the underlying influences that motivate everyone.

To begin with, concentrate on what the purpose of this get-together is. You might want to get information across, you might be engaging in training, or simply trying to influence the mood of a group. Although there are plenty of other labels attached, these three categories cover most large sessions. It's quite possible, of course, for a session to switch between categories during the event. For instance, a departmental away-day may start with information on the company, move on to a training session on a new way of working and end up with cheerleading to send the department out on a high. Even so, the different sections have different requirements.

In an information session you want the attendees to be motivated to listen to your message and to take it away in a form that will be remembered and used appropriately. Classic informing sessions are management briefings and press conferences. Some of the motivational factors apply also to the other categories. I have attended so many events (especially press events) where you are made to wait around for at least half an hour after the published start time, often kept out of the auditorium where the event is about to take place. This is not a good start to encourage constructive listening.

Once into the session, good use of support media (to illustrate rather than to be flashy for the sake of it) and an engaging speaking style make a lot of difference. If your presenter drones unmercifully, usually talking incomprehensible jargon, you will have lost your audience in minutes. Make sure you have a decent speaker, and run through the presentation in advance to catch glitches.

A great speaker or an exciting video can put across a message very effectively without anything else. Yet the retention capabilities of the brain will still start to limit what is taken in unless specific steps are taken. One requirement is frequent breaks, carving up the message into manageable chunks (it is also pretty demotivating if you are desperate to get to the bathroom). Another requirement for retention is the ability to revisit the input. For this reason, a good way to motivate the attendees to revise your information is to give them an interesting way of doing it. This might mean just having a handout of the slides, but this is the bare minimum (and an awful lot of packs of handouts spend the rest of their life on the shelf, never being looked at again).

Consider other, more fun ways to carry the message home. Can you put it on a laminated card to go in their personal organizers? Can you give away a proper book that puts across the message? Real books always have more impact than handouts. Can you give them the information to take away in a different medium? Beware, by the way, the illusion that high-tech is necessarily the answer. Although, for instance, you can build a very fancy CD ROM with your message presented as a dramatic multimedia presentation, a lot of people won't look at it. They might not have drives or, like me, they may be swamped with CD ROMs from different sources and never get round to do anything with your masterpiece.

Sometimes you can get more benefit from a more tangential approach. Give them something which is attractive in its own right that will remind them of your message. It might be a bag or a T-shirt with an appropriate message. It could be a penknife or practically any other gift that can have a few words printed on it. The important thing, though, is to judge your audience and the kind of give-away that is likely to appeal.

In a sense, training is a special case of informing, but it is different enough to treat independently. For our purposes the difference in a training session, whether it's a seminar or a workshop or a conventional training course, is the complexity of the message that has to be got across. Usually it will be more detailed and will often involve practical experience rather than just being talked at.

All of the motivational tricks that apply to informing can be brought over into training too, but some extra ones apply. Making the exercises enjoyable, and ensuring that the content is relevant to the training requirement are essential. Generally, hands-on experience in training is particularly motivational, though it can have a negative effect if it is very exposed – most people don't like their learning mistakes to be viewed by everyone. Because training often involves breaking the group into small teams, many of the team aspects of motivation discussed in the previous sections apply here too.

Although it is potentially a problem in all three forms of group exercise, training is particularly susceptible to boredom. There is a phenomenon where regular attendees of training sessions become fed up with the format. I have seen groups rebel because they had had enough of being broken up into syndicate sessions who then reported back to the full group – they wanted something different. Bear this in mind. If you do want to break up into teams, make them as different as possible. If you do want reporting back, don't make it a case of everyone giving a two-minute presentation, go for something outrageously different. This is particularly important if you are running a session over several days and want to keep the motivation level up.

A cheerleading session has pure motivation as its prime goal. You don't want to send people away informed or trained, but with a warm glow about your subject. A classic cheerleading event is a sales conference, where the salespeople (delicate flowers one and all) are encouraged and led on by the successes of others. Less obvious, but equally cheerleading in nature are celebrations. It might be your annual company barbecue, your Christmas party or a meal to celebrate completing a project – whichever, motivation is its *raison d'être*.

Motivating in a cheerleading session is usually blatant and works mostly at a gut level. Anything from actual cheerleaders to special effects, videos, lavish prizes and razzmatazz can contribute to a cheerleading session. This is fine as long as it is done in a style which is appropriate for the group taking part, and isn't seen as over-costly or celebration in a time of difficulty.

An unfairly large part of the motivational opportunity with any large group rests in the first few minutes of its existence. Luckily, through the flow of a day there are usually several 'first few minutes' – after the group has been broken up and re-formed, after breaks and meals. Setting the right tone in those first few minutes can make a lot of difference to motivation. One contributory factor has already been mentioned – getting started promptly. It is also very valuable to get started with a bang. Resist the temptation to drone through a summary of the day, safety regulations and how to find the toilets. A very short multimedia presentation can help introduce a positive, anticipatory state. Be intensely aware of the opportunities those first few minutes present.

When you are dealing with large groups, you are working at a particularly emotional level. Like any serious drama, you have to tread carefully to avoid flipping into farce. This is a particular danger if those attempting to put across the motivational message are more serious about it than those receiving the message. Grand spectacular can have superb results, but misjudged messages can have the opposite effect. Dressing up an unconvincing message with excessive razzamatazz can have the reverse effect to that intended. Those attending can go away thinking 'what a waste of money – so what?' This response is often seen in political events. Large-scale glitz works superbly when it is supporting a strong message – as smoke and mirrors to conceal an absence of message it is an effective (and expensive) demotivator.

COACHING

Why coaching?

It's not enough to give people leadership and the motivation to act. To get the best out of themselves they need a special kind of guidance: coaching.

How would you know coaching if it leapt up and bit you on the ankles? You have no doubt seen coaches at work. You will have been coached. You may even have coached others. Somehow, though, it's a subject that everyone knows about and yet very few people really *know*.

There's something about coaching that makes it close to the heart. Talk to anyone about it and they'll have an opinion or a story to tell. Talk to someone else and their opinion or story will be different. Indeed, their definitions of coaching will be radically different one from another. No two people mean the same thing when they talk about coaching. No two people have the same experience of it.

For many the word 'coach' is associated with sports and the development of top tennis players, footballers, athletes etc. This is not our area of expertise but many of the lessons in this book will be transferable. For many, 'coach' will bring to mind a personal coach who has helped with work, or a friend who has made some of life's obstacles easier. This is closer to the area we will be talking about, with more transferable lessons. We are focusing on the world of business, looking at one person in a business helping another to improve their performance.

The approach taken will vary from situation to situation. It will certainly involve guidance. It will certainly involve an examination of current performance and the factors that contribute to that performance. It will certainly involve planning changes in performance in a step-by-step manner. It will also involve some one-to-one work even if the coach is working with a group of people. Importantly, the role may or may not be identified as coaching.

We strongly believe that whatever role we play, we have the opportunity to coach others. We also believe that we get a great deal more out of life when we take this opportunity and work to improve the skill and ability of those around us. So whether or not you have the role of a coach at the moment, the coaching aspect of this course will be useful. It will help you to get more out of your life by helping others to get more out of theirs. That sounds altruistic and somehow holier than thou. It is not. You will be able to perform better if those around you perform better. You will be able to excel if you help others to excel.

A coach is not a teacher. A coach does not need to know more or be more highly skilled than the person they coach. Think of a sports coach. They are rarely as good as their star performers and yet they are valued and respected by those stars. They help improve performance by drawing out the factors that contribute to that performance, whether they know those in advance or not. This makes their role one of questioning. The most powerful tool that a coach has is the question. The right question asked at the right time can do more to move someone forward than any amount of teaching.

This brings us to another fundamental of coaching. Much of what is required is a systematic approach to uncovering what the person being coached knows already.

So, to summarize our approach to coaching: it is a systematic approach to improvement through questioning and guidance that focuses on incremental changes in current performance to reach a target level. Obviously, as with any definition, it is much more than that and at times much less than that. As you progress through the course your own definition will develop in relation to your own need to develop coaching skills. Feel free to add to or subtract from our view of coaching because for your circumstances your own definition will be more relevant.

The definition above is workable, but it feels far too dry. Coaching is about helping someone to make their dreams come true. No dry definition is going to sum up the emotions and the passions that this process can arouse. Dreams are at the heart of the process. We may occasionally forget that while writing, but ask you not to. Remember, everything you read about coaching is written in the context of helping someone's dreams to come true.

Who can coach?

Coaches are people like you or me. Some are highly skilled, others can make a difference just by asking the right question of the right person at the right time. There are individuals who are better suited to a coaching role than others, but anyone can improve their ability to coach. Some will make this improvement and still not enjoy or shine at the role. Only you can know whether or not this is something that will work for you. There are characteristics that are more likely to incline you to being a better or a worse coach.

Coaches like people. This is a massive generalization because I am sure that there must be excellent coaches who cannot stand being with others. The role of the coach is bound up with others. The coach earns merit through others, not through their own achievements. Someone who doesn't enjoy being with people would find these aspects of the role really tough.

Coaches learn. The coach's role is about questioning and observing and then looking for changes in behaviour that will lead to changes in performance. They must be people who enjoy learning in order to shine at this.

Coaches question, they rarely direct. The popular image of a coach may be the bully in the dressing room shouting abuse at the football team but such coaches are rare and, in my opinion, poor at their job. The most effective role for a coach to play is that of questioner and observer. When being coached we are all more likely to take advice that we have generated ourselves than advice that has come from someone else.

Coaches communicate. One skill that is as important as questioning is the skill necessary to get a point across. Communication (both ways) is at the heart of the coach's role. This would challenge someone who is a poor communicator.

Coaches give freely. Modern businesses are full of people who guard their small powers jealously. This may be in the form of authority or in the form of data and information. Such a person would find coaching difficult because it is inherent in the role that a coach will share what knowledge and ability they have in order to improve whoever they are coaching. They also give of themselves. They give their time, their effort and their ability in order to help others to improve.

Coaches do not seek the limelight. When you are working with someone in order to improve their performance you are preparing them for success, perhaps even fame. You will not be doing it in order to earn fame for yourself. A person who needs to be the centre of attention is unlikely to flourish in such a role.

Who can be coached?

For the partnership between coach and coached to work there needs to be a good coach and a receptive coachee (sorry, it's a horrible word, but we don't have a better shorthand. Continually writing 'person being coached' is tedious for both us and you). If you are coaching someone, what would you be looking for in them and how would you cope if it weren't there?

The first thing to look for is energy and commitment to the task. If this is missing then they will almost certainly pay lip service to the improvements that you plan but will not put in the time or effort required to improve. The next thing is an acceptance and understanding of your role as coach. If they do not understand how you'll be working together or understand but do not accept, then the partnership will not work.

Having got these, there are a number of lesser difficulties that might need addressing. These are best summed up by what might be said by the coachee.

'I really can't be bothered' – Probably the worst thing you can hear as a coach (apart from 'your house has burnt to the ground and your insurance policy has lapsed'). Coaching someone who will not put effort into their own improvement is a thankless and ultimately useless task. If you cannot turn this attitude around, stop coaching them. They will not improve until their attitude does. To work on their attitude, set very short-term improvement targets that they agree and then explain that you're only prepared to continue with the effort if they work too. If they don't reach the targets agree another set (make sure that they are an improvement on the current level but are also clearly achievable. If they do not reach these then stop coaching them. You'll be wasting your time not doing so).

'I already knew that' – This response is often used by people who mean more than this. They mean that they knew this and therefore don't intend to act on the knowledge. To overcome this you need to explain that most insights that a coach offers come from the person being coached. They are often things that are known but not acted upon. Once they show signs of acting upon their knowledge then they can play the smart-ass and tell you that they know it. Until they start acting upon it no amount of knowledge will be of any use to them.

'Now is not the right time' – There are people who want to improve themselves tomorrow. For some this might be quite genuine, now may not be the right time. For others this prevarication is merely a way of avoiding the effort whilst still feeling good about the potential. It's your judgement call. If the person you are dealing with is prevaricating you will need to push, but be careful not to push too hard. Remember your role as coach is to move at a pace that suits the coachee. Pushing is fine, bullying or taking decisions on their behalf is not.

'What makes you so damned smart?' – You may well come across people who resent the whole notion of being coached. They might not wish to be helped at all or they might have a very specific view of the qualities that they need in a coach. For some this may manifest as needing a coach who obviously excels in the area they are coaching. For some it may be that they want a particular type of person. Whatever the reason, if you have talked this through with the person you are trying to coach and they are still unhappy with the role then back away. You cannot force someone to be coached. At the heart of the role is the agreement between the two parties. If this agreement (explicit or implicit) is not there then coaching cannot work.

'Wouldn't it be better if I...?' – Then there's the person who has to gainsay every suggestion or strategy for improvement. Whilst being somewhat tiresome this can actually work to your advantage. If there is no good reason why their suggestion should not be used then going with it will give them an increased sense of ownership. If there is a good reason why yours is better (and your ego is not a good enough reason!) then explaining this is useful and may well be enough to bring them around.

'No' – There will come a time when someone will just refuse point blank to listen to a suggestion you have or to accept a target for improvement. When this happens and the negotiation and persuasion fails then the first step is to change approach. Would a different method work? Would a lower target be more acceptable? If there can be no compromise or if no common ground is found then you might have to cut your losses and back away from coaching this person. Accept that they will not be coached or find someone with whom they have more rapport.

'I'm bored with this, let's move on to something else' – Attention span is a critical factor in coaching. Developing someone takes time and effort. Some people are not suited to commitment to a long-term goal. For such people you might have to focus more on short-term deliverables. Celebrate intermediate targets reached. Set end goals that are actually steps on the way to a much longer goal. Persevere with these individuals because they are the ones most likely to surprise themselves when they do have help in applying themselves over a long time.

'I'll never be good enough' – In anyone's development there comes the long dark teatime of the soul (as Douglas Adams put it) where doubt creeps in. In fact doubt rarely creeps in. It usually marches in with cymbals clanging, drums beating and trumpets blaring. Short-term targets are good in these circumstances. 'OK, I'm not going to convince you that you can reach our long-term target of X but you can see that very soon we could reach Y. Let's go for that and worry about X later.'

'Yes I will. Sorry I didn't' – There are those circumstances where current failure is excused by future performance. I will be doing better. I will work harder. I won't make that mistake again. Very often this is true. They will do better. They will work harder. They won't make that mistake again. Sometimes this is just an excuse to get you off their back. If this is true then either you or they have misunderstood your role. You are coaching their performance, not your own. Any failure to meet targets is their doing. They have no need to make excuses or to make promises to you. A clarification of your role would help, as would a clarification of their role in agreeing targets.

'But I want it NOW!' – And finally those people who can't wait for the improvement to materialize. You develop and agree a set of targets that will take them from where they are to where they want to be and they then want to shortcut the process to get the results immediately. An approach that might work in these circumstances is agreeing a slightly more demanding set of targets and then monitoring progress against them. If they are committed enough to develop themselves to meet these targets then they may well get results faster than you had originally planned. If they do not meet these earlier targets then discuss with them falling back to your original plan.

Obviously these example issues are just that. They are examples. They do not cover the entire range of issues that you'll hit when coaching. Nor could they ever. Hopefully they will give you a notion of the role and the ways to develop it with the coachee. As your experience develops, so will your ability to handle situations not listed here.

A coaching model

In coaching someone you want them to adapt their performance. For that reason we have developed a simple model with the acronym ADAPT:

A – Assess current performance
D – Develop a plan
A – Act on the plan
P – Progress check
T – Tell and ask

Assess current performance – Before you can sensibly discuss an improvement in someone's performance you must assess for yourself where they are right now. With a sports person who competes as an individual the level is relatively easy to assess, merely look at their records and statistics. With a team player it is more difficult and in a business context it becomes more difficult still. You also need to understand for yourself how they achieve their current level. What style do they use? What tactics and strategies do they use?

Where are they most comfortable? Where are they least comfortable? Now all of this obviously means that the performance being improved must be measurable. In business life many aspects of performance seem unmeasurable. They are not. In my experience it is always possible to find a measure in one form or another if you are determined to do so. At times these might be crude approximations. At times they will be subjective. But they are there.

Develop a plan – The first stage of developing a plan to improve performance is to set the target for the performance level to be reached. How big an improvement does the coachee want? How big an improvement do you feel they can manage? Over what time scale could they achieve this improvement? The next stage is to break this target down into manageable time chunks. How far could you get in time X? How far in time Y? Finally, how far in time Z? At this stage keep the time scales short and the targets tightly focused. If necessary make a plan that gets only part way to the ultimate goal. Keep this goal in mind but do not be obsessive about planning for it.

Next, work on strategies for achieving this performance. Some may involve tuition, some may involve the coach observing and commenting on or questioning style, technique or approach. Some may involve observing experts in the area being coached. You may also involve the coachee in observing their performance in some way – feedback from others, audio tape, video tape or some other form of self-observation. Finally this plan needs to be formally agreed to by the coachee. They will have been involved in its development but there is something about the act of saying, 'Yes, I agree to these targets and this plan' that gives a level of formality that somehow improves commitment.

Act on the plan – Although this is the most visible part of coaching, it is usually the easy part. There is skill and some difficulty in observing and commenting upon performance or questioning another's performance in a way that focuses on the things they need to change. But most of this stage is about turning up and doing what is needed to get from one stage of the plan to the next.

Progress check – This is not so much a stage as a range of stages. Progress must be checked at each milestone but should also be checked on the way to the milestones so that failing to hit a target should never be a surprise. Ideally something can be done to improve the trend before the failure occurs. The progress check returns us to the point made earlier about the performance being measurable. If the measures used are imperfect then the rigidity with which they are applied needs to be relaxed. Don't be tempted to treat a subjective measure as a scientific benchmark.

Tell and ask – This section is the one whose name we're least happy with. It is about discussion of progress against performance measures and discussion of any future improvement desired (which will take us straight back to the start of the process). 'Tell' came first to make the mnemonic work, but in practice, asking should take the lead. Discussion is at the heart of coaching. The coach needs to understand the motivation of the coachee, needs to understand their performance and needs to understand how to question them in order to draw from them ways of improving their performance.

Once this model has been worked through and the coachee has improved their performance, you must decide between the two of you whether it is time to start the whole process over again. If you let it, the role of the coach can be a never-ending one.

INTERVIEWING

Conversations with a focus

The last of the people management strands is something of a Cinderella – yet interviewing is a skill that any good people manager needs to have mastered. Communication, as we have seen, underlies all of the practices in this book, and interviewing is a unique, very formalized style of communication that needs individual handling if it is to be carried out well.

Interviewing skills are essential for any professional, whether engaged in an interview-intensive occupation like recruitment, or in traditional line management. Yet all too many interviewers have had little or no training. An interview could be for recruitment or performance appraisal. It could be exploring the causes of a business problem or getting the truth from a potential supplier. The aim of the interviewing strand of this course is to provide the skills you need to interview effectively, whether you are starting from scratch or brushing up on a much-practised art. Generally recruitment interviews are used as examples, but the skills have a much wider application.

An interview is a conversation with a focus. It is designed to extract information from the interviewee. This isn't as simple as it sounds. In most business conversations the other parties will have their own agendas, and even if there is no attempt at concealment, few of us are good enough communicators to put across everything we need to say pithily and comprehensibly. It isn't enough to listen to what the interviewees want to tell you; the interviewer has to probe, to direct and to go beyond the words to get as close as possible to the truth.

Sadly, you are rarely given enough time to prepare for interviews. The need to interview might be dropped on you the night before. Many of us are expected to interview on top of our ordinary work. It's a crucial exercise, but one that inevitably gets pushed down the priority stack. Most interviewers outside a Human Resources department undertake the task occasionally, in the cracks between the other aspects of their job. It's not ideal, but it's the way things are. What's more, interviewing is a skill that many companies assume you will learn by osmosis. We were both lucky that the company we first interviewed for provided us with a training course, but that isn't the norm.

There is now a good body of research indicating that interviews alone are not highly effective as a recruitment selection method. Admittedly, some of those making this observation are responsible for the development and marketing of psychometric and other tests, but there certainly seems to be some evidence that many interviews are flawed. They remain, however, extremely popular, and most employers put a lot of faith in them.

Arguably this apparent paradox can be overcome by improving the quality of interviewing. Many of those who denigrate the interview have not had much experience of management. Interviews are certainly not perfect, but they give an essential insight into the nature of the interviewee that no number of tests and questionnaires can entirely resolve. However, most interviews could be improved greatly, which is in part the reason for existence of a course like this. It's also true that most interviews can be helped by supportive evidence from tests and group exercises, and that a small interviewing panel of (perhaps) three people will be much more effective than an individual interviewer. But we shouldn't be too hasty to knock the interview. Like all human processes it is flawed, but done well it delivers.

The structured interview

One form of interviewing that is growing in popularity in recruitment is the structured interview. This uses a set list of questions, delivered in exactly the same way with each candidate. The structure enables better comparison of applicants and, the theory goes, results in more accurate outcomes. It is indubitably a more scientific approach to interviewing. Nothing in this book either requires structured interviews or makes them unsuitable, but we have some doubts about their widespread use. There is nothing wrong with having a structured section in an interview, but in most circumstances, an organic interview that follows the interviewee's responses will produce more depth. This requires a different style of preparation and note taking if it is still to be thorough, but is still preferable if the interviewers are suitably trained and competent.

Information

Information is the currency of the interview. Your role as interviewer is to extract information from the interviewee. Note the crucial distinction between information and data. Data is a set of neutral facts. Take a recruitment interview. The interviewee's date of birth, his or her examination results, a list of employments – these are all data. Information tells you more; it is data plus interpretation, or data plus context. Information doesn't just tell you what your interviewee's exam results are, but why they are what they are, and what they signify for your requirement.

Some of the information and data you require will be taken directly from the interviewee in face-to-face conversation. It is certainly here that much of the interpretation and context will be applied to turn data into valuable information. But it would be very inefficient to extract every single fact from the interviewee on the spot. Some preparation, absorbing and putting the information you can obtain before the interview into context, will be very valuable in getting the most out of your limited interview time.

Environment

All too often, little thought is given to how the interview takes place and where it is located. It may be that your office, or the little interview room down the corridor, is the ideal place, but don't assume it. And when you have your interview set up, do you assume that all will be well with the environment, or do you take an active hand to make sure that it works for you and for your interviewee? The environment matters if you are to make the most effective use of your interview time.

Selling

It can seem strange that the selling is included as a factor in interviewing, but interviewing is a complex process (as is the case with practically any human interaction). Even if it were true that your only relationship with the interviewee was to pull information from them, you might like to sell them on the benefits of the interview to make sure they give you as much as they can. However, most interviews fit into a context beyond the information itself. A recruitment interview is not only about selecting a candidate for a job, it is about selling the company to the candidate. An internal performance appraisal is giving a message to the staff member (anything from 'we desperately want to keep you' to 'I think you'd be more comfortable working somewhere else'). An interview with a supplier is part of building a working relationship; similarly, a fact-finding interview will often be with people you need to work with in the future. Interviewing is always a two-way process.

Nerves

From the interviewee's point of view (particularly if this is a recruitment interview), you, the interviewer, are in a position of power. The interviewee will often be nervous, but will assume that you are calm and collected, without a care in the world. This isn't a bad thing – it doesn't help to be interviewed by someone who doesn't seem confident and assured. For many of us, though, it is going to be far from the truth. An interview, especially the first interviews you perform, can be as nerve racking for the interviewer as they are for the interviewee.

There are a couple of stress management techniques in the course to help you deal with these nerves, but the main weapon you have is your attitude. Think of all the positive benefits of doing the interview. It's a chance to talk to people – something most of us enjoy. It's a harmless situation from your viewpoint; you are in control. While keeping the professionalism and skills needed to make it an effective interview, try to think of it more as a structured chat.

Aggression

Some companies and individuals use aggression as part of their interview technique. In theory this is to see how the interviewee stands up under pressure. But in reality it's hard not to see many aggressive interviews as thinly disguised sadism, where the interviewer abuses his or her position of power.

This doesn't mean that you shouldn't be firm in an interview. We've all heard interviews with politicians where the interviewer hasn't stuck to the point, and it is painfully frustrating to have the politician evade the question without ever answering it. Nor does it mean you can't stretch the interviewee. An interview one of us used to perform for the Operational Research department at British Airways required the interviewee to answer an apparently simple technical question that tested his or her ability to think through what their knowledge really meant, rather than simply recite back what they had been taught. Interviewees have run out of the interview room in tears as a result of that question. But they had not been bullied or mistreated.

There's a need to remember that the way you treat an interviewee impinges on the selling aspect of recruitment. If I were a great candidate for a job and the interviewers bullied me, I would take great pleasure in telling the company's representatives what to do with their job when it was offered. Would you really want to work for a company that treats you like that? What does it say about how the company is likely to treat you in the future? There are perfectly straightforward mechanisms like role-plays to test how individuals react under pressure without abusing them in an interview.

Note taking

An essential in interviewing is being able to concentrate on the conversation – what the candidate is saying, how he or she is saying it. Yet at the same time, you want to be able to return to the detail of what was said after the interview. It is not practical to rely on memory for this. Particularly if you are involved in a series of interviews, the possibility of being clear exactly what was said in each one is almost negligible. Unfortunately, the need to concentrate on the interviewee and the need to take notes are in conflict.

In theory, perhaps the ideal is only to take steering notes yourself. These are the notes you will need to make sure that all the relevant questions are asked during the interview. Operating this way, you would either tape the interview and run through it later, or have someone else take detailed notes for you. Unfortunately, both these techniques are labour intensive, and interviews are often conducted with limited time scales and resources. What's more, someone else's notes will never represent exactly the same picture that you would have gained yourself. If you are to take the detailed notes yourself, find ways that you can do this with the minimum interference with your conversation. We will look in the course at making graphical keyword notes – it will also help if you can practise note taking without looking at the paper too often.

Recruitment precursors

While the focus of the interviewing aspects of this course is the interview itself, it is worth considering some of the surrounding paraphernalia that will influence the interview, particularly in the recruitment process. In many recruitment environments there are far more potential recruits than there are vacancies. Ideally everyone would be interviewed. The fact is, flawed as it may be, the interview is still an essential component of the ideal selection process. But it is neither practical nor cost effective to interview 1,000 candidates for a single job. Some form of sifting is required.

The starting point in using sifting has to be an understanding that it is going to fail you. Whatever technique you use to sift *will* remove some of the best candidates for the job. The hope is that there will be enough suitable candidates left – but don't fool yourself into thinking that you are being wonderfully scientific. Sifting is a pragmatic tool, and a very blunt one.

Some sifting techniques used by large companies verge on the ridiculous. A good example is handwriting analysis, which has no verified scientific basis whatsoever. Rather than spend money on handwriting analysis, you would be better picking every tenth application, or everyone whose surname begins with C (say) – it is just as likely to give a good result, and is both cheaper and quicker.

An apparently more logical sifting mechanism is academic results. You might, for example, insist that all applicants have a degree. This is not bad as sifting goes – many degrees indicate some ability to reason, and all show that the candidate has had the perseverance to attend the university or college for the required terms. However, there are some aspects of academic results that need closer examination. For example, a first class degree may indicate a candidate with limited social skills – a check on his or her wider experience would be worthwhile. Similarly, while a second degree or master's in a practical subject is promising, a doctorate needs to be treated with suspicion. A doctorate often shows a strong interest in knowledge for its own sake, which is rarely a good sign in a practical job. Narrow focus is all very well in academia, but can be dangerous in the real world.

If you have to sift before an interview, see if you can use a more human judgement. At least take the time to read the application and look for the signs of a good CV and form. These will be discussed more in the next chapter. This doesn't have to take long, and will beat any mechanical filtering.

What, though, of telephone interviewing? Is this a sensible compromise, perhaps for a second level of sifting? Again, approach with care. Telephone interviews can be valuable, but can also be extremely misleading. Unless you are interviewing for a position where good telephone skills are high on the requirements list, you are liable to bias the interviewing process unfairly to those who are very comfortable on the phone, a fairly small cross-section of the population. Make sure the interviewee has time to prepare – book a telephone interview, don't call out of the blue. As with aggression, remember the potential for projecting a negative image. Cold interview calls suggest that your company is disorganized or sneaky, neither exactly excellent sales pitches.

How many interviewers?

Generally the interviewee is a lone figure, unless this is the kind of interview that requires a professional adviser like a lawyer to be present. However, the interviewer has a wider choice. The interview can be a cosy one-to-one chat or an ordeal before a long line of panel members. The choice is yours.

To an extent this choice is limited by practicality. In many companies it simply isn't practical to have loads of interviewers, even if it were desirable. But there may still be a degree of choice. For an internal interview, perhaps assessing annual performance, there is rarely a need to have more than a single interviewer. But for a recruitment interview a larger interviewing panel is probably ideal. I would recommend from practical experience that three people works best: a human resources or personnel person, an interviewer who would either be the recruit's boss or is of a similar level, and a more senior interviewer, ideally with wide experience of interviewing.

In such a triumvirate, the human resources individual can provide technical guidance and observe human characteristics. The junior interviewer, who should be asking most of the questions, provides the contextual questions. And the senior interviewer has an overview and will add some more general business questions. When it comes to deciding on the outcome, such a group can come to a more measured decision, not overly influenced by a single person's biases.

If there are more interviewers than interviewees, care needs to be taken to make sure that the experience is not intimidating. A loose grouping for chairs, for instance, is less threatening than having the interviewing board ranged in a straight line behind a vast, imposing table.

Recruitment – alongside the interview

In recruitment, interviewing will often not be the only tool that is used. A corporate interview can involve a whole battery of tests, role-plays and group exercises. The aim is to get the best all-round picture of the individuals who have applied. Some of these tests are very valuable. Personality profiles, such as the Myers–Briggs Type Indicator, give a good guide to how an individual will interact with others in a team, as does the observation of a group or a role-play (however artificial the situation).

Reasoning tests can help indicate suitability for certain occupations. (These don't always have to be formal tests. When recruiting code breakers for the secret Bletchley Park centre, 'Station X', during the Second World War, the British government used expertise with crosswords as one of its indicators.) But it is probably unwise to put too much effort into this backup activity, because that's all it is. All the evidence is that it is the interview that will make or break the selection. If someone has a great interview, the interviewer will tend to ignore the test results. If it's bad, they're out, however good the tests and role-plays.

GETTING STARTED

With these four strands of leadership, motivation, coaching and interviewing fixed firmly in mind, let's move on to the course itself, a series of 30 units that can be undertaken on a weekly or daily basis – or however bests suits you. The next chapter gives a brief introduction to the layout, and provides a checklist to record progress.

2 Work plan

INTRODUCING THE COURSE

Each of the 30 units consists of five exercises or techniques. Exercises are designed to be performed immediately to help develop your management skills. They will normally take between 5 and 20 minutes to undertake. Techniques are additions to your toolkit that can be brought into play as and when you have a need for them. It is sensible to read through the techniques, and note when you might next find the technique useful, but it will not usually be practical to undertake the technique straight away. Some items are marked exercise/technique – these form general techniques, but should also be undertaken immediately as an exercise.

How you organize the course is up to you. You could take a day over each unit, or a week – or however long you like. It's up to you how long you want the 30 units to take.

Each unit also contains one or more unit books and many have Web links. The unit books are intended to help expand your horizons and give more opportunities for development of your people management skills. You aren't expected to read every book we recommend, but the more you can get in, the more effective the course will be. Most of our recommendations are available from public libraries, or you can build your own management library by buying them – there are links to online bookshops stocking them at our support Web site www.cul.co.uk/crashcourse.

Remember also the support Web site, www.cul.co.uk/crashcourse has links for many units, designed to extend your knowledge base into the Web.

The next short section provides a checklist to monitor your progress. You may also find it useful to make some notes on the exercise and technique pages to help record your progress.

When you have completed all the units, there is a final section that provides an opportunity to recap and to revisit the unit books.

CHECKLIST

Unit 1: A taster

- 1.1 Understanding your style ☐
- 1.2 Culture ☐
- 1.3 Creating a team ☐
- 1.4 Becoming a figure-of-eight person ☐
- 1.5 It's catching ☐
- Unit books ☐
- Web links ☐

Unit 2: Inspiration

- 2.1 Charisma ☐
- 2.2 Being an inspiration ☐
- 2.3 Getting *your* inspiration ☐
- 2.4 Learning to love your business and staff ☐
- 2.5 Learning to love your customers and suppliers ☐
- Unit books ☐

Unit 3: Leader as navigator – strategy and direction

- 3.1 Leadership and management ☐
- 3.2 Vision and mission ☐
- 3.3 Strategy ☐
- 3.4 Setting goals ☐
- 3.5 Developing a business plan ☐
- Unit book ☐
- Web links ☐

Unit 4: The murderous meeting

- 4.1 Meetings and how to chair them ☐
- 4.2 Meetings and how to develop them ☐
- 4.3 Meetings and how to kill them ☐
- 4.4 Visible improvement ☐
- 4.5 Break time ☐
- Unit book ☐
- Web links ☐

Unit 5: It's hard at the top: dealing with stress

- 5.1 Using stress ☐
- 5.2 Learning to relax ☐
- 5.3 Get fit ☐
- 5.4 Getting beneath anxiety ☐
- 5.5 Stop and think ☐
- Unit book ☐
- Web links ☐

Unit 6: Words, words – communicating

- 6.1 Conversations ☐
- 6.2 Networking ☐
- 6.3 Publish or be damned ☐
- 6.4 Eye eye ☐
- 6.5 Open questions ☐
- Unit book ☐
- Web links ☐

Unit 7: Knowledge is power

- 7.1 Technical competence ☐
- 7.2 Knowing your competitors and customers ☐
- 7.3 Knowing your people ☐
- 7.4 Knowing yourself ☐
- 7.5 Keeping abreast ☐
- Unit book ☐
- Web links ☐

Unit 8: Responsibility and influence

8.1 Taking responsibility ☐
8.2 Teaching responsibility ☐
8.3 How to be an ideal leader ☐
8.4 Saying 'No' ☐
8.5 Two-faced management ☐
Unit book ☐
Web links ☐

Unit 9: Reward and recognition

9.1 Arrivals ☐
9.2 Reward ☐
9.3 Recognition ☐
9.4 Somewhere to go ☐
9.5 Small gifts and big sums ☐
Unit book ☐

Unit 10: Injecting energy

10.1 Energy ☐
10.2 Leading a team over time ☐
10.3 Being obsessive ☐
10.4 Being ubiquitous ☐
10.5 Warm-ups ☐
Unit book ☐
Web links ☐

Unit 11: Embracing change

11.1 Creating change ☐
11.2 Change control ☐
11.3 Change as motivator ☐
11.4 Motivational marketing ☐
11.5 The hardest cut ☐
Unit books ☐
Web links ☐

Unit 12: Beating the system

12.1 Destroying the system from the inside ☐
12.2 Bureaucracy and how to develop it ☐
12.3 Bureaucracy and how to kill it ☐
12.4 Making it sane ☐
12.5 Doing yourself out of a job ☐
Unit book ☐

Unit 13: Messages – more communicating

13.1 E-motivation ☐
13.2 The genuine article ☐
13.3 Giving feedback ☐
13.4 Your body ☐
13.5 Non-verbal replies ☐
Unit books ☐

Unit 14: Delegation and trust

14.1 Delegation ☐
14.2 Responsibility ☐
14.3 Recognized authority ☐
14.4 Managing George ☐
14.5 Backing off ☐
Unit book ☐
Web links ☐

Unit 15: The right person for the right job

15.1 360 degree appraisals ☐
15.2 Appropriate appraisal ☐
15.3 Catch them doing it right ☐
15.4 What do they look like? ☐
15.5 Assessing test results ☐
Unit book ☐
Web links ☐

Unit 16: Difficult cases and troublemakers

16.1 Daggers drawn ☐
16.2 Confronting troublemakers ☐
16.3 The earnest objector ☐
16.4 Playing favourites ☐
16.5 Reluctance to improve ☐
Unit book ☐

Unit 17: Putting on a show

17.1 Risk and failure ☐
17.2 Energy transfer ☐
17.3 Lasers and dry ice ☐
17.4 Quality content ☐
17.5 Spice it up ☐
Unit book ☐
Web links ☐

Unit 18: You can't motivate

18.1 Contributors ☐
18.2 Do it themselves ☐
18.3 Perspective shift ☐
18.4 Personal projects ☐
18.5 Overcoming a lifetime of learning ☐
Unit book ☐

Unit 19: Training and learning

19.1 Developing others ☐
19.2 Train tracks ☐
19.3 Train strain ☐
19.4 Knowing what you know ☐
19.5 Learning and learning styles ☐
Unit book ☐
Web links ☐

Unit 20: The F word

20.1 Portfolio matching ☐
20.2 The tea bag ☐
20.3 Celebration time ☐
20.4 The F word ☐
20.5 Building relationships ☐
Unit book ☐
Web links ☐

Unit 21: Pitching it right

21.1 Stretch but don't stress ☐
21.2 Being realistic ☐
21.3 Being unrealistic ☐
21.4 Establishing pace ☐
21.5 'I can't do it' ☐
Unit book ☐

Unit 22: Coaching in all directions

22.1 Coaching outside work ☐
22.2 Coaching with others ☐
22.3 Coaching your boss ☐
22.4 Coaching your peers ☐
22.5 Coaching yourself ☐
Unit books ☐
Web links ☐

Unit 23: Modelling the role

23.1 Watch my feet, not my lips ☐
23.2 Honesty is the best policy ☐
23.3 Going the extra mile ☐
23.4 Love ☐
23.5 Role models ☐
Unit book ☐

Unit 24: Preparation for interviews

24.1 Understanding the job ☐
24.2 Sifting applications ☐
24.3 Information checklist ☐
24.4 Environment checklist ☐
24.5 Selling checklist ☐
Unit book ☐
Web links ☐

Unit 25: Notes and listening

25.1 Ask them ☐
25.2 What did I say? ☐
25.3 Checking for understanding ☐
25.4 Great note taking ☐
25.5 Using silence ☐
Unit book ☐

Unit 26: Decisions and choices

26.1 Decisions, decisions, decisions ☐
26.2 Setting criteria ☐
26.3 Simple option evaluation ☐
26.4 Sophisticated option evaluation ☐
26.5 Comparing apples and oranges ☐
Unit book ☐
Web links ☐

Unit 27: Coping with time

27.1 Diaries ☐
27.2 Mastering time ☐
27.3 Marking time ☐
27.4 Now is all you can do ☐
27.5 Quick results ☐
Unit book ☐
Web links ☐

Unit 28: Questions, questions

- 28.1 Personality and skills ☐
- 28.2 Business awareness and teamwork ☐
- 28.3 Leadership and manageability ☐
- 28.4 Self-starter and creativity ☐
- 28.5 Shocks and analytical thinking ☐
- Unit book ☐
- Web links ☐

Unit 29: Removing demotivators

- 29.1 Money, money, money ☐
- 29.2 Promises, promises ☐
- 29.3 The rumour mill ☐
- 29.4 No secrets ☐
- 29.5 Positive visualization ☐
- Unit book ☐

Unit 30: Subtle inspiration

- 30.1 Own pocket ☐
- 30.2 Taskforce opportunities ☐
- 30.3 What's in it for me? ☐
- 30.4 Ambience chasers ☐
- 30.5 On the up ☐
- Unit book ☐

3 The course

Each unit comprises a mix of exercises – activities to undertake now as you read the book – and techniques that can be used later, whether working alone or with others. Sections marked as exercise/techniques can be used straight away as an exercise, but also provide a technique to use later on.

Unit 1: A taster

In this first unit we get a taste of things to come, with exercises that explore your personal style and the way management is undertaken in your organization. Some of the techniques in this unit are intentionally high level – you may have to revisit some of them after taking on more of the course.

Do try out the exercises as you go. Put them off until later and you probably won't ever do them. Read through the techniques. Make notes about how and when you can use them. And make sure you give them a try in the next appropriate forum.

Unit books

There's no obligation to read all, or any, of the unit books, but you will find that they provide excellent support to the course and strengthen your management skills.

We start with an enjoyable trot through some straightforward but very worthwhile management experiences from executive turned TV presenter and troubleshooter, Sir John Harvey-Jones. His *Making it Happen* makes very useful background reading for this course.

Another book we recommend to get early on, which is simply a valuable teamwork resource, is *Instant Teamwork* by Brian Clegg and Paul Birch, containing a wide range of exercises to build energy and commitment in a team. Alternatively you can get the sister course to this, *Crash Course in Creativity*, which incorporates most of the *Instant Teamwork* techniques.

You can find more information on our unit books, or buy them, from our support site: www.cul.co.uk/crashcourse.

Web links

On general management at www.cul.co.uk/crashcourse.

1.1 Exercise: Understanding your style

Preparation None.
Running time Five minutes.
Resources None.
Frequency Once.

We start with a little navel-examining. Your existing management style will influence how well you perform and how others see you.

Tick the boxes below for the paired statements that match you best. Be honest: this is only for your benefit.

Leadership	Management
☐ 1. I can trust my staff	☐ 1. I need to closely monitor my staff
☐ 2. The carrot is more effective than the stick	☐ 2. Following the appropriate rules is an essential for discipline
☐ 3. I see myself as part of the team	☐ 3. I need to distance myself from the team to have clear roles
☐ 4. The successes of my team will reflect well on me	☐ 4. My successes will reflect well on my team
☐ 5. My key role is to give my team a direction and support them in heading towards it	☐ 5. My key role is to give my team clear and specific objectives and to monitor achievement of them
☐ 6. I expect my staff to put forward ideas without prompting and to contribute to decision making	☐ 6. Leaders have to take key decisions on their own

Both the leadership and management styles are appropriate for different situations, but the thesis of this course is that the leadership style has to come to the fore in difficult or fast-changing times. Our 'leadership' is sometimes called Theory-Y after Douglas McGregor's split of styles into Theory-X ('management') and Theory-Y.

Working on your own management style is central to our intentions, and can also have a very positive effect on the motivation of your staff – and often it is easier to change yourself than to change others.

You may find working through the paired statements that you have a mix of styles. This is not a bad thing: the good leader needs to be able to manage as well as to lead. However, it is probably worth highlighting those aspects in which you tend towards management as areas in need of the most development.

Personal Development	✪✪✪
Leadership	✪✪✪✪
Motivation	✪
Coaching	✪
Interviewing	✪
Fun	✪✪

1.2 Technique: Culture

Preparation Select a representative group of your people.
Running time Half a day to establish – years to change.
Resources Flip charts.
Frequency Regularly.

Culture means a wide range of things. It is one of those words that can subtly adapt its meaning depending upon how you use it. In this context we mean the culture of your organization – 'how we do things around here'.

The culture of an organization is one of the subtlest, least measurable and yet most important aspects of what makes it work or makes it fail. Finding out what the culture is and changing it are tough.

There are no easy tests to establish the current culture but a technique that can be valuable is to look at rules. Run a session with a cross-section of the people in an area and start by asking for ideas that would get you fired. These often start with the obvious, 'Switching off vital equipment' etc, but soon move on to the less obvious, 'Being caught in bed with the boss's partner' etc. The more of these that you uncover, the more feel you will have for what's going on.

The next question to ask the representative group is, 'What are the rules around here?' Again you will start with the obvious set of rules that come straight from the rule book but, with prompting, you'll move on to how we have to dress, the hours we're expected to work, the ways we're expected to behave.

Finally you could ask explicitly, 'How do we do things around here?' This is a tougher one to answer and so your focus group may dry up without prompting, so think in advance of some examples.

The outputs from these questions will give you the shape and feel of the culture of your organization. The next stage is to think about what you would like it to be. Describe for yourself your ideal picture of your organization working. Contrast that with the picture you got from the earlier questions. Look for major anomalies first and think about what would need to change to move to your ideal. You're in charge – change it.

This is a very heavy-duty technique to appear in the first unit, but though you may not be ready to use it yet, do bear in mind that it will often be necessary to work on organizational culture if you really want to change the management of that organization.

Personal Development	✪
Leadership	✪✪✪✪
Motivation	✪✪✪
Coaching	✪
Interviewing	✪
Fun	✪✪

1.3 Technique: Creating a team

Preparation None.
Running time Initially a few days, with some ongoing effort.
Resources People.
Frequency Regularly.

Whether you are dealing with three people or with three thousand there is work to be done in making that group into an effective team. The bonding process, the process of creating connections between the disparate individuals, is much more than identifying a set of jobs and popping people into the slots.

Traditional teambuilding exercises focus on stretching individuals until something bends or breaks, or on having a good time together. We have never believed in pushing people to or beyond their limits. Having fun is certainly a good thing, but this is only part of the answer. The key, rather, is a sense of connectedness between team members. Since most teambuilding takes place away from the office there is then also a need to take it back into the workplace.

Effective teambuilding can be broken down into four stages:

1. Breaking down barriers through energetic, fun, warm-up exercises (*some examples in our second unit book).*
2. Making connections by slowing things down and allowing more person-to-person, eye-to-eye, heart-to-heart contact.
3. Sharing or gift giving, where individuals or groups show the value of others.
4. Planning the transfer back into the workplace.

Probably the easiest way to get things going is through a teambuilding event of some sort that leads to an atmosphere of working for and in support of the team as a whole. The feeling generated by the teambuilding event would need to be developed through any activities planned in stage four above and anything else that you decide to do in support of the development of your team.

Personal Development	✪✪
Leadership	✪✪✪✪
Motivation	✪✪✪
Coaching	✪
Interviewing	✪
Fun	✪✪✪

1.4 Exercise: Becoming a figure-of-eight person

Preparation None.
Running time A few minutes.
Resources None.
Frequency Once.

In Gareth Hill's book *Masculine and Feminine* (now out of print), he develops some of Jung's thoughts on personality into a figure-of-eight diagram that sets the dimensions of Dynamic–Static (Doing–Being) and Masculine–Feminine alongside one another.

The masculine and feminine are personality traits and are not related to your gender. Look at the descriptive words above and ask yourself where you sit most comfortably. Where is your area of least comfort? Do you move freely? If not, which areas do you need to practise in order to be more willing to move into them?

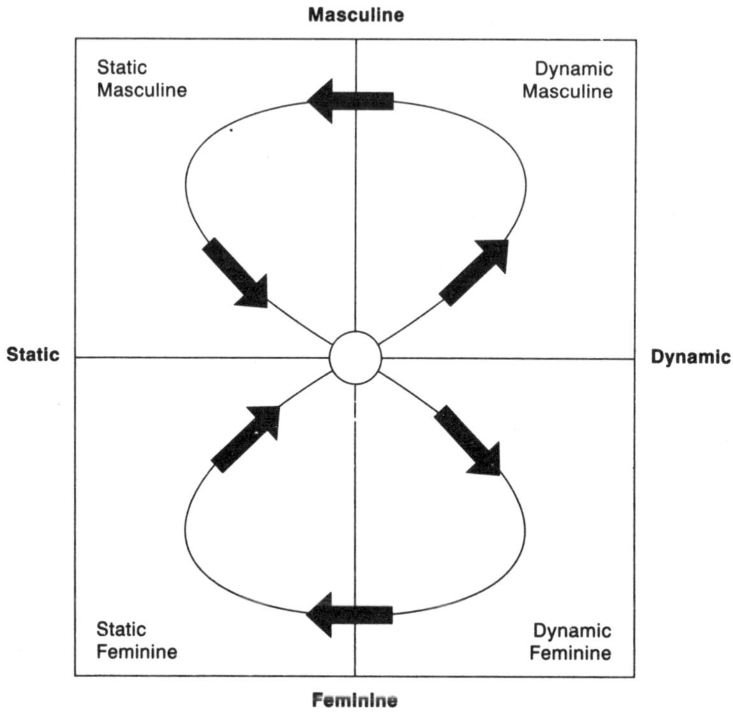

	Positive	Image	Negative	Image
Static Masculine	Ordered protective, responsible	King Arthur, Queen Elizabeth I	Dictatorial, controlling, killjoy	Traffic warden or petty official
Dynamic Feminine	Creative, transformative, positively destructive, tolerates ambiguity	Kali, Merlin, an artist	Madness, negatively destructive, chaos for chaos sake	Caligula, The Furies, The witches in *Macbeth*
Static Feminine	Nurturing, compassionate generous selfless	Mother Theresa, Father Christmas	Smother love, suffocating, addictive	Lady Macbeth Gollum in *Lord of the Rings*
Dynamic Masculine	Courageous, heroic, expansive, ambitious	Jason, Alexander, Emily Pankhurst	Aggressive, ruthless, tyrannical	Lucrezia Borgia, Attila the Hun

Movement through the quadrants follows the figure of eight. Most people have a preferred style. A well-rounded individual will be able to operate in all areas. Many people stick in a particular style and find it hard to move. Seeing the negative aspects of the current quadrant encourages you to move on. Seeing the negative of the next quadrant encourages you to stay put. The circle in the centre is seen as a particular area of risk. It is tougher to cross from top left to bottom right or bottom left to top right than from top right to top left or bottom right to bottom left. This may well be because both dimensions change at this cross-over.

By understanding your position and the elements that block you from moving through the quadrants you can help open up your capabilities.

Personal Development	✪✪✪✪
Leadership	✪✪✪
Motivation	✪
Coaching	✪
Interviewing	✪
Fun	✪✪

1.5 Exercise: It's catching

Preparation None.
Running time 10 minutes.
Resources Notepad.
Frequency Once.

The whole aim of this course is to help you to manage other people better. A key to this is motivation, and one of the best tips on motivation is noticing that it is infectious. If you are genuinely motivated in what you are doing, if it gives you real satisfaction and you are totally committed to it, it will rub off on those around you.

This isn't the place to discuss self-motivation and assertiveness in any detail. However, spending a few minutes looking at your own motivation will generate significant benefits. Spend a few minutes looking at what areas of work you prefer and have most appropriate skills for. Note down how motivated you are in the areas where you are trying to motivate others. Make sure you have that essential buy-in and enthusiasm. With it, you will succeed in motivating others.

The question arises, what happens if you aren't motivated yourself? Apart from looking at the possibilities of self-motivation, you have a number of options. Discuss it with those who have the opportunity to motivate you. Look at why you aren't motivated and see if you can remove the obstacles. If all else fails, find a way of doing something else. You can only keep up a façade of motivation for so long, and demotivation is even more infectious than motivation. You owe it to yourself to be doing something that excites you.

This is one of the most powerful techniques available in motivation. We aren't all capable of generating charisma, but everyone can provide enthusiasm and interest. This will communicate itself.

This technique works across the whole spectrum of audiences from individuals to huge groups. It is not an option.

Personal Development	✪✪✪
Leadership	✪✪✪
Motivation	✪✪✪✪
Coaching	✪✪✪
Interviewing	✪
Fun	✪✪✪

Unit 2: Inspiration

Leadership and management are matters of influence. Unless the people you are trying to manage are literally chained up and dragged around from task to task, you never have true control. Instead you are working indirectly. Because of this lack of hands-on, the ideal is that the people you manage should be inspired to do what you want them to do – the opportunities for this form the basis for the second unit.

Do try out the exercises as you go. Put them off until later and you probably won't ever do them. Read through the techniques. Make notes about how and when you can use them. And make sure you give them a try in the next appropriate forum.

Unit books

There's no obligation to read all, or any, of the unit books, but you will find that they provide excellent support to the course and strengthen your management skills.

The first of the two books recommended in this unit is Richard Branson's autobiography, *Losing my Virginity*. There's probably as much here about bad management as good (and I think Branson would admit as much) – but it's all good learning material. Crucially, Branson, unlike many other people at the top of organizations, is a leader who knows exactly how to inspire people.

The second book is Naomi Klein's very different book *No Logo*. This explores the impact of global brands on the world and suggests some alternatives. The main message of the book is not about leadership and inspiration – instead I strongly recommend that you read it seeing Klein as a potential leader, and noticing how she uses inspiration and enthusiasm to get her message across.

They're both quite chunky books, but don't be put off – you *can* make time for reading, and like all good managers, you will.

You can find more information on our unit books, or buy them, from our support site: www.cul.co.uk/crashcourse.

2.1 Technique: Charisma

Preparation Find or create a role model.
Running time Constant attention for the next year.
Resources None.
Frequency Regularly.

To be inspirational you need to attract the attention and following of others – in dramatic terms, to be charismatic. Charisma is often easier to define in its absence. We've all met managers who have had the charisma by-pass operation and don't even realize it. Charisma is a fundamental characteristic of the successful leader and yet it is tough to learn to be charismatic. There are, however, a number of characteristics of charismatic people that are easy to learn. Master some of these, act like a charismatic person, feel like a charismatic person, be seen as a charismatic person and, almost by accident, you will have become one.

Charismatic people make eye contact. Many who do not make easy eye contact with others find this difficult. Indeed they will look away, or close their own eyes without even realizing they are doing it. If you cannot see the reactions of the pupils of the person you are talking to, as you are talking to them, you are not making eye contact. If you are uncomfortable doing this with strangers, practise with people you know and trust and move outwards.

Charismatic people greet strangers confidently. Many of us are shy, embarrassed or overawed when meeting people for the first time. You must not appear to be so. You must be able to look them in the eye, smile and firmly shake hands (or greet in whatever way is culturally acceptable – kiss, bow, high five etc). If you find this difficult you might try imagining them naked. It probably won't help but it's almost always good for a laugh.

Charismatic people remember others – not only their names but also facts about people they have met. This is a tougher one to learn, but memory can, if necessary, be helped out by backups in a notebook or electronic organizer (particularly useful for birthdays, anniversaries and the like).

Finally, learn to walk, talk and sit like a charismatic person. Find yourself a role model that you can admire as a charismatic person and watch how they walk, talk and sit. Copy them. Ideally choose a role model who doesn't work too close to you. You don't want to be seen obviously aping the boss. Before long, if you play the role of a charismatic person, others will see you this way and you may even come to believe it yourself.

Personal Development	✪✪✪✪
Leadership	✪✪✪
Motivation	✪✪✪
Coaching	✪✪✪
Interviewing	✪
Fun	✪✪

2.2 Technique: Being an inspiration

Preparation None.
Running time Constant attention for the next year.
Resources None.
Frequency Regularly.

A charismatic person tends to be inspirational but this alone is not enough. What are the factors that cause others to be inspired by you? These are the qualities that would be worth a fortune if they were bottled. Short of finding the mythical shop that sells bottles of the stuff, we need to manufacture it for ourselves.

A first exercise is to learn how to be energetic. Energy is very inspirational (see Unit 10, which is all about energy). Apart from regular exercise, a key to energy is to raise the speed of your metabolism. A relatively simple way of doing this is to do some brisk exercise about 20 minutes after each meal. Just running upstairs or walking briskly between meetings is enough. What you must not do is to sit in meetings or work at your desk during this period. That will give your digestion the ability to slow you down to its pace instead of you speeding it up to yours. So, for the next few days, try this exercise. If it works for you, continue with it (be aware, though, that there is a danger of indigestion).

Another obvious but easily overlooked key to being inspirational is being good at what you do. There is nothing that inspires so well as a role model. Doing well and doing well with integrity are fundamental. Do not overlook the last sentence. Integrity is at the heart of being inspirational. You may have admirers if you achieve but bend your own and others' rules to breaking point, but you will inspire no one.

The counter side to this coin is spotting when others are good at what they do. Being aware of others and their effect on the business will be a real source of inspiration. Think about when you last made an issue of congratulating someone. Make a point of doing so today. Then again tomorrow. Then...

The final piece of advice is never stopping. Inspirational coinage has a very limited lifetime. You can't rest long on your laurels – to remain inspirational you will need to go on achieving. But that shouldn't be seen as a negative. Without that achievement, your life would be much less fulfilling.

Personal Development ✪✪✪✪
Leadership ✪✪✪
Motivation ✪✪✪
Coaching ✪✪✪
Interviewing ✪
Fun ✪✪

2.3 Exercise/Technique: Getting your inspiration

Preparation Various.
Running time 10 minutes.
Resources Wide range of inputs.
Frequency Regularly.

Inspiration is one of the magical words of our time. The picture of the artist or the poet waiting for inspiration to strike is a popular one. In truth, inspiration is one of those 'what goes around comes around' items in your life. If you feed the furnace it will heat the house. If you don't then you stay cold.

So, what does feeding the furnace mean? There are some obvious inputs. If you read a lot of business texts then you'll know something about modern business. If you read the newspapers regularly then you'll know what's going on in the world. But inspiration for a leader needs to be more eclectic than this. You should be feeding your soul as well as your brain. Attend the theatre or concerts regularly. Read a lot of novels as well as factual books. Read books that recapture the sense of amazement and wonder of childhood – in non-fiction, popular science is a great source, while science fiction and fantasy work well in fiction. Visit an art gallery. Indeed, you might make a particular point of visiting galleries with exhibitions of contemporary art since this is likely to challenge as well as to inspire.

Then, once you have done all of this you will need time for cogitation. That might be combined with jogging, working out in the gym or walking the dog, but it should be time for you and you alone.

So, list out now additional reading materials and additional inputs that you would like to have if you only had the time. Then make time and do them. You may not think so, but there are bound to be activities that you are involved in that contribute nothing to you, to your family, or to the world. If they were ditched they would create a hole that you could fill with inspirational activity.

Personal Development	✪✪✪✪
Leadership	✪✪✪
Motivation	✪✪✪
Coaching	✪✪✪
Interviewing	✪
Fun	✪✪

2.4 Technique: Learning to love your business and staff

Preparation None.
Running time Very little or, perhaps, a lifetime.
Resources None.
Frequency Regularly.

In trying to be inspirational you need to project a certain image to those you want to inspire. By far the easiest way to project such an image is to make sure that your targets are very important to you. In fact it would not be going too far to say that you need to love them.

If you are an entrepreneur and if your business has not taken over to the point that it is a millstone, you probably love it anyway. For those that aren't, taking a lesson from entrepreneurs could be a good start. What attitudes do they have that could teach others?

For a start, the product or service matters. It is something that they have staked a lot on and they are going to make it a success. What have you staked in your current business? What are you prepared to stake? The chances are, for most people reading this it's very little other than your time (and that often grudgingly). Can you change this? Can you stake more of yourself in this business? Can you move to a business that you can stake more of yourself in? Remember, staking yourself in the business has nothing to do with time. We have both, in the past, worked with many people who spent a long time at the office but cared nothing for the company, the product or the customers. Whether this is done in order to enhance their career, out of fear or for any other reason is irrelevant. Their stake in the business is small despite their time there being long.

The second point about entrepreneurs is that the money matters. The way the business is run, what is spent, and most importantly, what is wasted, is significant to them. If those who worked for large organizations (or even some impersonal small ones) thought about the business as though it was their own, there would be fewer resources wasted and business in general would be more efficient.

The technique in this section? Think like an entrepreneur. Act like an entrepreneur. If you can't find ways to love your current business then move on. Why should you be wasting such a significant piece of your life on something that you cannot love?

And then there's your staff. In many ways it is tougher to love your staff than your customers (see next technique). With the customers it is enough to have a generic and general sort of love. Your staff have the disadvantage of being here, where you can see them, all of the time. It's tough to forgive the foibles of those that you see a lot of.

Even so, you must learn to love those you lead if you are to be a successful leader. Once you do learn to do this – even if it is because you feel you must – you will then need to move to a position where the love is there because you want it, not because you need it in order to achieve results.

If the group of staff that you manage is small, you may be thinking by now of those in the group that no one could love, least of all you. If the group of staff that you manage is large then you will be having the same thoughts about entire sections of the company. Well, get rid of those thoughts. You cannot play favourites in this game. You must be fair and even-handed, and that applies to the ways that you love as well as the ways that you manage.

Spend time with your staff. Find out what their thoughts are. Find out what their needs and wants are. Find out how you are getting in the way of those needs and wants. Finally, find out how you can get out of the way and still achieve your vision. This is challenging stuff that cannot be completed quickly – luckily many of the techniques you will be picking up in parallel from later units will help along the way.

Personal Development	✪✪✪
Leadership	✪✪✪✪
Motivation	✪✪✪
Coaching	✪✪
Interviewing	✪✪
Fun	✪✪✪

2.5 Technique: Learning to love your customers and suppliers

Preparation None.
Running time Very little or, perhaps, a lifetime.
Resources None.
Frequency Regularly.

We want our customers to love us as a business so it is reasonable that we should love our customers.

Loving your customer is a little like the old adage, 'The customer is always right'. It holds true until it gets in the way. We've already said you should love your staff. There are often conflicts between staff and customers. How can you love them both? As an analogy (and not putting staff or customers into this category), think about loving your children. Those with more than one child know that they will sometimes fight. Sometimes you must arbitrate, sometimes you leave them to it. Ideally you encourage an atmosphere where they never feel the need to fight at all. Sorting out the squabbles does not imply loving one more than the other. It is a necessary part of the role.

So, how do you learn to love customers? It begins by ensuring that you have lots of contact. You can't imagine having a love affair, or a marriage, where your only contact with your partner is via third parties. For many leaders this is the relationship they have with their customers. Change that now by planning opportunities to meet with customers face-to-face. List them now.

The second thing you must do is to actively learn from that contact. If your lover or partner had an issue with your relationship and you listened to them talk about it and then ignored it, you wouldn't be surprised if it led to a deterioration in the relationship. Yet for many leaders this is how customers are seen. 'Let them moan and then take no action', as though the objective of feedback was to let them get it off their chest. No, the objective is to show how much they mean to you by doing something about it. So, when you do meet them, take notes, make commitments and carry them through.

Loving customers makes a sort of sense – but can you really extend this to suppliers too? For some businesses this relationship is based purely on price and contract. That is, specify the deliverables and the price and then establish contractual relationships that ensure delivery to specification and price. For many this is sufficient.

Some businesses, though, have established supplier relationships that are based on mutual benefit. These businesses have found that working with suppliers as partners offers a win–win that pays dividends to both parties. Some have gone as far as completely open book accounting and even sharing the vision and goals of the organization being supplied. How far you go with this is your choice. But if you see benefit in a partnership with suppliers then learning to love them is an added benefit.

Get to know their wants and needs. Make sure that they are absolutely clear about yours. Find ways of meeting their wants and needs and work with them to find ways of meeting yours.

One thing you must be clear about before you start to change the relationship with your suppliers. This is not a case of paying lip service to an ideal. It is not something that you do today and then change your mind about tomorrow. Be absolutely sure that you are comfortable with all of the implications of this change because it becomes pretty much irrevocable.

Personal Development	✪✪✪
Leadership	✪✪✪
Motivation	✪✪✪
Coaching	✪✪
Interviewing	✪
Fun	✪✪

Unit 3: Leader as navigator – strategy and direction

As was made clear in the first chapter, although this is a course on people management, the primary vehicle it is going to use is leadership. Where management focuses on tasks, leadership sets a direction, then supports staff in making progress towards that direction. Such an approach can't be undertaken unless you know where you are going. In principle you can manage without a clue of what it's all for. As a leader, though, you need to be able to explain and set the course. It's more challenging, but well worth the extra effort. This unit focuses on those direction-setting skills.

Do try out the exercises as you go. Put them off until later and you probably won't ever do them. Read through the techniques. Make notes about how and when you can use them. And make sure you give them a try in the next appropriate forum.

Unit book

There's no obligation to read all, or any, of the unit books, but you will find that they provide excellent support to the course and strengthen your management skills.

As a great manager you will need to set a direction, whether it's for a small team or a great organization. There's no one like Charles Handy for getting under the skin of the 'why?' of business, and in his *The Empty Raincoat* he looks at the changing shape of business, and its implications for the direction setters.

You can find more information on our unit books, or buy them, from our support site: www.cul.co.uk/crashcourse.

Web links

Links to sites on strategy and direction setting can be found at www.cul.co.uk/crashcourse.

3.1 Exercise: Leadership and management

Preparation Activity log.
Running time A few minutes.
Resources None.
Frequency Frequently.

Although we've already explored the distinctions between leadership and management in general terms, and looked at how you rated yourself on some key points, it's important to explore further the dimensions that make up these characteristics. And though our primary focus is on leadership, there are times when your management skills must excel. Times when you know exactly where you are going, but need to make sure you arrive on time.

It's convenient to think of the relationship between leadership and management on a three-dimensional grid. One dimension is task, another is people and the third is detail. There is a fairly clear line that goes diagonally across from a detailed high task and low people focus to a broad high people and low task focus. At one end of this line you are managing, at the other you are leading. Other areas of this chart would not be so clear. For instance, a broad task issue may be the leadership of vision, setting the direction for the business. Then again it may just be the management task of getting a clear picture before disaggregating down to lower-level tasks. Similarly, a detailed people issue may be the management role of making sure that pay and rations are taken care of or it may be that as a leader you need to get down into the detail to take the right leadership actions for individuals you lead.

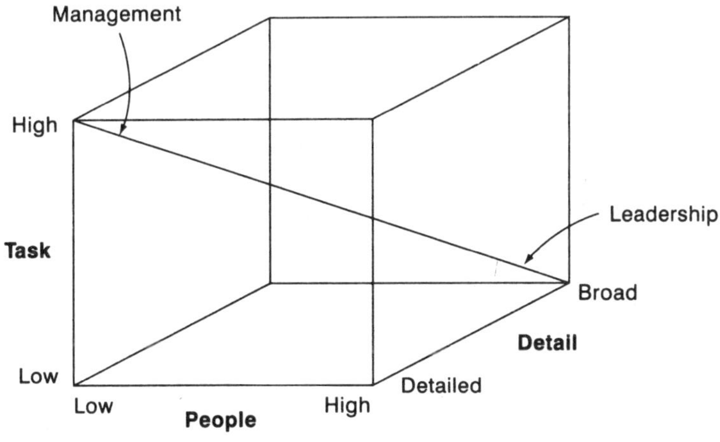

Go through the activities you have undertaken over the last week. If you have trouble remembering them, do this exercise next week after keeping a log. Evaluate for yourself what proportion of your time is management based and what proportion is leadership based. See where you feel more comfortable, and which aspects need most boosting.

Personal Development	✪✪✪
Leadership	✪✪✪✪
Motivation	✪✪
Coaching	✪
Interviewing	✪
Fun	✪✪

3.2 Exercise/Technique: Vision and mission

Preparation Collecting a range of magazines (possibly).
Running time 10 minutes to a few days.
Resources Input images.
Frequency Revisit every few years.

Vision is the drive and energy that you put into your business. It is the point that you give to the working lives of those you lead. It is the thing that gets you and your people out of bed in the mornings.

Now compare that to the vision statements that most businesses concoct.

If you don't have a driving vision and you go into work primarily for the wage, then you will never inspire others, no matter how lyrical the words. If you do then everything you do, every minute of the day, will convey this more surely than anything you could write.

There may be a need for writing down your vision. If your organization is large and you cannot be seen by all of your people then your example may not convey the message to all. Writing the vision and ensuring that it is communicated will help with this.

If you feel that you are driven by a personal vision but cannot articulate it, you might try this short exercise. Take a wide selection of magazines (including some you would not normally read). Go through them and rip out any images (or even phrases) that appeal to you. The appeal here is broad – forget about the vision for now. Take this pile of images and create a collage from them. This should be a mess of things that appeal to you. Now start writing words that describe the appeal. Analyse your thinking. These words will act as a guide to what is important to you. This guide should help you to sift a vision from the things that drive you. A vision should be short. Very short. Even a single word might be enough.

There is much similarity between the vision and the mission and the terms are often used interchangeably. The mission is finite. The vision endures as long as you are leader (or until a cataclysmic shift in the nature of your business causes a rethink). The mission is achievable but only just. The vision is phrased in a way that it is never reached. For some leaders the vision is the thing that drives them, the mission is the part of it they communicate.

Having a mission that is derived from an unreachable vision means that you can replace the mission once you reach (or get close to) the existing one. Think of NASA and their race to get a man on the moon. It drove everything they did. It defined them both internally and externally. Once they had achieved this they lost their way. It took some 30 years to get their act together again.

To create a mission, start with your vision. If you don't have and don't want a vision then you need to question why you're bothering with the mission at all. If it is just a feel-good thing or something that you think is expected of you then don't waste your time. Your people will watch what you do, not what you say or write. If you don't live the mission on a day-to-day basis it's a waste.

Make the mission a single sentence that describes a step towards achieving the unachievable. Don't worry if it seems almost impossible, this is a good thing. The time for more reality is when we move on to the goals.

Now make sure that every one that you lead knows what your mission is and knows why it is important to you. Weigh every decision you make against this or the vision. If they don't support it then they may be unnecessary. If they work against it then they are wrong.

Personal Development	✪✪✪
Leadership	✪✪✪✪
Motivation	✪✪✪
Coaching	✪✪
Interviewing	✪
Fun	✪✪

3.3 Technique: Strategy

Preparation Vision or mission.
Running time A few minutes to a few days.
Resources Business information.
Frequency Annually.

Giving direction through a clear strategy is one of the fundamental roles of leadership. There are entire volumes written about strategy. The strategy itself is rarely the problem. It is more often the will to implement it that lets down leaders.

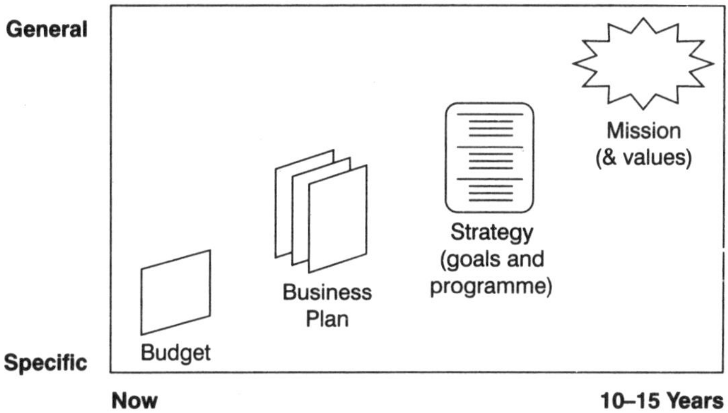

The first thing to develop is a mission or a vision (covered in the previous technique). This is the star that steers the business and sets your long-term aspirations. From this you develop a small set of goals. These should be clear, concise, measurable, have a definite timescale (usually five or more years) and should be discardable once the goal is achieved. Supporting each goal will be a more specific plan that will explain how the goal is made to happen. From the goals you can then develop a business plan. This will typically cover a three-year timescale and will be getting quite specific. At this stage you will be attaching people to the plan and assigning individual responsibilities. From the business plan you will be able to write your next year's budget.

If you have a small business, this level of strategy will feel like overkill. The fact is, it is just as critical to your success that you know where you're going in the long term as it is to a huge bureaucracy, but the planning will take less time for a smaller business. Schedule time now to go through the process of strategy development.

Many businesses go through a yearly round of developing strategy where last year's plan is either ignored or altered beyond recognition. This is a sign that you are not doing the job properly. What you planned last year should feed in to this year's plan. There will be changes, often huge ones. The world changes in ways that you cannot possibly anticipate. These changes should be alterations from last year's base, not a total rewrite. So, the final words – once you've written it, do it.

Personal Development ✪✪
Leadership ✪✪✪✪
Motivation ✪✪
Coaching ✪
Interviewing ✪
Fun ✪✪

3.4 *Exercise/Technique: Setting goals*

Preparation Collect current metrics for the business.
Running time From one day to many weeks.
Resources Metrics.
Frequency Annually.

We are now getting into areas of measurement and shorter timeframes. This makes goals easier to understand than other aspects of strategy. They should cover a time period of three to five years. This is long enough that you have time to make radical change but short enough that you have half a chance of predicting the future.

More than about seven goals becomes unmanageable. Organizations that have more than this either forget the goals completely or rank them in order of importance and focus on the top few. Aside from this, if you have more than seven goals you are likely to find them conflicting with one another too often to be useful.

Each goal should be a single, measurable statement, aimed three to five years in the future, that seems to be half possible, half impossible. By this I mean that you should reckon on a 50/50 chance of success (and a 50/50 chance of failure). Goals that are obviously achievable are a total waste of time. This is management, overseeing what would have been done anyway, not leadership. Goals that are obviously impossible become demotivators.

Yet again, once you have developed the goals your key task is communication: making sure that all the measurements that all people throughout the organization use are aligned with the goals.

Immediately you will hear the cry that these goals are not applicable in this or that area because it is different from the rest of the organization. There are three possible reasons for this. Firstly, they have misunderstood their role. Help them to understand. Secondly, you have not got a complete set of goals. Change them. Thirdly, it is a genuinely stand-alone part of the business that needs its own goals. Re-create it as a separate company.

Spend 10 minutes now trying to assess what your goals have been up to now, then another 10 minutes deciding whether you need to change some (and how they should be changed). You will spend considerably more time on your goals, but it's important to start immediately.

Personal Development	✪✪
Leadership	✪✪✪✪
Motivation	✪✪✪
Coaching	✪✪✪
Interviewing	✪
Fun	✪✪

3.5 Exercise/Technique: Developing a business plan

Preparation A developed set of goals.
Running time A few hours to a few months depending upon the business.
Resources Goals.
Frequency Annually.

Finally, we get to an area of strategy that most people are comfortable with. We understand business plans, we use them (and frequently ignore them) all the time.

At an organization level, as opposed to a project level, a business plan lays out the next two or three years in some detail. It gives a significant amount of detail for the first year and this decreases through the life of the plan. At a project level a business plan is equivalent to the financial side of the project plan and won't be covered here.

Not only are there fairly tight measures in a business plan, there are also specific responsibilities. Without accountability the measures are useless.

It is impossible to predict beyond the present year and yet years two and three of the plan should still be specific. Without this, the only changes your business will be able to achieve are those that can happen within a one-year time span. You might have to change your business plan after year one (indeed I will confidently predict that you will have to change it) but you will still have taken a first year's moves towards your three-year (or longer) change needs.

As an immediate exercise, study your current business plan (if it exists and if you can force it out from where it's acting as a doorstop) and write down those actions that are happening in year one that are specifically aimed at change in years two, three and beyond. If these do not constitute at least half of the actions in the plan then your focus is too short term and you need to change it.

Personal Development	✪✪
Leadership	✪✪✪✪
Motivation	✪✪
Coaching	✪
Interviewing	✪
Fun	✪✪

Unit 4: The murderous meeting

One of the greatest single tests of your ability to manage others is the effectiveness of your meetings. Meetings are invaluable – for all the benefits of modern communications, you can't beat face-to-face for many interactions – yet speak to anyone who works for a large organization and they will tell you they spend much too long in meetings that don't achieve anything. To be a great manager you are going to have transform those murderous meetings into their more compact, constructive relatives.

Do try out the exercises as you go. Put them off until later and you probably won't ever do them. Read through the techniques. Make notes about how and when you can use them. And make sure you give them a try in the next appropriate forum.

Unit book

There's no obligation to read all, or any, of the unit books, but you will find that they provide excellent support to the course and strengthen your management skills.

Managing meetings is just one aspect of time management – and good time management is an essential if you are to survive as a manager. A short book, packed with bite-sized techniques to enhance time management (ideal when you haven't the time to time-manage), is Brian Clegg's *Instant Time Management*. (Alternatively, many of these techniques and more appear in the sister course to this, *Crash Course in Personal Development*, also by Brian Clegg.)

You can find more information on our unit books, or buy them, from our support site: www.cul.co.uk/crashcourse.

Web links

Links to help with meeting management can be found at www.cul.co.uk/crashcourse.

4.1 Exercise/Technique: Meetings and how to chair them

Preparation Some additional work ahead of meetings.
Running time Less time than you currently waste.
Resources Information.
Frequency Regularly.

For the next week, follow these meeting guidelines. As an immediate exercise, you can check out the meetings you have coming up and make the necessary preparation.

Before the meeting

1. Try cancelling if there aren't clear benefits.
2. Objectives: what will be different at the end of the meeting as a result of it?
3. Attendees: groups of three to six work best.
4. Participants' preparation: tell them now rather than at the meeting.
5. Write an agenda. Link and order subjects. Allocate times to the agenda according to the importance of subjects, not their urgency. Keep the meeting short.
6. Other preparation: Is the venue right? Is the equipment there? Do you need to make special arrangements, such as parking or access for anyone?
7. Communicate with the participants. Do they need to attend? Ask for additional agenda items.

During the meeting

1. START ON TIME!
2. Write up the objectives.
3. Draw attention to the times on the agenda. Reinforce the finish time.
4. Concentrate on the process (how the meeting is running), as well as the content (what is being said).
5. Stick firmly but not doggedly to times on the agenda. Allow time at the start and end for social chit-chat.
6. Make sure that everyone has his or her say and that everyone has understood what has been said.

7. Stay focused. Take subjects out of the meeting.
8. Summarize and record specific actions and deadlines.
9. Arrange another meeting if you have to. Ideally, don't.

After the meeting

1. Write the list of actions and deadlines.
2. Do not include those things that you wish had been said.
3. Publish within 24 hours.
4. Follow up on important action items before the deadline to check for problems.
5. If it is not remembered after the meeting then it never happened. Short meetings and clear concise action lists help memory.

Personal Development	✪✪
Leadership	✪✪✪✪
Motivation	✪✪
Coaching	✪
Interviewing	✪
Fun	✪✪

4.2 *Exercise/Technique: Meetings and how to develop them*

Preparation Depends upon the development you choose.
Running time Less time than you currently waste.
Resources None.
Frequency Regularly.

The previous exercise is written from the perspective of chairing meetings. You will also attend meetings. As an immediate exercise, ask yourself how usefully your time is spent when you do so. Check through the 'other people's meetings' you have in your diary and rate them. Quite probably, many will be of limited value to you. If so, you need to do something about it.

A good start might be to send the meeting-chairing guidelines from the previous exercise to the chairs of other meetings you attend. They might listen, they might not. Even if they don't, they'll understand where you are coming from when you intervene.

Next, when you get an agenda for a meeting, make sure it has times for each item. If it doesn't, call up the organizer and ask for them. Next, be clear that you understand what each item is about. Ask yourself whether you need to be there at all. If you are there for only one item, ask that it be first and that you can then leave.

At the meeting, if there was no agenda, get one written up at the start. Make sure that there are times for each item and that everyone understands the purpose of it. Help the meeting to keep to time with continual reminders. If it overruns by a significant amount then leave.

This may seem like managerial detail rather than leadership overview but it is this dross that is currently filling your days and preventing you from doing what you should be doing. One of your early tasks as a leader is to take charge of your time so that as much as possible is spent doing what you should do, not what others want you to.

Personal Development	✪✪
Leadership	✪✪✪✪
Motivation	✪✪
Coaching	✪
Interviewing	✪
Fun	✪✪

4.3 Exercise/Technique: Meetings and how to kill them

Preparation Very little.
Running time Less time than you currently waste.
Resources None.
Frequency As required.

You waste time at meetings. In some organizations, the time wasted is truly worrying. It is truly amazing how unavailable many managers are. In a recent example where one of us was working with the Board of a UK insurance firm, he was told that, despite the importance of the work, the first date they could all make available was in September. This was in January! This is an extreme example but no one can sensibly do business this way.

There are two types of meeting to kill – yours and other people's.

Your meetings are easy. Go through the meetings you are organizing and ask yourself what the purpose of the meeting might be. Is it intended to give information, to get information or to reach a decision? In many cases it will be a muddle of the three. In some cases it will be none of them and you'll be wondering why it hasn't been killed already. Traditional meetings are inefficient mechanisms for giving information. If necessary, arrange a short presentation session, but ideally disseminate the information another way – a way that allows others to choose when and how they absorb it. Getting information is much better done on a one-to-one basis and need not take very long at all. Decision making usually requires people to meet (as long as they are genuinely needed for the decision). But making decisions does not take long. It is not making them that absorbs time.

For other people's meetings you may not worry about killing the meeting, just avoiding it. If there are no political repercussions just don't go. If there are, find a way around them, ideally by killing the whole meeting. If you have an altruistic streak, or if your business is being damaged by your meeting culture, then you might want to help kill other meetings. Spend time with their organizers questioning the purpose and looking for alternatives.

As an immediate exercise, check all the meetings currently in your diary and assess whether they should survive. But this is only a start – new meetings will continue to evolve and need suppressing.

Personal Development	✪✪✪
Leadership	✪✪✪✪
Motivation	✪✪✪
Coaching	✪
Interviewing	✪
Fun	✪✪

4.4 Exercise: Visible improvement

Preparation None.
Running time Five minutes.
Resources None.
Frequency Once.

The reason the good manager can happily kill off many formal meetings is that almost all the effective face-to-face communication is done in informal meetings, often the casual opportunity to catch someone and get your message across. Yet too many managers lock themselves away all day, making such informal communication almost impossible. Spend a few minutes checking through your diary. Are there times blocked off when you will be available in your office? Are there times when you are going to walk around the staff and give them the opportunity to talk about issues – and give them a pat on the back?

Unless you give these activities specific slots in your diary, or make sure you build them around 'natural' breaks like visiting the coffee machine, meetings will displace them. If your company makes it easy for you to be in an open plan area with your team, give it a try. Give visibility a chance.

Management by walking about (MBWA) was very popular in the 1970s and 80s, but has become slightly unfashionable. The existence of other management techniques does not reduce the power of MBWA – and it has the advantage of giving you control of the visibility agenda, rather than leaving it to people to come in to your office to see you. However, a total open-door policy makes time management impossible. You have to be able to shut yourself off to deal with personal matters, to think and to be productive. Being visible isn't about being accessible 24 hours a day.

Visibility says a lot to the staff – that you value them – as well as making it possible to eliminate many long-winded formal meetings. Look for different ways to be visible. Eat in the same place as your team. Try to get in a bit early, so someone who wants to see you can just pop in before the day's work begins. Don't consider this an interruption – it's why you're there.

Personal Development	✪✪✪
Leadership	✪✪✪✪
Motivation	✪✪✪✪
Coaching	✪✪
Interviewing	✪
Fun	✪✪✪

4.5 Technique: Break time

Preparation Schedule breaks.
Running time Five minutes.
Resources None.
Frequency Regular.

In any group sessions – meetings are just one example – careful management of breaks is essential. Regular breaks will restore drooping attention, remove distractions (like the need to go the toilet) and improve motivation to get on with the agenda. Such breaks should be scheduled, but if possible be prepared to modify them in response to the mood of the group. This is easy with a small meeting, but less practical with a group of 400, where you will need on the whole to stick to a schedule.

A common mistake with breaks is to make them too infrequent and too long. It's much better to have chunks of effort lasting 40 minutes to an hour with five-minute breaks than a whole morning concentrating and then a long gap. Be particularly careful with the lunch break. This is very dependent on the location and the group. It should not be too long, as people can become bored or drift back to work (if appropriately located), never returning to the session. However, people will need time to eat and have a few minutes away from it all. A good rule of thumb is to allow enough time to get everyone through the feeding process, plus 15 minutes spare time.

Sometimes breaks will be resented. Everything is going so well that people don't want to stop. They want to get on with it. Persevere with the breaks nonetheless. However much they feel that they are progressing, short breaks will help things go better, and keep on going well. They improve creativity and stop the group getting into a rut. Without breaks, individuals get stale, group morale tails off and the outcome is rapidly diminishing motivation. Whatever the pressure to keep going, make sure breaks occur.

Personal Development	✪✪
Leadership	✪✪✪✪
Motivation	✪✪✪
Coaching	✪✪✪
Interviewing	✪
Fun	✪✪

Unit 5: *It's hard at the top – dealing with stress*

Stress is a feature of life. It's not something we want to be totally without – it's the edge that drives us on to achieve. But too much stress, negative stress, is detrimental to your health and your performance. This unit looks at dealing with stresses both you and those you manage will face.

Do try out the exercises as you go. Put them off until later and you probably won't ever do them. Read through the techniques. Make notes about how and when you can use them. And make sure you give them a try in the next appropriate forum.

Unit book

There's no obligation to read all, or any, of the unit books, but you will find that they provide excellent support to the course and strengthen your management skills.

Stress is a big topic that we can touch on only briefly here. A straightforward but effective book giving more information on stress management is Cary L. Cooper and Stephen Palmer's *Conquer your Stress*. Alternatively, if you like the *Crash Course* approach, you will find plenty of stress management material in the sister course *Crash Course in Personal Development* or condensed in *Instant Stress Management*, both by Brian Clegg.

You can find more information on our unit books, or buy them, from our support site: www.cul.co.uk/crashcourse.

Web links

Stress management Web site links can be found at www.cul.co.uk/crashcourse.

5.1 Exercise/Technique: Using stress

Preparation None.
Running time Five to twenty minutes.
Resources None.
Frequency As required.

This piece is actually a series of short activities rather than one single exercise. In all leadership roles, however large or small, there is a degree of stress but it need not be a problem.

One of us recently attended a seminar run by Adrian Nicholas. Adrian makes a living by jumping out of aircraft. He holds various world records for his free diving but also works underwater as a cave diver, has been a rally driver and has even been to the North Pole. As he says, he has been in more high-stress situations than most of us could dream of. His main piece of advice was, 'If in doubt, breathe out.' One of the first things that happens when you get stressed is that you get controlled by your breathing rather than vice versa. Breathing out (and then remembering to breathe thereafter) brings the control back to you.

Another way to control stress is to use the adrenaline by having a regular, physical workout. This could be a trip to the gym. It could be taking part in a sport. It could be a brisk walk with the dog. It could even be work in the garden. Whatever it is, make sure that you break sweat and make sure that you stop thinking about your problems at work.

One of the most direct ways of tackling stress is to get on and do the things that are causing it. The reason that I say this is that much stress is created by anticipating the things that cause us problems. We worsen this by putting off these activities. This causes the stress to build. Once you get on and do it, the stress goes away.

A final broad consideration is looking for areas where you feel out of control and finding ways to reduce that out-of-control feeling. Almost all stress seems to be linked to the degree in which we believe ourselves to be in control, so this has a huge potential for a lever to work on your stress.

As an immediate exercise, think through your life, looking for those 'least in control' situations and see how you can make some modifications.

Personal Development	✪✪✪✪
Leadership	✪✪✪
Motivation	✪✪
Coaching	✪
Interviewing	✪
Fun	✪✪

5.2 Exercise: Learning to relax

Preparation Setting some time aside.
Running time Only minutes but quite often.
Resources None.
Frequency As required.

When you are stressed a few things happen in your body. The first is that you drug yourself. Adrenaline washes around your body getting you ready for intense physical activity that doesn't happen. Next, you release endorphins into your blood. These are morphine-like drugs that are intended to stop you feeling the pain that your body is convinced is about to happen. Whilst this is going on, your brain processing speed is moving up and up until, very often, it gets to so many cycles per second that it is no longer functioning. This is the 'rabbit in the headlights' phase.

Set some time aside now to start. First, learn to breathe. Despite doing it all your life, the chances are you haven't got it right yet. Use your diaphragm, not your chest. You'll know that this is happening when you take a deep breath, with your hand on your stomach, and your stomach moves more than your chest. Spend a little time every so often taking deep breaths in through your nose, holding for a second and then sending deep breaths out through your mouth.

Next, sitting in a comfortable chair, starting with your toes and working slowly upwards, tense and relax muscles. Feel them relaxing and remember that feeling. Your aim is to be able to replicate that at any time. It is particularly important to concentrate on relaxing your shoulders, your hands and your stomach.

Then spend time burning off the adrenaline through physical activity.

Finally, consider seeking some outside help. Not the services of a shrink (though live like you want to live), but any outside agency – a gym, a church, a good wine bar – that can help you with your personal brand of relaxation.

Personal Development	✪✪✪✪
Leadership	✪✪✪
Motivation	✪
Coaching	✪
Interviewing	✪
Fun	✪✪✪

5.3 Technique: Get fit

Preparation None.
Running time A few hours a week.
Resources Gym, dog or none.
Frequency Regularly.

First, let's stress that this is not about becoming an Olympic athlete. Fitness here means being fit for purpose. That is no different for you than for a product you might sell. In this instance it means being fit enough to do your job. The more sedentary your job, the more you'll need to work on your fitness in order to do it.

The first thing to establish in order to become fit is an attitude of mind. Push yourself to do a few things that stretch you physically a little. Walk a few places that you might have taken the car. Take stairs instead of lifts. At the weekend work a little harder at something physical like gardening, or walking the dog. As with all advice about fitness, if you suspect that any of this will put your body under stress – ie if you are overweight or have a physical problem – consult your doctor for advice.

Next think about (and then DO something about) a regular programme of physical activity. Join a gym or take up the sport that you dropped when you were younger – cricket, football, hockey, netball. If it's darts then think again, this probably doesn't qualify. Swimming is an ideal form of exercise in that it is relatively gentle and uses a large amount of your body. Many pools offer early morning sessions for people on their way to work.

Schedule the activity in a way that you will continue it. On the way to work, on the way home from work or at lunchtime are timings that work well. Make sure that you have at least two sessions a week. Any exercise is better for being lighter but repeated more frequently rather than heavier and less often.

Personal Development	✪✪✪✪
Leadership	✪✪✪
Motivation	✪
Coaching	✪✪
Interviewing	✪
Fun	✪

5.4 Exercise/Technique: Getting beneath anxiety

Preparation None.
Running time An hour.
Resources None.
Frequency As required.

Stress doesn't only have an impact on you – it is just as much a problem for your staff. There are times when a person that you are managing will be anxious. This is particularly obvious when you are coaching an individual. There are whole ranges of causes for this anxiety. Some of them will be associated with the coaching process and some of them with the field being coached.

Generally those associated with the coaching process will be addressed by discussing what you will be doing, how you will be going about it and by being open to any questions that the coachee may have. Those anxieties associated with the field being coached are harder to deal with here because the approach that you take will depend upon the cause of the anxiety. Often that cause is not obvious because the anxiety itself may reflect something that is not known even by the coachee. We are not suggesting that you set yourself up as a psychoanalyst, but you will have to be very empathetic and may have to spend time digging beneath the surface to uncover what's going on and the reasons behind it.

One way to practise this is to deal with your own anxieties. You may have some about the whole coaching process. Whether or not you are currently engaged in coaching someone, take a few moments to write these down now. Once you have done that, look at the first one and ask why it is an area of concern. Write down the answer(s). Now look at them and ask in turn why they might be. Write down the answers. Keep on asking why until you reach a point where the answers seem trivial or unhelpful. Now move on to the next concern and so on. Once you have completed this, look at the whole list and hunt within it for the underlying fears that drive the anxieties you may feel. This may not be obvious but dig in there because finding them can make a significant shift. If this process works for you then you might try it with your coachee.

Personal Development ✪✪✪
Leadership ✪✪✪
Motivation ✪✪
Coaching ✪✪✪✪
Interviewing ✪
Fun ✪✪

5.5 Exercise/Technique: Stop and think

Preparation None.
Running time An hour or two.
Resources Diary, pen and paper.
Frequency Every couple of months.

In any aspect of management it is possible to get onto a treadmill that carries us forward with its own momentum.

Build a personal review with yourself into your diary every couple of months. This review is to look at what you are doing, how you are doing it and to think through whether it is still giving you the buzz you would like it to.

Sit down alone with a pad of paper, a pen, a cup of tea or coffee and plenty of time. Now list for yourself all of the things you are currently doing that you love. This list is not related solely to work, all of your life should be included. Now write down all of the things that you do that feel like chores – the things that you feel you have to do.

Now, with the first list take each of the statements and write, 'I choose to <whatever the statement is> because…'. Write here why you choose to do this and list as many 'because' statements as you can.

With the second list take each of the statements and write, 'I have to <whatever the statement is> or else…'. Write here what will happen if you don't do this. Write as many 'or else' statements as you can.

Work through each of these statements and, as objectively as you are able, write next to each statement the letter T, the letter F or a question mark: T if the statement is absolutely true; F if the statement is false or true only in part; question mark if you don't know. Now for all F statements rewrite a statement that is objectively true.

The reason for this writing is to give you ammunition to think through your life and to address anything in it that you would like to change.

This is a very valuable exercise when dealing with stress as there is a strong link with control. When you have found areas in need of change you may then need to establish a personal goal to make that change happen – a personal process similar to the business planning we have already encountered.

Personal Development	✪✪✪✪
Leadership	✪✪✪
Motivation	✪✪
Coaching	✪✪✪
Interviewing	✪
Fun	✪✪

Unit 6: Words, words – communicating

In essence, management (and particularly leadership) is founded on communication. Communication is the primary channel through which management is achieved. We have already looked at one, very specific aspect of communication – the concept of the meeting. In this unit we widen your communication requirements to cover more of the management role.

Do try out the exercises as you go. Put them off until later and you probably won't ever do them. Read through the techniques. Make notes about how and when you can use them. And make sure you give them a try in the next appropriate forum.

Unit book

There's no obligation to read all, or any, of the unit books, but you will find that they provide excellent support to the course and strengthen your management skills.

Communication is at the heart of management, which becomes very clear in Peter Block's classic text, *The Empowered Manager*. The word 'empowered' may seem dated now (this book dates back to the 1980s), but the content of the book is still as valuable as it was when it was first published.

You can find more information on our unit books, or buy them, from our support site: www.cul.co.uk/crashcourse.

Web links

Online guide to communication can be found at www.cul.co.uk/crashcourse.

6.1 Exercise/Technique: Conversations

Preparation Try the exercise.
Running time A few minutes quite frequently.
Resources None.
Frequency Regularly.

Informal, face-to-face communication carries significantly more weight than any formal methods. Research carried out at MIT has shown that around 80 per cent of key implemented ideas are developed in informal meetings. Tactics for using the conversations you have are an essential part of your leadership armoury. Before you go rushing off to plan every 'chance' conversation for the next few days, it is also true that being seen to be selling a viewpoint is one of the fastest turnoffs in a conversation. Yes, another contradiction to overcome as a leader.

So, if selling a particular viewpoint and planning chance meetings isn't advisable, what can be done to enhance this valuable communication vehicle? In a word, preparedness. To use chance conversations to maximum advantage you must be prepared for them to happen. This means that you need a few, a very few, key messages that you want to drive home every opportunity you get.

A colleague once told me that he used the elevator test. If he could get his message across to someone he was sharing an elevator with then it was short enough. What would your key elevator message be?

Having thought this through, develop more in order to have a range of messages. People don't choose parrots for their leaders. You need to be seen to be thinking about this stuff.

Now you have the messages you must maximize the number of chance encounters. This is the tough part because the only way you can do this is to get up off your butt and walk out amongst your people. The more you are out of your office, the more face-to-face communication you are doing. The more of this you do, the more you are doing your job.

Personal Development	✪✪✪✪
Leadership	✪✪✪
Motivation	✪✪✪
Coaching	✪✪
Interviewing	✪✪✪
Fun	✪✪

6.2 Technique: Networking

Preparation None.
Running time 10 minutes to several hours.
Resources Contact list.
Frequency Regularly.

A few years ago management guru Tom Peters spent a lot of time on the topic of managing yourself. He claimed that there are two fundamental tools for this – your résumé and your Rolodex. In other words, what you have achieved and who you know. This is truer for a leader than for anyone else. You need a strong network to support and help the work that you are doing.

The way that your network changes over time is a key measure of its success. Who are you adding and where are they from? If your key contacts are from within your organization then you are being too insular. If they are from within your industry then you are still being too insular. You need to find ways to expand your network beyond its current limitations.

Every day you should be adding a new contact (OK, let's average that to five a week) and at least two-thirds of those should be from outside your organization and with a fair proportion from outside your industry.

How can you make this happen? The obvious first answer is to get out more. Spend time at conferences. If they are conferences that are nothing to do with your industry, so much the better. Use these conferences as opportunities to chat to people and to swap business cards. If your card is memorable this will help you to stick in their mind. One of the authors used to have the job title Corporate Jester (for British Airways) – that was memorable. Now his cards are printed on playing cards.

After you have met people, follow up on those you like. Invite them to dinner or arrange to meet them for no better reason than to get to know them better. It is not only fun, it is great for your network and your personal development.

If you are the sort of person who finds this sort of socializing difficult then push yourself. Push at the point that you meet them in the first place and push again to make the follow-up happen. It becomes habit forming and consequently easier over time.

Personal Development	✪✪✪✪
Leadership	✪✪✪
Motivation	✪
Coaching	✪
Interviewing	✪
Fun	✪✪

6.3 Technique: Publish or be damned

Preparation None.
Running time 10 minutes.
Resources None.
Frequency Regularly.

Face-to-face may be hugely important, but it isn't your only mechanism for communication. On a regular basis spend a few minutes thinking how you can make use of your company publications as a way to get the message you want into the organization. It doesn't matter what level you are in the organization, these publications give you a valuable platform. Bear in mind that 'publications' covers a multitude of vehicles. It can be a company magazine or newspaper, departmental or team equivalents, bulletins, newsletters and increasingly the in-house version of the Intranet, an intranet.

Describing individual, team and company successes can be very positive for those involved, provided the publication is not seen as a vehicle for company whitewash, only ever carrying good news. Publications also give staff an opportunity to contribute letters and comments. Combine this with editorial action on comments to give the best motivational effect.

Internal company publications traditionally have a low impact because they are bland and careful, putting across the company line. Consider starting a publication with an action orientation that is edgy in tone, giving a strong voice to the staff. Any publication that can be seen as 'ours' is much more likely to be read – both to get your message across and to provide motivation. It should not be allowed to be a simple 'moan sheet', which is anything but motivational – perhaps a good model would be the TV consumer rights programmes, where the goal is not to moan but to get a result.

In considering conventional publications, don't forget the bulletin board. This could be a literal notice-board, but is more likely to be an electronic one, like a Web discussion or a Lotus Notes database. Such a discussion needs to have regular management input, picking up concerns and responding to them. Because of the time constraints, such electronic publications are the best approach for large groups, though for sessions lasting more than a half day it is also possible to put together a paper publication which may give more lasting impact.

Personal Development	✪
Leadership	✪✪✪
Motivation	✪✪✪✪
Coaching	✪✪
Interviewing	✪
Fun	✪✪

6.4 Exercise: Eye eye

Preparation None.
Running time Five minutes.
Resources A mirror.
Frequency Once.

Eye contact is a fundamental component in face-to-face communication. Spend a couple of minutes on your own with a mirror. You will feel silly, but don't let it stop you. Before you start, produce a few keyword notes of a script, assuming you were having to tell someone that they had performed well, but because of external circumstances they were going to have to do even more. Now deliver this message to yourself in the mirror. Try to keep good eye contact with yourself. This does not mean staring constantly into your eyes (this is off-putting – look away occasionally, but naturally), but make sure that you are looking into your eyes when you make your key points, and for most of the time.

After this exercise, try to be conscious of your eye contact when you are talking to people. Don't be tempted to look away when the message is bad. Poor eye contact means that you will be interpreted as being devious and not believing in what you are saying. You will be seen as being uncomfortable in their presence. Good eye contact reinforces the message and signals your commitment.

You can only communicate well with visible sincerity. No matter how much you genuinely believe in your message, if your eyes say you don't, the message will not be believed. By enhancing your eye contact you will do wonders for your ability to motivate.

Eye contact is also important when dealing with teams and groups. Here you will have to scan, trying to spread your eye contact across the group. This can seem artificial (for you) to begin with, but it does work. Watch a good speaker in action. Look also at other aspects of body language that can enhance motivation (these come up in a later unit).

Personal Development	✪✪✪✪
Leadership	✪✪✪
Motivation	✪✪✪✪
Coaching	✪✪✪
Interviewing	✪✪✪
Fun	✪✪

6.5 Exercise: Open questions

Preparation None.
Running time Five minutes.
Resources Someone to talk to.
Frequency Regularly.

Closed questions are ineffective in any communication, something that becomes particularly obvious when you are involved in an interview. It can turn the process into a nightmare. This exercise is particularly helpful for interviews, and is phrased in terms of them, but applies to any verbal communication. Closed questions are the sort of questions that prompt a one-word answer, giving hardly any information. Any closed question can be asked in an open form, inviting a fuller answer. So, for example, instead of asking 'did you enjoy your last job?' (answer: 'yes' or 'no'), you could ask 'how do you feel about your last job?' In theory you could get the answer 'good', but you are much more likely to get revealing detail.

Re-phrase these closed questions as open ones:

1. Did you enjoy your last job?
2. Is our company better than its competitors?
3. Were you fired from your last job?
4. Are you happy with our terms and conditions?
5. How many jobs have you had?

Don't read on until you have had a go.

That last question doesn't solicit a 'yes' or 'no' answer, but it's still closed. Even professional interviewers can fall into the trap of asking closed questions. Keep an eye out for them in TV or radio interviews.

If you do get a 'yes' or 'no' answer to a question, give yourself a moment's silence. Many people will then naturally begin to expand on their answer. In an interview, experienced interviewees will be aware of the danger of closed questions themselves, and do the opening up for you. During that pause, re-phrase the question as an open one. If the interviewee doesn't open it themselves, either re-ask in the open form or just say 'could you tell me a little more about that?' or 'could you expand on that?'

Note a second advantage of the open question that may well have emerged from your re-phrasing. The question 'were you fired from your last job?' is a loaded one. If instead you asked something like 'what prompted you to leave your last job?' you get more information, but also don't irritate the candidate by implying that they might have been fired if they weren't.

If you are doing interviews, try to spot any closed questions you tend to ask. Pick up on them and consciously look for alternative phrasings to make them open. Occasionally you may use closed questions intentionally to test a candidate's verbal skills.

Personal Development	✪✪✪
Leadership	✪✪✪
Motivation	✪✪✪
Coaching	✪✪✪
Interviewing	✪✪✪✪
Fun	✪✪

Unit 7: Knowledge is power

Francis Bacon, the Elizabethan politician, scientist and writer, made the observation *nam ist ipsa scientia potestas est* – knowledge itself is power – and Bacon was a pretty canny operator. In managing people you need to wield a form of power, but the traditional powers of authority through position, of reward, and of punishment seem to hold less sway in a modern organization. One of the most effective forms of power is knowledge.

This isn't putting knowledge forward in some Machiavellian sense – get the goods on your staff, then you can blackmail them into performing well – but rather that knowing your company, your staff, your competitors and more will all place you ideally to get things done.

Do try out the exercises as you go. Put them off until later and you probably won't ever do them. Read through the techniques. Make notes about how and when you can use them. And make sure you give them a try in the next appropriate forum.

Unit book

There's no obligation to read all, or any, of the unit books, but you will find that they provide excellent support to the course and strengthen your management skills.

There has never been a time when it has been more possible to have a knowledge base at your fingertips. Thanks to the Internet, very little information need escape your grasp as long as you know how to seek it out. Yet the e-world is still a trap for the unwary, hence our recommendation of *The Professional's Guide to Mining the Internet*, by Brian Clegg. This is a handbook of the skills you need to get the information you want, rather than a simple guide to Web sites, so particularly suited to the task.

You can find more information on our unit books, or buy them, from our support site: www.cul.co.uk/crashcourse.

Web links

Links to Web sites to help you build your knowledge management can be found at www.cul.co.uk/crashcourse.

7.1 Exercise/Technique: Technical competence

Preparation Little.
Running time A lifetime.
Resources Skills.
Frequency As required.

There are two conflicting schools of thought on a leader's need to be technically competent. One says that you must be better at the jobs your people do than they are themselves and the other says that the leader has no need to be able to do the jobs of their people in order to lead.

Perversely, we believe that there is a grain of truth in both of these and that both of these views are wrong. It simply is not true that in order to lead it is necessary to be able to do jobs better than your people. You have employed them for their skills and, in a larger organization, the range of skills you have employed will be vast. However, having worked in computing roles in the past, we have seen many systems constrained to the lowest common denominator, which is often the manager's ability to understand the technology.

It is also a fact that you cannot lead effectively unless you understand the pressures and the limitations placed upon your people. In many instances this knowledge will come about as a result of talking to them. In some instances you may decide to do their job for a while in order to experience these pressures and limitations. The watchword here is humility. If you are to try the jobs of your people it must be from the perspective that you do not and cannot know it as well as they do. Of course, humility isn't enough. They won't stand for simple humble too long – it had better get its finger out and become competent but not expert.

As an immediate exercise, rate yourself against your staff on the technical competence needed to do their jobs. Their jobs, not yours. If you are higher than them then you should be developing them hard. If you are lower then you'd better be far higher on leadership skills.

Personal Development	✪✪✪
Leadership	✪✪✪✪
Motivation	✪✪✪
Coaching	✪✪✪
Interviewing	✪
Fun	✪✪

7.2 Exercise/Technique: Knowing your competitors and customers

Preparation Learning to use the Internet.
Running time 20 minutes.
Resources Internet access, press sources.
Frequency Regularly.

According to Francis Bacon, knowledge is power. Given the information sources that you have at your fingertips you should be an immensely powerful individual. The reason you are not comes in two parts. Firstly, you haven't bothered to collect the information that you could. Secondly, you already know what isn't available. Or at least, you think you know.

A first source of information should be the Internet. Being at least competent and probably expert at finding things on the Internet is a non-optional management skill for the 21st century. (If you don't feel you have the expertise, make sure you read the unit book.) Being too busy or too important may be an adequate reason in your mind for being a dinosaur but there are many people who would disagree. Trawl through your competitors' Web pages. Put their names in search engines and see what is thrown up. As an immediate exercise, do this for your top two competitors.

Although much will be on the Web it's still worth getting hold of the press releases of your competitors and having press cuttings provided or searching the press yourself.

Then there is the information you can glean from your competitors' products. What is their pricing strategy? Where are their products heading? How is their design compared to yours? What are the key similarities and key points of difference? Even in a commoditized marketplace you can make these comparisons. And no product *need* be a commodity as long as you can package, price or distribute it differently.

Finally, don't forget trade organizations and industry conferences. It is amazing how much people are willing to tell you about their strategy as long as you are prepared to ask questions and read between the lines.

Customers also will tell you a great deal about themselves if you are prepared to ask in the right way.

There are two factors that will affect their willingness to help. Firstly, what's in it for them? Secondly, how easy do you make it? If there is a significant cost involved in giving the information or there's no obvious payback, why should they waste their time? Obviously you can weight this relationship by bribing them – offering immediate payback in a tangible way. But the ideal should be to get the information flowing to you at no effort to your customers and without the need to bribe.

SuperQuinn supermarkets in the Republic of Ireland springs to mind. They have customer suggestion boxes that are full to overflowing every day. This is because they guarantee that every suggestion will be read the following morning by the meeting of the senior managers and that they will implement as many as they can as quickly as they can.

How can they afford to spend their time reading all of these suggestions? Well, if you had this free data flowing in about your customers' needs and wants you'd have to be a fool not to spend your time reading it. If you had the opportunity to duplicate this you'd have to be a fool not to take it up. Oh, you do have the opportunity and you haven't taken it up – sorry.

Finally, as well as asking them on paper, consider the other listening posts you can create. Your staff will know a lot about what works and what doesn't work for customers, particularly those staff with daily, face-to-face contact. You yourself could learn more by spending time working on the face-to-face contact. Any opportunity, any time, take it.

Personal Development	✪✪✪
Leadership	✪✪✪✪
Motivation	✪✪
Coaching	✪✪
Interviewing	✪✪
Fun	✪✪

7.3 Technique: Knowing your people

Preparation None.
Running time A few minutes.
Resources None.
Frequency Regularly.

If it is important that you know your customers, how much more important is it that you know the people who represent you to the customers? Your staff provide the face of your organization. You must know the face that they are presenting. To know this you must know how they see and hear you (and your messages) and how they see the products and services you offer.

Some of the listening posts used for customers could be duplicated for staff. For instance, a suggestion box that guaranteed that you would read the inputs on a daily basis and would implement as many as you were able could be a huge source of information. The difficulty with this is that it is a promise you cannot afford to renege on.

A regular staff input survey is another source to consider. Asking a structured set of questions can give you an overview of the feelings of your staff but it will not be a great source for a detailed picture. Asking the same questions time on time gives you a chance to compare how things are changing between surveys.

Talking to your staff is essential. In a large organization, pre-arranged sessions every so often might work but there is nothing quite as effective as just getting out and about and talking to people. If you are doing this to spread your messages then you might want to stop and listen awhile as well as talking.

The real message is that any opportunity you can create to get input from your people direct, rather than filtered through managers or staff representatives, is an opportunity that you should seize with both hands.

Personal Development	✪✪
Leadership	✪✪✪✪
Motivation	✪✪✪✪
Coaching	✪✪✪
Interviewing	✪
Fun	✪✪

7.4 Technique: Knowing yourself

Preparation None.
Running time As long as it takes.
Resources Yourself.
Frequency Regularly.

Knowing yourself sounds easy but anyone who has started the journey to self-discovery will know that it is a very, very long road. Indeed it is probably never ending. Yet it is very difficult to lead others effectively until you have a reasonable understanding of yourself. Not a complete picture, but better than most others know themselves.

This is a piece of self-development that really does benefit from outside help. It is possible to undertake on your own, but so much more difficult that you have to ask why you would want to make it that tough. Mind you, it is also true that even with some outside help, most self-discovery is a singular and personal process.

A good place to start is with a standard battery of psychometric tests. Understand from these what your behaviour preferences are and what impact these might have on others. Once you've done this, be prepared to treat the results lightly. These things are indicators. They are neither rigid science nor religion. If taken too seriously they can mislead and misdirect.

Another good place is to talk to family, friends and colleagues about what you do well and badly in interacting with others. If they are willing to be open with you they could be a great source of insight. If they are not willing to be open with you then you might glean some insight from this.

Looking inside yourself is a useful approach. Whether you do this through meditation, psychoanalysis or just some personal deep thinking is your business. You will need to think hard about your drivers and your motivation. Accept at the start that you are neither the hero you would like to be nor the demon you fear you might be but that you are both an ordinary and an extraordinary person.

Personal Development	✪✪✪✪
Leadership	✪✪✪
Motivation	✪✪✪
Coaching	✪✪✪
Interviewing	✪✪
Fun	✪✪

7.5 Technique: Keeping abreast

Preparation None.
Running time A few minutes to an hour a day.
Resources Learning sources.
Frequency Daily.

A key to business success in the 21st century is an ability not just to access information but to do something with it, quicker and more effectively than your competitors. There are those who argue that this skill is being made redundant by computers – they will be able to sift and sort information so fast that you will not need to know anything except how to switch them on. Whilst this may be true in the future (a pretty distant future, we suspect), our view is that information overload will get worse before it gets better.

How can you know more? How can you absorb more than you already do?

The first thing to do is to set aside more of your time for learning. It may seem occasionally that we are asking you to create huge amounts of time out of nothing but luckily we will be covering delegation in a later unit – if your people are doing all of your work you should have plenty of time.

The next thing to do is to get better at using that time. You can do this in four ways. Firstly, read faster – train in speed reading or simply push yourself to get through more in less time. Secondly, remember more – learn better ways of note taking or practise recalling items that you have read in order to improve retention. Thirdly, read more digested material – if someone is going to go to the trouble of digesting business or news items then it seems impolite not to read them. Finally, expand your view of learning to include listening to educational radio shows, browsing on the Internet or attending lectures.

Personal Development	✪✪✪✪
Leadership	✪✪✪
Motivation	✪✪
Coaching	✪✪
Interviewing	✪✪
Fun	✪✪✪

Unit 8: Responsibility and influence

Responsibility and influence are twin tools without which good management is pretty well impossible to achieve. The act of managing people implies taking on responsibility – but responsibility is also a mechanism you can use to get buy-in from others. By giving them responsibility (provided they also get the appropriate recognition) you are enhancing their jobs and their lives.

Responsibility is easy to take on when it is matched with authority – the ability to make your point of view a de facto law. But in modern organizations it is more likely to be set alongside influence. Everything from flatter organizations to more flexible working implies you are less likely to be in authority and more likely to be expected to influence others.

Do try out the exercises as you go. Put them off until later and you probably won't ever do them. Read through the techniques. Make notes about how and when you can use them. And make sure you give them a try in the next appropriate forum.

Unit book

There's no obligation to read all, or any, of the unit books, but you will find that they provide excellent support to the course and strengthen your management skills.

No one knows better how to influence people than a great marketer, and Jay Abraham, author of our unit book, *Getting Everything You Can Out Of All You've Got*, is one of the best. Although this book is aimed primarily at the direct world of commercial marketing, every lesson strikes home with equal force in the business of marketing your ideas to those you have to influence. Don't be put off by its brashness – this book is an essential part of any good management library.

You can find more information on our unit books, or buy them, from our support site: www.cul.co.uk/crashcourse.

Web links

Read more on responsibility and influencing at www.cul.co.uk/crashcourse.

8.1 Exercise/Technique: Taking responsibility

Preparation None.
Running time Whenever you are leading.
Resources You.
Frequency Daily.

Many years ago we both attended some training at which we were given a piece of advice that keeps coming back to haunt us. We were told that every time one of us points our finger at someone else, there are three fingers pointing back at us. Yes, it's trite and cutesy but it sticks in the mind to a degree that verges on frustration.

As a leader, when one of your people screws up it is your fault. When one of your people does well, they get the praise. Before you start bemoaning the injustice of this, remember that you have a choice. You are playing this role because you have chosen to. You could back out of that choice at any time.

One of your main roles as a leader is to take the flak that would hit your people and to redirect the praise that might miss them. This calls for a combination of tough skin and open heart that is very difficult to maintain. Yet again, nobody said it was going to be easy.

As if this wasn't tough enough, taking responsibility doesn't stop there. You are responsible for everything your organization does, whether it falls into your area of official responsibility or not. If, for instance, a customer calls and their problem sits elsewhere in the organization, the last thing you should do is tell them that. Take responsibility for the problem and sort it out for them. This is easy to see when the customer calls directly but when a problem occurs elsewhere that is less directly linked to an individual customer your knee-jerk reaction should be to ask how you can fix it. If something isn't working in your business it is your problem. No arguments, no prevarication – fix it.

As an exercise, collect together a sample set of customer complaint letters and e-mails (if such things exist in your area of responsibility). Identify the proportion of them that would have been mollified, or even delighted, by being sorted out by the first person they contacted. Find a way to spread this learning.

Personal Development	✪✪
Leadership	✪✪✪✪
Motivation	✪✪✪
Coaching	✪✪
Interviewing	✪
Fun	✪✪

8.2 Technique: Teaching responsibility

Preparation None.
Running time Considerable.
Resources None.
Frequency Regularly.

It is not enough to take responsibility. As a leader you also need to teach it. There is something faintly contradictory about saying that every problem is your problem and then teaching others to think in the same way. It is a necessity. You cannot solve all of the problems of the world on your own. You need help.

Being seen to take responsibility for everything around you will have two opposite effects. On the one hand you will act as a role model and encourage others to do the same. On the other hand you will cause others to feel that they need not bother because it is now your responsibility.

There is a place for formal training in taking responsibility. How far you go down this path will depend upon the culture and resources of your organization.

Whether you train or not, you need to spread the word that taking responsibility is everyone's job. You need to find ways of increasing the role model aspects of your behaviour and decreasing the nannying side. The very best way to do this is to have a few discussions with people after you have sorted out a problem and ask them why they hadn't. Do not be tempted to do this before sorting it out because this defeats the point you are trying to convey.

So, each and every time you sort out a problem, find someone else who could have done it and discuss the situation with them. Make it clear that this issue was your responsibility but it was theirs also.

Personal Development	✪✪
Leadership	✪✪✪✪
Motivation	✪✪✪
Coaching	✪✪✪
Interviewing	✪
Fun	✪✪

8.3 Technique: How to be an ideal leader

Preparation Work through this course.
Running time Most of your time.
Resources None.
Frequency Regularly.

Much of this course is aimed at offering advice that will allow you to fulfil the aim of becoming an 'ideal leader'. This section contains a couple of principles that don't fit easily elsewhere, sitting over and above specific tips and techniques.

The overarching message is that leadership is about challenge and support. The very best leaders are those who make impossible demands and then offer impossible levels of support to help their people achieve.

The terms *challenge* and *support* need some explanation. They are subject to such a breadth of definition that they need to be fairly carefully handled.

Challenge: This is not meant to imply that you challenge in an aggressive manner. It is not the notion of challenge normally associated with confrontation. It is more meant to imply that you have impossible targets to achieve. The managerial approach to this would be to break these targets down into a work plan and evaluate what could realistically be achieved in the timescale. The leadership approach is to say that they are impossible but that the future of the business depends upon them, so we either throw in the towel now or we commit to making them happen.

Support: This is not meant to mean nannying or being overly gentle with people. It is meant to imply that in order to achieve impossible targets people need every obstacle that can be removed from their path to be removed. The managerial approach to this would be to offer a realistic set of resources in support of those meeting the targets. The leadership approach is to ask what you need to make this happen and then find ways of getting it there. It is about being there at all times for your people in a way that they know means that they can lean on you if they need to but that they won't if they don't.

Personal Development	✪
Leadership	✪✪✪✪
Motivation	✪✪✪
Coaching	✪✪✪
Interviewing	✪✪
Fun	✪✪

8.4 Technique: Saying 'No'

Preparation None.
Running time Half an hour to a lifetime.
Resources None.
Frequency As required.

Most people who become leaders have little trouble in saying no to others. This lack of assertion often does not apply. Some, however, find themselves in a leadership role and then find that their job is impossible because they have agreed to things they should never have said yes to.

If there is even the remotest chance that this describes you then read on.

There are many reasons why people find saying no difficult. They mostly stem from being brought up to be polite and accommodating. Learning to be assertive and realizing that you have the right not to do as others want you to is a huge step towards making this easier. There is something about the socialization process of girls in many families that makes it even tougher for women managers and leaders to be assertive than men.

Here are some quick tips:

- Accept that you have the right to say no and that anyone who pushes or manipulates you to try to change your mind is infringing your rights.
- Accept that others have the right to ask you for help but that you can choose to give it or not according to your needs, not theirs.
- If you anticipate a particularly tough negotiation, visualize it going your way. Role-play the conversation that you want to have and make sure that things go as you want.
- Learn to be persistent in asking for what you want and saying what you are prepared to offer. Repeating yourself (even over and over and over again) can be a useful technique.
- Be prepared to offer or accept compromises that give you what you want, even when (or especially when) they give the other party more too.
- Stay calm. You are sticking to your rights, what need do you have to get angry?

If you have a severe problem in this area take some assertiveness training. It will pay huge dividends. If you have a minor problem then train yourself by reading books about assertiveness.

Personal Development	✪✪✪✪
Leadership	✪✪✪✪
Motivation	✪✪
Coaching	✪✪
Interviewing	✪
Fun	✪

8.5 Exercise: Two-faced management

Preparation None.
Running time Five minutes.
Resources Notepad.
Frequency Once.

This is a one-off exercise, but you are likely to have to undertake the real thing a number of times. It reflects the way that most of us are in positions of influence, rather than true authority (and arguably that's not a bad thing unless you are divine and/or omnipotent). Imagine that there was a new policy in your company that you didn't agree with. Come up with a specific example for the exercise (there may be something already under way in your company). First, spend a couple of minutes planning your upward-pointing campaign. What could you do to encourage your bosses not to go ahead with this action?

Then take a couple of minutes on your local campaign. Assume that the policy has gone through despite your best efforts. How will you sell it to your staff, despite your opposition? Is there anything you can do to shield them from its excesses? Make sure that you don't sell it by distancing yourself from the company – setting up an 'us and them' position is only effective in the short term. Long term it demotivates. Your staff might find it easy to identify with you when you blame 'them' but they won't respect you for it.

This is a difficult one for honest managers. After all, it seems to require you to be two-faced. This is particularly difficult when you consider how important it is to be genuine with your staff if you are to motivate them. The paradox is that in both stages you are doing your best for your staff's motivation, in the first place by trying to stop the unfortunate development occurring and then by helping them to accept the inevitable. It might seem also that it will damage your status with your superiors, but it may actually have a positive effect.

Personal Development	✪✪
Leadership	✪✪✪
Motivation	✪✪✪
Coaching	✪✪
Interviewing	✪
Fun	✪

Unit 9: Reward and recognition

There's a touch of 'what's in it for me' in everyone. Okay, there may be some things we do out of a deeper sense of what's right, but a fair amount of what happens in the working environment is still driven by the urge for reward. As a good manager, though, it's important to remember that reward is not all about money – in fact money is a relatively small part of the overall package with which you can reward an individual for a job well done. In fact one aspect of being rewarded is so valuable (while at the same time, so cheap – the accountants love this one) that it has to be pulled out in its own right. Recognition.

It doesn't matter how much you pay someone for doing a job, if you then take all the credit, he or she will be rightly irritated. Recognition for our successes, whether it's a simple pat on the back or a Nobel prize, can be a very useful adjunct to the more tangible aspects of reward.

Do try out the exercises as you go. Put them off until later and you probably won't ever do them. Read through the techniques. Make notes about how and when you can use them. And make sure you give them a try in the next appropriate forum.

Unit book

There's no obligation to read all, or any, of the unit books, but you will find that they provide excellent support to the course and strengthen your management skills.

Reward and recognition are at the heart of motivational theory. The unit book is on motivation, but it's anything but a piece of dry theory – and may well surprise you. In fact Charles Handy's *The Hungry Spirit* looks at the motivation of us all in a new world where old values have gone, if they ever existed (he wryly points out that even in the era of the 'job for life' few organizations lasted as long as an individual's working lifetime). It's a brilliant book that ought to be enforced reading for anyone who has been on an MBA or manages a company.

You can find more information on our unit books, or buy them, from our support site: www.cul.co.uk/crashcourse.

9.1 Technique: Arrivals

Preparation None.
Running time Five minutes.
Resources None.
Frequency Regular.

There's something very motivating about arriving. If you are always on the road, but never get anywhere, it can be very depressing. All too often work involves projects with long timescales, or even no completion date because it's a task that continues forever.

To introduce a motivating element, make sure that there are regular arrivals for individuals and teams. When considering a project, look for milestones along the way. When considering an endless project, find measures that can give completion for a particular section. How you mark arrivals can vary enormously, depending both on the type of work involved and the people. At one extreme it can be simply ticking a box. At the other it can be an out-and-out party. The important thing is that there are arrivals that the individuals involved recognize as worthwhile.

I've often used the example of electronic commerce firm Entranet, where the managing director tries to make sure that there's an arrival every day. It might be an article about them in a newspaper, or the delivery of a new drinks machine, or the completion of a major project, but there is some arrival. Some people feel that this is too often, and too mechanical. There is a danger that arrival becomes routine, but that needn't be the case if it is handled properly. For many it might be more appropriate to have a couple of arrivals a week, but this does not in any way invalidate the daily arrival as a worthy model.

Bear in mind, by the way, that arrivals are diluted by distance, which is why they are not particularly effective at a large group level. But made personal or relevant to a team that the individual associates strongly with, they can be a great, low effort motivator.

Try starting with one a week – everyone ought to be able to manage this level.

Personal Development	✪
Leadership	✪✪✪
Motivation	✪✪✪✪
Coaching	✪✪✪✪
Interviewing	✪
Fun	✪✪✪

9.2 Technique: Reward

Preparation None.
Running time An hour or two.
Resources Rewards.
Frequency As required.

Although, arguably, reward could refer to any positive gain in response to a task that has been carried out, it has long had the association of money, and for the purposes of this technique we will consider it only to refer to tangible reward, with recognition, which is often cheaper and more effective, handled separately.

The first and most obvious reward that you offer is the pay packet. How much do you pay your people in relation to the average for your sector? We are a firm believer in the adage, 'Pay peanuts, get monkeys.' In general, if you show that you value people by paying a reasonable wage then they appreciate it. Naturally this is not enough on its own and you'll need to do a whole range of other things in this book to reap real rewards. This need not mean that you are at the top of the tree for pay. Make sure that you are being fair and then motivate using something other than money.

The next elements of reward are those payments that happen, contractually, for extra time or unsociable hours; overtime payments, shift payments and the like. In recent years there has been a trend in some industries to reduce or remove these payments and yet still push people to work overtime. Naturally this causes resentment and that is not a good basis from which to lead. Again, fairness would be the watchword here.

Finally, reward could include money that you pay for anything else that your staff do. Payment for good ideas, for instance. However, it often seems the case that these are situations where recognition is a far, far better tool.

Personal Development	✪
Leadership	✪✪✪
Motivation	✪✪✪
Coaching	✪✪
Interviewing	✪
Fun	✪✪

9.3 Technique: Recognition

Preparation None.
Running time One minute.
Resources None.
Frequency Regular.

One-to-one recognition is something that can be given with little or no notice. A simple comment can have a totally disproportionate effect on motivation. It's hard to believe, but extra cash in the pocket doesn't motivate as much as genuine recognition.

When a particularly good job has been done, try to arrange for casual recognition from someone important in the company. Certificates and awards are very nice, but they don't have the same impact as personal contact outside of a formal environment.

It's important that the person giving the recognition is respected by the recipient. If a technical expert is complimented on technical ability by someone he or she believes has no technical knowledge, the result may well be ineffective. The response is coloured by the thought 'but what does he (or she) know?' Respect multiplies up the value of recognition, so you need to know enough about the person being recognized to have a fair idea of whom he or she would respect.

If handled well, you can get extra benefit from a 'chance' meeting with a senior person in the company. If, say, a director comes up to the person to be recognized in the corridor and says 'great job, Phil', there's the added benefit of literal recognition. The individual is extra-motivated by knowing that a director knows him (assuming he is called Phil!). This technique has to be used with care – the senior person needs to be good at appearing to know (or even better, actually knowing) staff before they are let loose.

Feel free to attempt recognition with larger groups, but bear in mind that recognition has a weaker but still valuable effect as the numbers involved get larger and larger. The more personal, the better.

Personal Development	○
Leadership	○○○
Motivation	○○○○
Coaching	○○○
Interviewing	○
Fun	○○○

9.4 Exercise/Technique: Somewhere to go

Preparation None.
Running time 10 minutes.
Resources None.
Frequency Occasional.

We are all driven by the desire to get somewhere. The destination differs wildly from person to person, and often is not clear, but the need is there. If you want someone to be motivated in their job, they need to feel that they have somewhere to go – that they aren't in a dead-end job.

Actually getting advancement is, of course, an effective source of motivation, but most long-term value comes from the feeling that there is somewhere to go, and there is a realistic opportunity of getting there. After all, job changes will rarely happen more than once every few years, but opportunities to use the motivational power of possible future advancement occur every day.

Take a few minutes to look at the possibilities for advancement with someone you'd like to motivate. It's important to be realistic about timescales and not to raise false hopes in this process. If you find that there aren't enough prospects within a timescale that is meaningful for the individual, arrange a second session, before which you can come up with something helpful. If you can't find anything, perhaps this is a hint that you ought to help this person to look for opportunities outside your company. Better that than keep them inside, disillusioned and bitter.

The easy mistake with this technique is to assume that advancement means promotion. Increasingly, with flatter organizations, promotion is less common. Instead advancement can also be seen as taking on new roles – but they should be clear-cut new roles, with new challenges and different prospects.

A useful precursor to looking at advancement possibilities is to have a session with the individual looking at their personal goals. This will give both of you a better picture of the advancement that is most likely to motivate.

Advancement within the company is a personal goal for almost everyone. By making it explicit it becomes a powerful motivator – provided reality makes a reasonable match to expectations.

Personal Development	✪
Leadership	✪✪✪
Motivation	✪✪✪✪
Coaching	✪✪✪✪
Interviewing	✪
Fun	✪✪

9.5 Technique: Small gifts and big sums

Preparation None.
Running time 10 minutes.
Resources Budget.
Frequency Occasional.

Let's spend a few minutes thinking about the value of incentives. While they pall with over-frequent use, generally the thought of an incentive is motivational. In fact, most of the motivation comes from the anticipation, rather than the delivery of the incentive itself.

One clear area where this applies is in lump sum bonuses. I have consulted for a company that seriously felt that bonuses in the region of £100–200 (perhaps 0.2 to 0.3 per cent of annual salary) would be motivational as an annual lump sum bonus. Such a bonus verges on the insulting. If that's the amount of money you want to spend, you'd be much better using an appropriate gift, personally chosen to suit the individual. Yes, it's a real pain for the manager, but it gives it significantly more value. Properly chosen, the gift will seem much more worthwhile than the cash, because it adds a degree of opulence most people wouldn't normally bother with. £200 is not much when you see it as cash alongside an annual salary. But it's a lot for a watch or for dinner and a room at a hotel – the result being a gift that's really appreciated.

Don't fall into the trap of giving gift vouchers or a 'staff reward catalogue' to choose from. These are just a particularly weak form of money. The whole point of giving a gift rather than money is that it is personal and that it allows for more luxury than the individual would choose for themselves.

If you do want to give cash, and have a meaningful impact, a lump sum should be at least a week's salary and typically closer to a month's. Alternatively, you can go for a more substantial gift such as a car or a luxury holiday.

You might not have the control over the budget that would allow large incentives yourself. This doesn't mean that you can't lobby for them. One of the best ways of doing this is to move to a company reward scheme in which a reasonably high proportion of the salary is given as a performance bonus. If you don't have such a scheme (for all staff, not just managers), start lobbying for one.

One way you can provide the potential anticipation of a big incentive within the capability of any budget is to use lottery tickets as quick 'thank-you' motivators. You may need to check with your company to make sure that the legal people don't have any objection to this.

You may not be able to give major incentives all the time, or to many people, but bearing in mind it is the anticipation rather than the delivery of the incentive that improves motivation, the occasional big incentive can be valuable, as long as everyone genuinely has a chance of getting them.

Personal Development	✪
Leadership	✪✪✪
Motivation	✪✪✪✪
Coaching	✪✪
Interviewing	✪
Fun	✪✪✪

Unit 10: Injecting energy

At first sight it might seem that a manager has a low energy job. He or she just sits around and tells everyone what to do. But this misses out on our view of the leadership-oriented manager, whose prime roles are direction setting and supporting the staff in heading off in those directions. Just getting the direction across can involve a lot of energy on the leader's part, while providing support requires a constant flow of energy from the leader to the led – if anything this is a job that can suck you dry, rather than being low in effort. But once again, we never said it was easy.

Do try out the exercises as you go. Put them off until later and you probably won't ever do them. Read through the techniques. Make notes about how and when you can use them. And make sure you give them a try in the next appropriate forum.

Unit book

There's no obligation to read all, or any, of the unit books, but you will find that they provide excellent support to the course and strengthen your management skills.

Many books on motivation are packed with energy, and a good example is Richard Denny's *Motivate to Win*. It's charismatic, personal and fun.

You can find more information on our unit books, or buy them, from our support site: www.cul.co.uk/crashcourse.

Web links

Links to sites with ideas for energy boosters at www.cul.co.uk/crashcourse.

10.1 Exercise/Technique: Energy

Preparation None.
Running time Variable.
Resources Time.
Frequency Daily.

Leaders are like that bunny in the battery commercials. Not cute, pink and fluffy (necessarily) but they just keep on going and going and going and going.

This level of endurance and commitment is part of the inspiration that you will be offering. How can you create this additional energy to make sure that you are there whenever you are needed?

The first thing to do is to make sure that you are physically and mentally fit. You can't be a source of energy for yourself and others if you are half-asleep. This isn't the place to go into health – but all the common-sense things about sleeping, eating the right things and exercising apply.

It's important to be able to energize yourself and others that you are doing what you love. If the work that being a leader in this role entails does not give you a real buzz then you're in the wrong job. If you don't leap out of bed in the morning ready to face the challenges then you're in the wrong job. Mind you, if you don't dash home every evening, eager to get on with your life, then you're also in the wrong job (or possibly the right job but the wrong life).

In an attempt to evaluate what would make this job perfect for you, try thinking of the absolute ideal job for you. It might be real and it might be fictional. List all of the attributes of this job. We mean *all* – cover at least an A4 sheet and ideally more. Now, for each of those attributes, list the equivalents in your own. What needs to change? There's probably something. So, how do you change it? It may mean changing jobs. It probably means changing the shape of the job that you do.

Personal Development	✪✪✪✪
Leadership	✪✪✪
Motivation	✪✪✪
Coaching	✪✪✪
Interviewing	✪✪
Fun	✪✪✪

10.2 Technique: Leading a team over time

Preparation None.
Running time Variable.
Resources A team.
Frequency Daily to weekly.

There are many texts on teamworking or leadership that make you feel that it's like climbing a mountain. You have a peak to ascend but once you have reached the top, that's it, your task is done. Unfortunately, leadership isn't like that. It's more akin to climbing an infinite mountain with no summit. The climb goes on forever and you never reach the top. You cannot ever sit back and say, 'My work here is done.'

Okay, that's not entirely true because there will come a time when you want the challenge of a steeper slope and you choose to hand this one on to someone else. That doesn't mean that you've reached the top, just that the gradient isn't challenging enough.

The main tool that you have for providing motivation and enthusiasm is the vision. That isn't to say that you wave this in front of people and tell them to be enthused. Rather this drives your energy and enthusiasm and that transfers into the business. If you find this waning, stop and ask yourself why. Is the vision no longer inspiring? Is the business no longer a challenge? What more do you want in your life and what do you need to do to get it?

Assuming that you are still inspired by the vision then your leadership task is to move towards it. Having a really tough mission to try for is one step. If you get close to this then change it. Having the ideal mix in your team is another. As your needs change, so should the team. The communication that keeps them focused is key.

Having done that, much of your role is to get out of the way and let them achieve. Keep up the challenge, keep up the support. Continually monitor the temperature. Continually monitor success. But mostly, step back.

Personal Development	✪
Leadership	✪✪✪✪
Motivation	✪✪✪✪
Coaching	✪✪
Interviewing	✪
Fun	✪✪

10.3 Exercise: Being obsessive

Preparation None.
Running time Half an hour.
Resources Pen and paper.
Frequency Once.

In the exercise at the start of this unit we looked at what might be a perfect job. Now we're going to take that a little further and try to get an understanding of what it is that drives you, the ultimate source of your energy.

If it is the bottom line of the business that is all-important to you, then your obsessions will vary according to the current mood and flavour of the business gurus. If it is something deeper than this, you may well find business and leadership success despite the ups and downs of the latest fads.

To identify the source of your passion you need to decide what it is that gets you out of bed and doing something. For some it is the thought of earning money, which will later be spent on something enjoyable. For others it is something much deeper. If you have trouble with this, try applying the vision and goals exercises in Unit 3 to yourself rather than to the business.

Having identified your passions and your principles it is worth taking some time to decide how much they contribute to or detract from the success of your business. If they detract from the business, what could you alter in order to change this? It is possible, for instance, that one of your personal beliefs is to give back to society in the form of charity or direct help. This will detract from the bottom line but, with the correct tax treatment and some use of PR, could actually contribute. It is perfectly OK to have principles and passions that do not contribute as long as you are truly in charge of the business. If not then you need to consider the owners (shareholders?) whose wealth you are using.

The final element of being obsessive is to make every judgement from a position of principle and for everything you do to be driven by your passion.

Personal Development	✪✪✪✪
Leadership	✪✪✪✪
Motivation	✪✪✪
Coaching	✪✪✪
Interviewing	✪
Fun	✪✪

10.4 Technique: Being ubiquitous

Preparation None.
Running time 10 minutes.
Resources Time.
Frequency Regularly.

The very best leaders can be a pain in the neck for their people because they are forever popping up all over the place. They are well informed – in fact they are absurdly well informed. They seem to be driving every major initiative. Mostly they are clearly at the heart of the drive of the business. In short, they get everywhere all of the time.

This is obviously impossible. So, how can you give this impression? In effect what you need to do, bearing in mind that you only have a finite amount of energy, is to distribute it where it will have the most leverage.

You need to plan very carefully where you go and what you do when you are there. It is relatively easy to be ubiquitous in a small company. In a large one you must make sure that you spread yourself evenly and thinly.

Take out your schedule for the next two months and look at how your time is spent relative to the geography of your people. If you are spending a significant proportion of your time in one place, this should be because the significant majority of your people are there. If this is not true then work to balance where and when you carry out business in order to even it up.

The next thing to ensure is that you are seen. When you travel to other locations it is useless to lock yourself away in an office. Walk the shop floor and meet people. Shorten the formal meetings and hold more informal ones.

Finally you need to ensure that you are absurdly well informed about the goings on in the company. Think through how you could establish a series of listening posts that will get you this information. Once you have them, think through how you will bring your information into informal conversations. It is important not only to be everywhere and know everything but to be seen to be everywhere and to know everything.

Personal Development	✪
Leadership	✪✪✪✪
Motivation	✪✪✪
Coaching	✪✪✪
Interviewing	✪
Fun	✪✪

10.5 Technique: Warm-ups

Preparation None.
Running time Five minutes.
Resources None.
Frequency Occasional.

A warm-up technique can be invaluable for injecting energy into a group. This is one of many that you will find in the literature. (See *Instant Teamwork* by Brian Clegg and Paul Birch in our recommended books, for instance.)

Get the entire group standing up. If you are performing this exercise as a delaying tactic (eg to keep motivation up while an auditorium is prepared), explain that there has been a delay, so you are going to warm them up first. Ask them to get together in teams whose surnames start with the same letter (with a smaller group, make this surnames A to C etc as appropriate – you will need to prepare this ahead of time). If they haven't achieved this after two minutes, stop them anyway. Now get them teamed up with people who drive the same make of car. After a minute or so, stop them again. Finally, ask them to join people with the same colour of underwear.

Allow more time for the first session, because it becomes easier with practice. Initially there will be some tentative asking around, until someone takes the initiative and stands on a table, shouting their selection at the top of their voice. An excellent aspect of this exercise is that the bigger the numbers are, the better. We have used it with several hundred people to great effect.

You can use almost anything to group people, though ideally it should have relatively few options (age, for instance, is too broad). Colour of underwear is a great finisher, because it has a slight frisson of naughtiness, leaving the participants on an energetic high. Don't be tempted to replace it with something tamer, whatever the audience.

The principal purpose of a technique like this is to inject energy into a group, but it can also be used to keep motivation up if, for example, an event is late starting and the attendees aren't to become irritated.

Personal Development	✪
Leadership	✪✪✪
Motivation	✪✪✪✪
Coaching	✪✪✪
Interviewing	✪
Fun	✪✪✪✪

Unit 11: Embracing change

There's one thing that divides management and leadership time after time. Management is about more of the same. Leadership is about change. This arises from two different aspects of change. Leadership implies heading off in a new direction, and hence requiring change. But there is also the requirement to help out individuals who have difficulty with change in general, or the specific changes that are required to achieve your goals. Here we see the leader as a shepherd, assisting the sheep to keep up with change – perhaps even to enjoy it.

Do try out the exercises as you go. Put them off until later and you probably won't ever do them. Read through the techniques. Make notes about how and when you can use them. And make sure you give them a try in the next appropriate forum.

Unit books

There's no obligation to read all, or any, of the unit books, but you will find that they provide excellent support to the course and strengthen your management skills.

One of the best ways to understand how to do something well is to learn from doing it badly, and the first of this unit's books is a delightful catalogue of disaster, including the mishandling of change, choreographed skilfully by engineer turned cartoonist Scott Adams, in his take-off of blockbuster management texts, *The Dilbert Principle*.

A much more serious lesson from the mismanagement of change is found in Paul Carroll's excellent biography of a business, *Big Blues: The Unmaking of IBM*. As it happens, the mighty computer company that Carroll covers did manage to bounce back to some degree (though never to be what it once was), but that doesn't detract from the lessons it provided in its disastrous initial response to a changing world.

You can find more information on our unit books, or buy them, from our support site: www.cul.co.uk/crashcourse.

Web links

Links to sites with more on coping with change can be found at www.cul.co.uk/crashcourse.

11.1 Technique: Creating change

Preparation Reading on creativity and change.
Running time Half an hour to a day.
Resources Information sources.
Frequency Regularly.

Much of what we've been talking about has involved change happening in your organization. To be sure, much has also involved changes in you, but those are your problem: we'll look at the organizational change here.

Change is an odd thing. There are sayings around like, 'The only person who welcomes change is a wet baby' and yet anyone who lives without it feels as though they are stagnating. There is a general feeling of fear around change. It often feels as though we have lost something and yet it takes time to realize what we have gained.

The shape of the business world means that change is inevitable. It always has been but the periods between changes are becoming shorter and shorter until it seems a continuous process. As leader you have two jobs in this process. First, designing the shape of the changes and second, making them happen.

To design the shape of the changes you will need to become creative. Don't worry: this is far easier than you might imagine. The sister course to this, *Crash Course in Creativity* (Brian Clegg and Paul Birch), is designed to give you exactly the skills you need to be able to manage creatively with change. The techniques available to help with creative idea generation and problem solving are easily learned and implemented.

Making change happen is tougher. The reason for the change will be obvious to you. It will be far more obvious to others why they should not. Convincing people to change has two elements: showing them the negatives of where they are and showing them the positives of where they could be. Okay, so there's more than just showing them. They will cling like limpets to what they know and will avoid what they don't. You have to be pretty damned convincing.

Once you have started the process of change, monitor it and ensure that it moves continually forward. Given half a chance inertia will creep in and the change will halt.

Finally, given the nature of change we described earlier, you will need to be starting the next one before this one is even under way.

Personal Development	✪
Leadership	✪✪✪✪
Motivation	✪✪
Coaching	✪✪
Interviewing	✪✪
Fun	✪✪

11.2 Technique: Change control

Preparation None.
Running time 15 minutes.
Resources None.
Frequency Occasional.

Having considered the basics of making change happen, you may also have to act to overcome the impact of change on staff. Change is an immensely powerful force, which can motivate or demotivate. It is one of the most common causes of demotivation. When, for example, the banking industry in the UK went through a major change in the 1990s, most branch staff were significantly demotivated. Grouping the branches under a central customer service office cut down on direct customer contact. The pressure to sell insurance turned them into salespeople. But it wasn't what they had joined the bank to do. Three factors caused the demotivation, all of which need to be considered in change. The staff blamed the fresh young managers, because they had no experience of working in a branch. They blamed the move away from customer contact, and they blamed the move to selling, both of which damaged their relationship with customers that might have gone back 20 or 30 years.

If the banks had given more thought to motivation, they would have spotted this coming. Where there is a major change, perform a back-of-an-envelope risk assessment. Will it mean a change in management structure? How will you assure that new managers understand the grassroots business? It can help a lot to give them practical experience at the coalface before expecting them to command. Think particularly about the human impact, which is where most demotivation comes from. Bank employees really resented having the relationship with customers taken away from them.

It's impossible to foresee every risk, but a quick session before embarking on a project can be well rewarded. You aren't going to cushion your staff entirely from all change – and some of them will enjoy it. But by reducing the negative impact a lot can be done.

Try to catch the risks before they happen, but if you have to act in retrospect, be generous with accepting fault and being seen to make a difference.

Personal Development	✪
Leadership	✪✪✪
Motivation	✪✪✪✪
Coaching	✪✪
Interviewing	✪
Fun	✪✪

11.3 Technique: Change as motivator

Preparation Background information.
Running time 30 minutes.
Resources Team meeting.
Frequency Occasional.

Change, we have seen, is often a demotivating factor. We all find comfort in 'the way things have always been' and tradition. Change undermines the status quo and makes us feel uncomfortable. Yet without change there is inertia and boredom – and like it or not, change is here to stay, and ever accelerating.

It is possible to use change as a positive agent for motivation. Often the gut reaction of staff to change is to try to counter it – to say how it has been tried before, or it will never work, or they didn't join the company to do this sort of thing. Turn the situation around. Explain the need for change, then consult them as experts in what to change and how to make it work. Don't make the possibility of it not working an option – look for ways to make things succeed.

Initially you will get the knee-jerk responses, asserting that the change won't work. Some people will never come round to change but by squashing any negatives at this stage you will have a good chance of carrying most of the staff with you. Next you will probably be given the solution of throwing a lot of cash/people/resources at the problem. As new governments soon discover, this is rarely an acceptable long-term measure. Point out the implications of huge spending and help the staff to move towards solutions that fit within the financial (and other) constraints you may have. Now you should begin to get some effective suggestions. Even if you don't, the simple process of being consulted and taken seriously will help motivation.

This approach turns change into a motivational factor, a rather handy development given the certainty of change in the business environment. Try this approach of turning the factor on its head and getting staff to make it work with other demotivators.

Personal Development	✪
Leadership	✪✪✪
Motivation	✪✪✪✪
Coaching	✪✪✪
Interviewing	✪
Fun	✪✪

11.4 Exercise/Technique: Motivational marketing

Preparation None.
Running time 10 minutes.
Resources Ability to produce posters etc.
Frequency Occasional.

All a company's marketing, from direct advertising to subtle PR, is intended to motivate. Given the apparent power of marketing, it seems reasonable that it should be turned on internal motivation and coping with change. If you need to support a major change, taking a marketing approach is highly beneficial. You will usually need to involve professionals – the 10-minute running time on this activity is only to consider the option. You won't motivate with an amateurish poster or poorly written messages.

Motivational marketing should be used infrequently, and ought to be regarded as a last resort. However fun it might be, marketing emphasizes the distance there is between you and those being motivated.

As an exercise, think through the changes that might be happening in your business in the next year. Highlight those where some motivational marketing might be valuable, and outline the principal negative reactions you may have to work against.

This approach needs careful handling. One person's motivational slogan can be another's joke. Take a couple of specific examples. A large company, aiming to produce a warm glow in its staff, produced a glossy poster with the slogan 'What was the highest mountain before they discovered Everest?' This was supposed to show how easy it is to jump to the wrong conclusion – the 'correct' answer being 'Everest'. The trouble is, all it ever did for me was to suggest that the true correct answer was 'the highest known mountain of the time' – because perception is more important than absolute reality in such circumstances.

Another example was a department with a bad image, which tried to improve motivation using arty posters carrying slogans like 'I'm improving customer service'. This resulted in a series of pirate posters with negative slogans like 'I'm going downhill fast' accompanying the picture of a skier. Poster campaigns reinforce a message, but don't turn things around – in fact in isolation they are a negative force. Also, when money is tight they can be seen as a waste of money.

Personal Development	✪
Leadership	✪
Motivation	✪✪✪
Coaching	✪
Interviewing	✪
Fun	✪✪

11.5 Exercise/Technique: The hardest cut

Preparation Staff interviews.
Running time 10 minutes.
Resources Notepad.
Frequency Occasional.

This toughie faces everyone who totally changes the direction of a group. You might be a new manager, or there might be a major switch in strategy. If this isn't your circumstance now, try the exercise anyway, but use a major hypothetical change. The exercise involves thinking through what you would do – the reality takes much longer.

When you have got to know the staff, and the staff understand the changes they are facing, talk to them individually. Make sure they appreciate the need for change, and how it will affect them. As a result of these interviews, and picking up general talk in the group, you may find, especially in a long-established group, that some individuals simply won't buy in.

The caring manager's view is that with lots of attention, these people will come round. Unfortunately, experience shows this isn't the case. Some (hopefully only a few) people will continue to undermine the new direction, demotivating everyone around them. This is an example where the leader's view is harsher than the manager's. The manager, seeing people as interchangeable components, says, 'I can make them work that way.' The leader, recognizing real differences between people, says, 'I've given them every chance, but they are sabotaging the change.' And the leader gets rid of them.

This sounds brutal. It doesn't have to be. A properly managed career session will help the individual in a new direction, and they should be given every support, but they must not be allowed to remain and destroy motivation. Don't let this process drag on either. If they are still there after six months, you have failed.

We have both managed changes of this sort several times. Each time this part of the exercise has been most painful – but has proved necessary. This is nothing less than essential surgery, yet most of us don't learn this until we've made the mistake of trying to manage without it. Apart from this aspect, being an agent of change can be very exciting.

Personal Development	✪
Leadership	✪✪✪✪
Motivation	✪✪✪
Coaching	✪
Interviewing	✪
Fun	✪

Unit 12: Beating the system

Systems are wonderful things, but they take on a life of their own. When you manage people effectively you sometimes will find that you bump up against the system. Often it will be that a process designed for a very sensible reason simply doesn't apply in a particular case. Or, all too often, you will find that a system has grown from being something that makes things happen to something that is self-justifying and has no benefits.

We are not suggesting that you should abandon systems, nor that you should break every rule going just for the sake of it. However, the leader will always exhibit a degree of pragmatism. You should be prepared to challenge rules and systems and ask 'why?' If there's a sensible answer, then comply. If there isn't, perhaps it's time to ignore or dismantle the system.

This is potentially a high-risk strategy. Some organizations can't cope with individuals they regard as 'mavericks'. Where this is the case, the organization itself is a system in need of change – but bear in mind that a system under threat can become defensive and expel you.

Do try out the exercises as you go. Put them off until later and you probably won't ever do them. Read through the techniques. Make notes about how and when you can use them. And make sure you give them a try in the next appropriate forum.

Unit book

There's no obligation to read all, or any, of the unit books, but you will find that they provide excellent support to the course and strengthen your management skills.

Few management gurus have excelled more at pushing the message of beating the system than Tom Peters. At one time Peters was a disciple of the system, but he broke away and the individualism of his later books is much more one that's appropriate to modern management. Probably the best balance comes across in *The Tom Peters Seminar*, subtitled *Crazy Times Call for Crazy Organizations*.

You can find more information on our unit books, or buy them, from our support site: www.cul.co.uk/crashcourse.

12.1 Technique: Destroying the system from the inside

Preparation None.
Running time An hour or two.
Resources Access to your organization's systems and processes.
Frequency Annually.

You are responsible for the bureaucracy and the inefficiencies in the area you lead. It's no use bleating on about the demands of the parent company or the needs of the wider organization. If there is something going on that doesn't add directly to the achievement of your vision then it is getting in the way and it is your fault.

The title of this section is deliberately provocative. We have long held the view that part of the role of a leader is to encourage an underground movement that will question the leadership and be a real thorn in their side. It sounds perverse to suggest that you should have a hand in creating problems for yourself, but this is one of the few ways that you will generate real questions. Real questions, from people who share your vision but not necessarily your ways of going about them, are the ones most worth hearing. So, one way of destroying the system is allowing or encouraging the creation of a dissenting voice.

Another way is to hold a high-profile event aimed at identifying and removing wasted activities. If you add up the minutes taken to generate the product or service you offer and then the minutes available from your total workforce you will find a huge discrepancy – often twice or three times the time available to time needed, and sometimes far more. All of this difference happens because of systemic inefficiencies. Some of these are unavoidable (or would cost more to remove than they are worth). Many of them can and should be expunged.

Having done these you need some way of every employee being able to question wasted time. Ultimately, the ideal would be a culture that said, if you don't think it adds to the vision don't do it. This would put the onus on you to explain those things that do add but not obviously.

Personal Development	✪✪
Leadership	✪✪✪✪
Motivation	✪✪✪✪
Coaching	✪✪
Interviewing	✪
Fun	✪✪✪

12.2 Exercise/Technique: Bureaucracy and how to develop it

Preparation Collect a week's in-tray and example customer communications.
Running time An hour or two.
Resources None.
Frequency Annually.

Bureaucracy is a dirty word in most businesses, usually with good reason. Bureaucracy can be a real plus for your business if it is handled right and if it is treated with a high degree of caution.

In order to complete this exercise and the next, you will need to save a week's worth of the mail that travels through your in-tray. In our electronic world you will also need to file all incoming e-mails temporarily in a particular folder. This could be the originals or could be copies. You will also need to collect together as many samples as you can of the bureaucracy that you send to your customers.

Having collected this material, go through it item by item and identify any input that is required from you in association with this item. What is the information that you are being asked for? What action are you being asked to take? When you are asked for this, are there more efficient ways (for you) of providing it than the one being requested?

Now look through the information you are asking for from your customers. Ask yourself the same questions. How could you make their lives easier?

As a case in point, you might want to look at the various bookstores on the Internet. They don't use paper but still need the bureaucracy. They all need to ask you for a certain amount of information but some will ask this every time you make an order. Others will store this information and allow you to insert it automatically using a password. The most advanced, and the one that each of us uses most often, assumes that you are the only person to use your PC and allows you to buy with a single click. The item is charged to your usual card and sent to your usual address. It makes buying from them worryingly easy!

Personal Development	✪
Leadership	✪✪✪
Motivation	✪✪✪
Coaching	✪
Interviewing	✪
Fun	✪✪

12.3 Exercise/Technique: Bureaucracy and how to kill it

Preparation Exercises 12.1 and 12.2.
Running time An hour or two.
Resources None.
Frequency Annually.

There are times when bureaucracy exists only for the benefit of the bureaucrats who generate it. This sort should be killed as soon as possible. Any leader worthy of the title will spend time rooting out the career bureaucrats from within their organization in order to minimize future paper generation.

Even before you root them out you should get rid of their paperwork. After conducting the previous exercise, ask yourself what would be the effect on you of doing nothing with this form or paper. What would you lose as a result?

If you can see no benefit to it then send it back to the originator with a request to justify your return of the information. What is in it for you?

If you can see benefit to providing a subset of the information then do so and ask the person generating it what is the benefit to you of providing the rest.

Obviously, for internally generated bureaucracy the question needs to ask for the benefit to you and to the business as a whole.

For those pieces of bureaucracy that are information providers rather than requesters, ask yourself what benefit you gain from the information – all of it, item by item. If none then send it back and explain that you don't want it any more. If it is internally generated then send it back with a request to justify why it is produced and what it adds to the bottom line. From experience of running departments that are responsible for providing information within a large organization, it seems best to stop the production of all regular reports and only to reinstate them for those who complain. Every time we know this has been done it was surprising for all involved how many of them were never missed by their recipients.

This exercise is labelled 'annually' because you will find that bureaucracy is like an invasive weed – it always grows back.

Personal Development	✪
Leadership	✪✪✪
Motivation	✪✪✪✪
Coaching	✪
Interviewing	✪
Fun	✪✪✪

12.4 Exercise/Technique: Making it sane

Preparation None.
Running time 10 minutes.
Resources None.
Frequency Occasional.

The previous exercises have very much dealt with bureaucracy on your own level – now it's time to take the fight to your team. Fix up two diary sessions now – one with the team that works for you, the other with your peers. This should be a deliberately short session – half an hour at most. Ask everyone to come along with their top two examples of bureaucracy that wastes time but seems not to achieve anything. Get them up on a board, pick out the most irritating collective examples and develop some solutions.

Someone (not necessarily you) should be tasked with attempting to get the solution in place and reporting back at an agreed timescale.

Simply recognizing the existence of bureaucracy and attacking it helps, but getting something changed has the most positive benefit. In some circumstances the apparent bureaucracy will have a sensible and unavoidable reason behind it (for example a legal safety requirement). If so, the outcome should be to make sure everyone understands just why it is really necessary. Other examples will be capable of simple reform. But don't ignore the class of problem that it isn't possible to change in the short term (or from your position) but which can simply be avoided by cheating. There's nothing wrong with going round the bureaucracy to get something done, provided it really is bureaucracy.

This is a great target, as beating a piece of bureaucracy both helps improve motivation and has a positive effect on the running of the company.

Personal Development	✪
Leadership	✪✪✪
Motivation	✪✪✪✪
Coaching	✪
Interviewing	✪
Fun	✪✪✪

12.5 Technique: Doing yourself out of a job

Preparation None.
Running time An hour or two for the initial exercise.
Resources Pen and paper.
Frequency Every few years.

This is a very special case of beating the system. It stems from our personal belief that the most successful people in large organizations are those that strive continually to do themselves out of a job. If you don't subscribe to this notion, it will seem counter-intuitive. How can you be successful if you are unemployed? In reality those that are successful in doing themselves out of a job are almost always kept by their company because they are seen as successful and most smart companies want to hang on to the successful.

If your company isn't this smart then do you really want to work with them? We should point out at this stage that this approach has always worked for us but that we accept no liability for any loss of income or employment caused by following our advice.

Break your job down into sub-tasks. Which ones do you feel that others are able to do immediately? Which ones do you feel that others could do with some development? Are there any tasks you do that no one else can do? If so then you are in a very dangerous position. Yes, you are secure in your present role but you can never change role or move on because you can't hand this task over to anyone. Now is the time to start planning ways to do this.

Assuming that there are no tasks that cannot be done by someone else then you need to draw up a plan to hand over everything you do to someone else. An alternative is that you talk this over with your boss and point out how you could save them some cost – yours.

Personal Development	✪✪✪✪
Leadership	✪✪✪
Motivation	✪✪
Coaching	✪✪
Interviewing	✪
Fun	✪✪

Unit 13:
Messages – more communicating

We have already stressed the significance of communication to the management task – now we need to come back to it because there was so much to cover that it can't be fitted into a single unit. As Captain Kirk used to say, open a comms channel…

Do try out the exercises as you go. Put them off until later and you probably won't ever do them. Read through the techniques. Make notes about how and when you can use them. And make sure you give them a try in the next appropriate forum.

Unit books

There's no obligation to read all, or any, of the unit books, but you will find that they provide excellent support to the course and strengthen your management skills.

This unit's books look beyond the usual components of communication to those that are most powerful but least noticed. Non-verbal communication is immensely powerful (try saying 'I agree with you' while shaking your head to prove this – the non-verbal will take priority). In *Body Language*, Alan Pease gives a valuable lesson on how we go beyond words in getting the message across.

If you would like to put non-verbal communication into its wider context, try Desmond Morris's classic *Manwatching*. This coffee-table book looks visually dated now (itself an interesting observation on non-verbal communication) but it's great for putting human interaction in its place without being over-technical.

You can find more information on our unit books, or buy them, from our support site: www.cul.co.uk/crashcourse.

13.1 Exercise/Technique: E-motivation

Preparation None.
Running time Five minutes.
Resources E-mail.
Frequency Regular.

Making sure that people get the right message is an essential part of management. E-mail may be one of the newest means of communication, but it is intensely valuable to the motivating manager. E-mail's principal benefit is immediacy. You can have a message in front of someone halfway round the world in minutes. This means that if you want to give someone a quick thank-you, you can do it almost instantly – and the motivating power of a thank-you is greatly enhanced by timeliness.

E-mail is also a very rich means of communication. In all but the most steam-driven e-mail technology you can include pictures, attach documents and send a very sophisticated message to many people at once, which will help increase the chances of getting your message across and not leave anyone in demotivating ignorance. Try to make your e-mails personal, though: this always gives them extra impact.

As a quick exercise, find at least two people to send a 'thank-you' e-mail to right now. If no one is obvious, flick through your contact list for people who have done something for you recently, or you feel have not had enough contact from you recently.

Beware the negative aspects of e-mail, though. E-mails are so quick to send that you can have one on the way before you've really thought about the content. Always read through your e-mails before sending them.

The ease of sending e-mails to many people at once can itself generate a problem. No one likes being flooded with junk mail. Don't copy people in to a document just on the off-chance that it will be useful – but make it very easy for anyone appropriate to receive a copy. One way to avoid this overkill is to make receipt of the messages active rather than passive. Put them onto a bulletin board, or use an e-mail list manager where potential recipients can choose to receive mail (or not) on a subject and can browse through an archive of earlier mail.

Good use of e-mail is a powerful tool in enhancing communication and hence motivation. Of course you still need good content to go along with the enhancements.

Personal Development	✪✪
Leadership	✪✪✪
Motivation	✪✪✪✪
Coaching	✪
Interviewing	✪
Fun	✪✪

13.2 Exercise: The genuine article

Preparation Produce scenarios.
Running time 10 minutes.
Resources Sounding board.
Frequency Twice.

Communications is a key factor in motivational management. How well you communicate will often determine how well you can motivate. The most powerful means of communication for these purposes is direct, face-to-face. Unfortunately, it is difficult to judge how good you are at this.

Produce a few short scenarios of motivational communication. Try one where you congratulate someone on an excellent piece of work, one where you go through a mistake someone has made, one where you discuss life goals (what someone really wants to do) and one where you welcome a group of people to a company event. Find a sounding board – someone to listen and note how you come across. They should check how genuine you seem, your body language (don't fold your arms, for example), your eye contact, your tone of voice (watch out for dropping your tone at the end of a sentence) and the way you speak – anything that can alter motivation.

After the session get some feedback. Look for areas to improve. Put together an action plan – and book your sounding board for a review.

There's an old (if not very good) joke along the lines of 'when you can fake being genuine you've got it made'. What you say is important, but the way you say it will have an equal impact. It's not enough to be genuine, you've got to put it across. Many of us, for instance, find it difficult to praise and resort to a joking delivery and reduced eye contact. Praise that sounds as if you don't mean it is totally wasted.

Getting honest but constructive feedback on how you come across is very valuable. Without it, it's almost impossible to be sure what your messages really say.

As a variation, you could try videoing this exercise. Almost everyone cringes at the sight of themselves on video – go beyond the personal embarrassment to the specifics of your performance.

Personal Development	✪✪✪✪
Leadership	✪✪✪
Motivation	✪✪✪
Coaching	✪✪✪
Interviewing	✪✪✪
Fun	✪✪

13.3 Technique: Giving feedback

Preparation None.
Running time Half an hour to prepare, as long as it takes to do.
Resources Person being coached.
Frequency Regularly.

Feedback is a type of communication that the good manager is often involved in giving – and one of the hardest forms to carry out well. It is particularly relevant to the coaching aspects of a manager's job.

Feedback should never be a surprise. In the coaching relationship feedback is a way of life. It is happening all the time and is two-way. Feedback can take the form of a casual observation, a thought-through, longer discussion or a formal session. It is always done from a position of trust and even love. It is never an opportunity to dump on the coachee. The bottom line is that it is happening all the time.

Part of the feedback process is signalling areas of concern soon enough that when they become issues neither you nor the coachee is surprised. When they form part of the discussion the attitude will be that this was expected.

To prepare yourself for giving feedback, sit down and list those areas that you feel need to be discussed. Decide for each of them how big they are. For the smaller ones make a decision to talk about them informally sometime. For the larger ones schedule some time with the coachee to discuss them explicitly. From now on this needs to be the way that you are working. Any issue that you become aware of needs to be raised. As you become aware of it, note it down and decide what is the most appropriate form of feedback. Schedule time to make this happen.

When scheduling time, remember that there are two sorts of feedback. There's the stuff we all like where we get praised and there's the stuff that few of us like where we get to hear some of our faults. Do not mix the two. If you give bad feedback followed by good, the recipient gets so mired in the bad that they don't hear the good. If you give good feedback followed by bad, the earlier stuff is discounted as sweetening the pill. As an old saying goes, 'Everything before the "but" is bullshit.'

Personal Development	✪
Leadership	✪✪✪
Motivation	✪✪
Coaching	✪✪✪✪
Interviewing	✪✪
Fun	✪✪

13.4 Exercise: Your body

Preparation None.
Running time 10 minutes.
Resources Mirror, clipboard, large book, pen.
Frequency Once.

Another specialist form of communication you will need to become expert in is the interview. The interview is a two-way process of communication, not a one-way flow from the interviewee to you. All the time as you speak to the interviewee, you are putting across non-verbal messages. It is important that you do so in a controlled way, rather than accidentally.

Get hold of a mirror and get it propped up so that you can see your face and your upper body in it from a comfortable seating position. Get hold of a clipboard, a large book and a pen. Spend a few minutes talking to yourself (as interviewee) in the mirror – bearing this in mind, you need to find a location where you won't be observed. During this pseudo-conversation, try to notice as much as possible what you look like in the mirror. At different points in the conversation, make some notes on the clipboard, look up something in the large book, yawn and grimace.

We all have habitual actions when in conversation, some of which may be giving entirely the wrong message to an interviewee. Be aware of your posture. Just being too slumped can make you seem bored or not interested. Facial expressions that might be designed to suppress a yawn or deal with an itchy nose can seem dismissive. And too much time looking away from the candidate – whether at your notes or other documents, or even at the ceiling or out of a window – can again signal a lack of interest. It may be your tenth interview of the day, but it's the candidate's first and only chance. Don't let the way you look and the messages your body gives put them off. Instead make sure you give good encouraging signs – frequent (but not staring) eye contact, smiles, nods, leaning forward a little in your seat. Make sure also that you look relaxed. Don't cross your arms across your body – open up to the candidate.

Giving the right non-verbal communication is very important, as anyone can be put off by negative signals.

As a variation, you could conduct the exercise with a stooge instead of a mirror. Get feedback on how he or she felt.

Personal Development	✪✪✪✪
Leadership	✪✪✪
Motivation	✪✪✪
Coaching	✪✪✪
Interviewing	✪✪✪✪
Fun	✪✪

13.5 Exercise: Non-verbal replies

Preparation None.
Running time 20 minutes.
Resources TV.
Frequency Once.

The previous exercise concentrated on the non-verbal messages you were giving out. Be very aware also of the non-verbal communication from others. If you stick to words alone, you are ignoring a large part of the information being communicated to you (this is one of the reasons that face-to-face meetings are often so much better than telephone calls).

Over the next week, when watching TV, look out for interviews. Watch the interviewee's body language. What message is coming across from his or her posture, facial expression and non-verbal sounds? Make quick notes on four or five different interviewees.

Some basics to look out for. How does the person sit? Are they slumped (low energy) or upright? Are they leaning forward (showing interest) or leaning back (detached)? How do they use their hands (watch out for cultural variances here)? Is their facial expression at odds with what is being said? Is there good eye contact, keeping in touch with the other person much of the time, but dropping away regularly so that it does not become a stare? Does the interviewee seem evasive or wary? How can you tell? Are there sympathetic responses? Is the interviewee reflecting the interviewer's posture? Is the interviewee smiling and nodding acceptance? Does the interviewee use regular non-verbal sounds to put across agreement and understanding?

One thing to be aware of here – non-verbal communication is an important part of your conversation, and is particularly useful when formally interviewing, but don't regard it as some sort of visual lie detector. Most candidates for professional roles will be familiar with the basics of body language, and will make a conscious effort to look convincing. It isn't always easy to force a particular non-verbal message, but it is often possible. Even so, this is a major part of the communication process, and it is certainly harder to fake the whole spectrum of non-verbal communication than it is to lie verbally.

To miss out on the wide bandwidth of non-verbal communication would be a great shame. Make sure you find out a little more about it.

Personal Development	✪✪✪
Leadership	✪✪✪
Motivation	✪✪
Coaching	✪✪
Interviewing	✪✪✪✪
Fun	✪✪

Unit 14: Delegation and trust

A lesson that some managers find very hard is accepting that you can't do everything yourself. This is a particularly difficult problem if you are an entrepreneur who has built up a business from nothing – it's awfully hard to let go. Yet the more your responsibilities grow, the less able you will be to take them all on effectively.

Our difficulties with delegation are usually centred on trust. If we believe that someone else can be trusted to undertake a task and trust them not to make a mess of it (and perhaps not to do us out of a job) then there's no reason at all not to delegate. A leader has to be able to turn his or her back on 'the troops' and trust them to get on without delivering a virtual knife between the ribs. And one thing is certain about trust – if you don't trust people, they certainly will prove they aren't worthy of it.

Do try out the exercises as you go. Put them off until later and you probably won't ever do them. Read through the techniques. Make notes about how and when you can use them. And make sure you give them a try in the next appropriate forum.

Unit book

There's no obligation to read all, or any, of the unit books, but you will find that they provide excellent support to the course and strengthen your management skills.

When giving seminars, one of us regularly comments 'If you only ever buy one management book, the one I'd recommend is *Maverick!* by Ricardo Semler.' This amazing story of the transformation of a Brazilian engineering company shows just how much can be achieved when trust is established (and, by the way, how hard it is for both sides of the management divide to accept trust). By the end, Semler's white-collar staff were setting their own salaries – now that *is* delegation and trust.

You can find more information on our unit books, or buy them, from our support site: www.cul.co.uk/crashcourse.

Web links

Links with information on delegation and trust can be found at www.cul.co.uk/crashcourse.

14.1 Technique: Delegation

Preparation Think about what you do with your days.
Running time From half an hour to a day.
Resources Diary.
Frequency Regularly.

Delegation is your most effective leadership tool. It is the ultimate win–win because it frees up your time and develops the people to whom you delegate. It is also an extremely tough thing to do. Strange that. Most of us would imagine that getting rid of work would be ridiculously easy.

Delegation is about trust. There is an obvious trust question – can the person that you are delegating to actually do the job? There are a number of other trust questions that are less obvious. Can this person do the job as well as I could? Will they show me up by doing better than I can? If they can do it so well, what am I here for?

Delegation is about time. It is not only about saving time by doing it, it is about creating time in order to be able to do it. It takes time to delegate and you are too busy to think about it right now. You intend to though, don't you? Maybe when your retirement party is over, you may make time to think about it. You must stop the merry-go-round now and make time to think this through:

- What do you do with your day?
- Why do you do it? (Stop altogether)
- Why do you do it? (What does it add to customer?)
- Why do you do it? (Give it to someone else)

There will be a large number of activities that you guard jealously and say that others can't do ('They don't have the skills', 'It's too important', 'It's too trivial to bother', 'They are too busy already'). All of these can be delegated. You may need to think harder about how you manage it but they can be delegated. What you keep for yourself is about strategy and inspiration. Those must be done by the leader.

One way of delegating the significant stuff without taking too much risk is to use delegation as a coaching opportunity. Look at the significance of each area and try to find a few significant tasks and a few trivial tasks that you can delegate. The reason I'd suggest this is that delegating all of the significant stuff leaves you with all of the trivia. Now talk to the person to whom you're delegating.

For this to work well you need to be explicit with them about the reasons for doing this and your expectations of them. As with all coaching, very specific targets, ideally within tight time boxes, are essential.

The key difference between coaching and delegation is that the negotiation of the targets is tighter when delegating. If you are coaching someone for personal development and they wish to take a leisurely path then, as their coach, you can question and challenge but the decision is theirs. If you are delegating and the person to whom you are delegating wants to take a leisurely path then the chances are that you can't afford to delegate to them.

Now is the period of monitoring performance against targets and correcting any shortfalls. If the targets are being missed by a long way then you will either have to help in a more active way or take back the task. The bottom line is that this form of delegation is a genuine win–win if it is working but if it is not then the buck stops with you.

Personal Development	✪✪✪
Leadership	✪✪✪✪
Motivation	✪✪✪
Coaching	✪✪✪✪
Interviewing	✪
Fun	✪✪

14.2 Technique: Responsibility

Preparation None.
Running time Five minutes.
Resources None.
Frequency Occasional.

It seems crazy at first, but you can actually increase the motivation of your staff by giving them extra work. Most of us have enough of a craving for power and being seen to have authority that being given clear responsibility for something will act as a motivator.

In the previous exercise we looked at delegation from the point of view of freeing up your time. Now revisit the responsibilities in your gift. They don't have to be major, but rather a good fit to the individual. Could you delegate one or more of those responsibilities to someone who will be motivated by it? Try to hand over responsibility for at least two tasks or areas.

Responsibility has to be handled with care, as it can be a big source of discomfort. Giving someone extra responsibility when they are already overloaded causes highly demotivating stress. Some very capable people actually dislike responsibility. They are happy continuing to be a highly productive part of the team and don't want responsibility imposed on them. This can be hard to understand for most managers, for whom responsibility tends to be a primary driver.

Unfortunately, just asking someone if they really want the responsibility isn't enough either, because there is often a culture that someone who refuses to take on responsibility is a non-effective team member, who should be downgraded. If you are genuinely offering responsibility as a motivator, make sure there's an escape clause with no penalties attached.

Giving someone responsibility can give a wide range of opportunities to expand – from leadership and decision making to risk taking and managing their own time. Provided the responsibility is not accompanied by an excessive burden of stress, it's a great motivator.

Personal Development	✪
Leadership	✪✪✪✪
Motivation	✪✪✪✪
Coaching	✪✪✪
Interviewing	✪
Fun	✪✪

14.3 Technique: Recognized authority

Preparation Consider your authority.
Running time 10 minutes.
Resources Staff.
Frequency Occasional.

This technique appears confusingly similar to the previous one, but is in fact quite separate. The other technique is about increasing an individual's responsibilities – the tasks and work areas they will ensure get completed. Authority is the accepted ability to take decisions and to authorize (or not) action. As such, authority is a special case of responsibility, but it needs to be considered separately.

Although companies are increasingly less authoritarian, to delegate a degree of authority is still one of the most powerful recognitions you can give to a more junior member of staff. It might involve going to a senior decision-making meeting on your behalf. It might involve taking a decision at a technical or business level. In effect, when you delegate authority you are giving others the ability to act on your behalf, as if they were you.

Because delegation of authority implies a high degree of trust, it will have an equally high associated motivation – provided that the individual wants this responsibility and that you genuinely do trust them. If you delegate authority and then constantly look over their shoulder, they will soon lose any motivational value. Beware re-making the decisions for them every time.

The personal benefit of effective delegation of authority is that it stretches elements of a rare resource (you) well beyond their natural limits. From the point of view of those receiving the authority it shows very strong trust and gives a degree of power, both of which can be highly motivational to the right individuals.

Personal Development	✪
Leadership	✪✪✪✪
Motivation	✪✪✪✪
Coaching	✪
Interviewing	✪
Fun	✪✪

14.4 Exercise: Managing George

Preparation None.
Running time Five minutes.
Resources None.
Frequency Once.

Are you frustrated by your manager not doing things or causing problems? If not, skip this one. If you are, you have a responsibility but no authority, always a difficult position.

Don't let it drag on. Put together an action plan for changing your relationship by upward motivation. In effect you are going to be doing some upward delegation and building of trust:

- Are there opportunities to get on a better social footing? It might help relationships, plus you could even get to like him/her.
- Can you openly discuss things? Don't assume you can't have a discussion on the meta-level of 'how we do things round here'.
- Find out what motivates your manager. If he or she has a real dislike of paperwork, but you need to get things signed, make it ridiculously easy to do. If he or she is constantly interfering, find a way of providing the detail without direct involvement.

Why 'Managing George'? One of us was once managed by George (name changed to protect the innocent). I enjoyed being managed by George. But everyone else got extremely frustrated. 'How do you cope?' they would say. It was partly because I liked George – you can cope with a lot when you like someone. And the rest was motivation.

Some of it came from George. He was prepared to give you a task and let you get on with it, making sure you got the reward if it went well. Some came from me. I realized early on that George would only do something if *he* was interested in it. Tell him he had to do something (because the system required it) and he would go out of his way not to do it. Despite being aware of this, I regularly fell into the trap of forgetting motivation and trying to play it by the book – but the failures from this approach were infrequent enough for me to be quite happy being managed by George.

Motivating upwards is never easy, but particularly so with a George. (Don't forget George's demotivators too.) Even so, the benefits are even greater in such a position.

Personal Development	✪✪✪
Leadership	✪✪✪
Motivation	✪✪✪✪
Coaching	✪
Interviewing	✪
Fun	✪✪

14.5 Technique: Backing off

Preparation None.
Running time Less than five minutes.
Resources None.
Frequency Occasionally.

If your management role includes coaching relationships, there often comes a time when you find yourself taking on the role of task-master. You are pushing, cajoling, even bullying the person being coached. This is far from ideal. Your role is to agree a set of targets and then to act as conscience, questioner and guide. You should make sure that the responsibility is passed to the person being coached, rather than kept to yourself.

If you find yourself bullying or cajoling then you need to ask yourself whether it is time to back off. A good quick check for this is the ICE scale. Mark from 1 to 10 the following scales:

I – Ideas – I have ideas that will help me to be more of a coach in this role.
C – Coaching – I am operating in a coaching role.
E – Enjoyment – I am enjoying what I am doing.

A low Coaching score will determine whether or not you need to look at the ideas you may or may not have. Obviously, if you are operating successfully as a coach then you do not necessarily need ideas to improve this. Despite this, if you have some, why not give them a go? A low Enjoyment score (whether you are operating as a coach or not) will indicate that something is wrong with your role. A high Enjoyment score combined with a low Coaching score implies that you are enjoying not being a coach – again, question your role. A low score on all measures indicates that it is time to back off and give yourself and the coachee some space. If you are reluctant to do this you could read through the book and see whether this generates any ideas that will bring your Ideas score higher.

Often you will have dropped into this bullying mode as a result of lack of trust. Coaching is a participative process. It is not about the coach telling. It is not about the coachee doing as they are told. It is about discussion and questioning. For this to work well both parties need to be able to communicate well with one another and need to have trust. The coachee needs to trust that the coach has their best intentions at heart and needs to trust in the coach's ability. The coach needs to trust that the coachee will do as they agree and will be honest about the results.

For the most part trust develops over time. To an extent it can be helped along. At the simplest level is the coachee's trust in your ability as a coach. It is fairly clear that if you continually apologize for your lack of experience or question your own judgement then you will undermine trust. It is useful to keep at the front of your mind that you need not give advice. If you question and play back effectively then you will find that the coachee advises themselves. Using lots of phrases like 'What I hear you say is…' and 'so it seems that you are suggesting that you…' means that you have no need to question your judgement since you are merely acting as a sounding board.

If this sounds like copping out then you are taking too interventionist a view of the coach's role. Very often (though not always) the coach is just a sounding board.

The next level of trust is the personal one. You need to have established ground rules with your coachee about confidentiality and other minefield areas. You then need to stick to them religiously. Even a slight slip in this area is a major betrayal of trust. Guard against it. Beyond this, their level of trust of you will depend upon how trustworthy you seem. There's little that a course like this can do for you if you come across as someone you wouldn't buy a used car from.

Personal Development	✪✪✪
Leadership	✪✪✪
Motivation	✪✪
Coaching	✪✪✪✪
Interviewing	✪
Fun	✪✪

Unit 15: The right person for the right job

Fitting people to jobs and tasks is something that leaders may feel that they don't need to do. If you have been clear enough about what is required, perhaps you should be able to stand back and let everyone else take on the parts that best suit them. And they should then be able to assess how well they've done.

There are two problems with this picture. One is that, though this is probably the ideal, you've got a lot of work to get from the way things are to that, and people will need help along the way. Secondly, even if everyone is genuinely working in this manner, it's easy for some things to slip between the cracks. You will need to be fielding any missed opportunities and helping with assessment, which always benefits from wider input.

Do try out the exercises as you go. Put them off until later and you probably won't ever do them. Read through the techniques. Make notes about how and when you can use them. And make sure you give them a try in the next appropriate forum.

Unit book

There's no obligation to read all, or any, of the unit books, but you will find that they provide excellent support to the course and strengthen your management skills.

One of the most important requirements in getting the right people working effectively is having an understanding of how teams work. Without it, it is difficult to make anything happen. Meredith Belbin practically defined how individuals function in teams in his *Team Roles at Work*. It's not a light read, but an essential part of gaining the knowledge.

You can find more information on our unit books, or buy them, from our support site: www.cul.co.uk/crashcourse.

Web links

Links to information on selection can be found at www.cul.co.uk/crashcourse.

15.1 Technique: 360 degree appraisals

Preparation Finding a suitable 360 degree feedback mechanism.
Running time Varies from minutes to a day or more.
Resources Feedback forms or other mechanism.
Frequency Six-monthly or annually.

360 degree appraisals are an important way of understanding how you are seen compared to how you see yourself. You need to find an appraisal tool that you can use to help you to understand yourself, your strengths and your weaknesses as a leader.

360 degree appraisal is simply asking anyone you work for, some people that you work with, some people that work for you and yourself, what you are good at and what you are not so good at. The methodologies used for doing this vary widely.

There are many instruments on the market that will assist in this. If you work for a large organization, they probably already have one. At the lowest end these will consist of other people listing what you do well and what you do badly. At the highest end these will be packed with pseudo-science and norms and all sorts of spurious statistics. There are a few fundamentals that we feel are important.

Firstly, any 360 degree feedback should be anonymous. This is a big advantage in having it conducted by an outside agency. They can be more convincingly detached than your secretary or your HR/Personnel manager. Secondly, the feedback should be primarily directed at leadership. There are many ways of measuring that are directed at middle management. Much of what you would discover from this would be useless. Thirdly, it should cover a range of attributes. Fourthly, an ideal feedback exercise would be able to take you to the next stage of deciding whether or not you wished to change as a result of the feedback and, if you did, how you would go about doing so.

Bear in mind, finally, that you aren't the only one who can benefit from such an appraisal – it needs managing up and down the chain.

Personal Development	✪✪✪✪
Leadership	✪✪
Motivation	✪
Coaching	✪✪
Interviewing	✪
Fun	✪

15.2 Technique: Appropriate appraisal

Preparation Review past period.
Running time 30 minutes.
Resources Assessment method.
Frequency Occasionally.

If you are frustrated by bureaucracy, you may feel that a formal appraisal system is pure paper pushing. You are probably right – yet unless we regularly assess progress against objectives, measure successes and note room for improvement, it is easy to decide that nothing really matters, inducing a demotivating spiral of doubt. Ideally appraisals should be informal, accurately spotting the moment to check on progress, always catching the staff member doing something right, always discussing ways to improve in a timely way. Sadly, even a manager with the best of intentions is unlikely to deliver on this promise. Reluctantly we have to turn to a formal system. But make sure that it is used properly.

Formal appraisal should be given the highest priority – all too often it is put off because the manager is too busy. Before the appraisal, the manager and staff member should have prepared, pulling together achievements and opportunities for improvement. If the appraisal is driven by a form, don't let the form dictate too much. Be prepared to work round the tick boxes and definitions, as long as the outcome is correct. Oh, and make sure that any outcomes are followed up in the following period.

Appraisal is extremely important, but can be glossed over because the manager has a lot of them to do, or is uncomfortable talking about performance. This is one of those areas where comfort has to be sidelined. However bad the message, make the items the staff member takes away positive. Not failures, but agreed actions for improvement.

Although most companies recognize the essential nature of assessments, few give them enough real importance (as opposed to the appearance of importance). By making them truly important, you can have a very positive effect on motivation.

Personal Development	✪✪
Leadership	✪✪✪✪
Motivation	✪✪
Coaching	✪✪✪
Interviewing	✪
Fun	✪

15.3 Exercise/Technique: Catch them doing it right

Preparation None.
Running time A few days elapsed time.
Resources None.
Frequency Regularly.

A piece of advice both of us have been given separately in the past is 'Catch them doing it right'. Often this seems to fly in the face of most management thinking, which is still far too often about spotting errors and correcting them. Such traditional thinking is more about catching them doing it wrong and putting that right than catching them doing it right.

The advice we were given assumed a number of things: firstly, that people fundamentally want to do a good job; secondly, that they sometimes need help understanding what doing a good job looks like; thirdly, that praise is a far more powerful weapon than criticism. Put these together and you come up with a philosophy that says that if you catch people doing it right and let them know that, they will remember this and will strive even harder next time. Indeed, as a management style this is very akin to coaching. As a coaching style it is almost axiomatic.

So, what are you going to do about this? Here's an exercise that you might want to try that will take a few days but is well worth persevering with. For the next few days (or for the next few days of contact time with your staff), keep a record of the number of times you manage to catch them doing something right and the number of times you manage to catch them doing something wrong. The very nature of the exercise means that you will tend towards catching them doing it right rather than wrong. Whilst you are doing this, notice how your management style changes with each attitude.

At the end of the few days sit down by yourself and think through how well you are able to focus on the positive rather than the negative. Think through how well your staff responded. Think through how you felt about this style. If your feelings were generally positive then you might want to build this into your toolkit as a regular activity.

Personal Development	✪✪✪
Leadership	✪✪✪
Motivation	✪✪✪✪
Coaching	✪✪✪✪
Interviewing	✪
Fun	✪✪✪

15.4 Exercise: What do they look like?

Preparation None.
Running time Ten minutes.
Resources Newspaper.
Frequency Once.

A surprisingly large part of our appraisal of another human being depends on appearances. It is useful to get a handle on this before attempting to appraise others, particularly when meeting them for the first time, such as in a job interview. Go through a newspaper and find half a dozen pictures of individuals with very different modes of dress, hairstyle and so forth. Look at each in turn, imagining that this person has turned up for a middle management interview that you are conducting. What do you feel about the individual? Would you start off favourably or unfavourably inclined towards them? How much do you think their appearance would influence an otherwise average interview?

There is no doubt that physical appearance has a big influence on us. What is important is that you analyse your own reactions, understand them and keep them in balance in a real interview. Beware of any bias as a result of physical attractiveness or unattractiveness to you of the individual. This isn't always a matter of tending to favour a physically attractive candidate; sometimes an interviewer will underrate an attractive candidate in an attempt to seem unbiased. Your reaction to choice of clothing, hairstyles and colouring, body piercing and tattoos should reflect not your own personal inclinations, but the requirements of the job.

To insist that a telephones sales operative dresses in business attire is as bizarre as the way that early radio announcers were required to wear dinner jackets to make a broadcast. However, staff exposed visually to customers (external or internal) will need to have an appropriate dress sense. And it is reasonable to make some assumptions about how seriously the candidate is taking the interview from the way they have attempted (or not attempted) to match your company's public persona. Famously, at a first meeting of representatives of a joint venture between Apple Computer and IBM, the laid-back anarchistic Apple staff wore suits and the tight-laced East Coast IBMers wore jeans and T-shirts. Both made the right decision – they were matching the perceived dress style of their new partners. The meeting (if not the joint venture) was a great success.

In the end, while a candidate's appearance at an interview is important, the measures you use in assessing their appearance should depend on the job requirements and your company's desired image, not any personal preferences.

Spend a few minutes thinking about the different styles of dress you adopt when in a range of work and social activities. Why would you choose a particular way of dressing? What does it say to other people? What message would you give if you dressed up or dressed down? If you regularly wear dress that stresses form over function (for example, the totally impractical tie) ask yourself if it adds to the comfort and practicality of your dress. If the answer is 'no' consider finding ways to dump it.

Personal Development	✪✪✪✪
Leadership	✪✪✪
Motivation	✪
Coaching	✪
Interviewing	✪✪✪✪
Fun	✪✪

15.5 Exercise/Technique: Assessing test results

Preparation None.
Running time 10 minutes.
Resources None.
Frequency Once.

Sometimes our assessments of staff are influenced by the outcome of tests. If you are interviewing for a large firm, the chances are that you will have to merge the output of your interviewing with the results of one or more test results. You may also be using tests to assess how well a particular team will function. A typical professional battery of tests might include verbal reasoning, personality profile, numerical skills and any technical aptitude required.

Put together a list of five significantly different jobs with which you are familiar. Against each, list any tests that you think would be useful. For each job/test combination, note down how you would use the outcome of the test in coming to a decision about this individual. Perform this exercise before reading on.

The most important consideration when dealing with test results is not to be blinded by science. Don't let the fact that these results have concrete numbers against them give them an unnecessary gloss and importance. Test results should support the interview, but never supplant it. Also beware of the bullshit factor. Some tests are only in existence in order to make the people who write or run these tests money. Perhaps the classic example is handwriting analysis, which has never been shown to have any scientific validity. If your organization uses such tests, take action to have them stopped.

Good applications of a test result are directing and fine-tuning. If you know from your interview that you are going to offer an individual a position, but have several posts that might be appropriate, tests such as a personality profile can help assess how the individual would fit within a particular team or working environment. If, on the other hand, you have one post and several candidates who were all excellent in interview, you may need test results to push you in one direction or another.

To some extent you might use test results to filter – for instance, requiring a certain level in a reasoning test – but in general the interview should have more weight. Anyone can make a mistake in a test, but in a good interview few can appear totally different from their actual performance.

Tests are very valuable, but shouldn't be overrated. Understanding how to make best use of the results is important if tests are part of your interviewing armoury.

It's a good move to try performing the tests yourself (and look at your results) before making decisions on others based on those tests.

Try taking the following:

- A psychometric test – How well does it match up to your expectations? What does it say about you?
- A reasoning test – How does the result compare with your job requirements?
- A use of English test – What are your weaknesses when it comes to written communication?
- A lateral thinking test – How do you cope with less predictable and structured demands?

Personal Development	✪✪
Leadership	✪✪✪
Motivation	✪
Coaching	✪✪
Interviewing	✪✪✪✪
Fun	✪

Unit 16: Difficult cases and troublemakers

There's a management equivalent of the old moan 'this shop would be great to work in if it weren't for the customers'. Being a manager would be a piece of cake if it wasn't for the staff. Unfortunately, in both cases it's the apparent cause of discomfort that is the whole reason for the job's existence.

Still, the fact remains that we will all come across particularly difficult individuals, people who seem to go out of their way to make things difficult, at some point in our management career. It's worth being prepared for these people, rather than expecting them to simply go away and stop bothering us.

Do try out the exercises as you go. Put them off until later and you probably won't ever do them. Read through the techniques. Make notes about how and when you can use them. And make sure you give them a try in the next appropriate forum.

Unit book

There's no obligation to read all, or any, of the unit books, but you will find that they provide excellent support to the course and strengthen your management skills.

Sometimes, when dealing with difficulties, the best thing to do is to take a complete break, and Gary Larson's mind-boggling Far Side cartoons achieve this like no other humorist's output can. There are a whole host of Far Side collections, but try *Last Chapter and Worse* as an excellent example of the genre.

You can find more information on our unit books, or buy them, from our support site: www.cul.co.uk/crashcourse.

16.1 Exercise: Daggers drawn

Preparation None.
Running time 10 minutes.
Resources Notepad.
Frequency Once.

This is a preparatory exercise for a situation that you may never encounter – but if you lead teams on a regular basis you almost certainly will. Sometimes two individuals or even sub-groups within the team build up ill-feeling against each other. The reasons are as diverse as people themselves. Such a problem could be caused by a simple clash of personality, by differences of opinion over strongly felt areas or by sexual or racial tensions. Once such a situation is having an effect on the motivation of the staff you cannot afford to let it ride, you have to intervene.

How you intervene inevitably depends on the nature of the problem. Consider these three cases. Spend a couple of minutes jotting down what you would do in each case before reading on:

- Paul is getting on Sue's nerves. Sue likes to work head-down, quietly. Paul is always chatting and asking Sue about things. Sue's motivation has gradually dropped further and further.
- Bill and Tim are IT specialists. Bill, who is an expert in programming languages, is recommending adopting a new type of language across the company. Tim, who is a business computing expert, disagrees, thinking that the recommendation is too theoretical and not based on pragmatic application.
- Mandy is Simon's team leader. Although Mandy is married, she has become increasingly fond of Simon and is beginning to make sexual overtures. Simon is not happy with this situation.

Don't read on until you have written down some thoughts.

In the first case it may be enough to talk with Paul, but such behaviour is deep rooted and he may be unable to stop it. Monitor the situation and look at ways of putting other people between them.

There is a danger in the second case of underestimating the strength of feeling involved. After all, we are only talking about a programming language. Yet I have been on the receiving end of almost incoherent insults and ranting as a result of challenging the technical opinion of an expert with a pragmatic concern. Give the two cooling-off time. Talk to them separately, then bring them together. If sparks still fly you may need to take action to insulate your more technical people from the world, leaving the more pragmatic ones to interface, but there is a real danger here of an ivory tower developing. Usually technical disagreements can be overcome, but never underestimate the strength of feeling just because you don't feel it yourself.

The third case is particularly difficult. It will often be better for all concerned if it is possible to move one or both of the individuals into different teams (it might be necessary to move both to avoid it seeming a punishment). This sounds radical, but the potential consequences of no action are terrible.

Don't agree with our assessments? That's fine. There is no magic answer, nor will the same answer work with everyone. But whatever answer is adopted, it is better if you have some practice at thinking through these situations before things happen for real.

Most teams get by with a small amount of ill-feeling. No group of people is going to agree about everything, and there will always be petty arguments and small emotional responses. While it may be appropriate to intervene in some of these, it isn't always necessary. The two danger signals are very obvious bad feeling (shouting, physical action etc) and differences which continue to irritate over several days.

Personal Development	✪✪✪
Leadership	✪✪✪✪
Motivation	✪✪✪
Coaching	✪
Interviewing	✪
Fun	✪

16.2 Technique: Confronting troublemakers

Preparation None.
Running time 10 minutes.
Resources None.
Frequency Occasional.

Every now and then you will come across a motivational troublemaker. This is not someone who goes around smashing things (though such activity doesn't encourage motivation), but someone who constantly undermines morale. They are usually very cynical, suspicious of the company's motives and willing at every opportunity to share their discontent.

We have known very good managers who have a blind spot about motivational troublemakers. They see them as a challenge to try to rehabilitate, treading very carefully around the troublemaker's sensitive areas. Unfortunately, during the rehabilitation process (which rarely succeeds), the troublemaker will have been undermining the motivation of everyone within earshot. It's a painful possibility, but it is sometimes necessary to encourage a motivational troublemaker into a different job. Of course this must be entirely consistent with legal restrictions on constructive dismissal etc. The ideal approach is to find another area where the troublemaker would rather work.

There's an interesting dilemma when finding the troublemaker a role in a different part of your company. On the one hand you wouldn't want to drop a disaster on a colleague without warning them. However, you also don't want to put the troublemaker into a new position where he or she may flourish with a label that says 'don't trust me' attached.

The ideal is probably to find a job in which the troublemaker would be so motivated that he or she doesn't want to upset others, but this can be difficult.

There's an element of being cruel to be kind here. The fact is, with a real troublemaker, you can make a significant improvement in motivation of a whole group of people by encouraging an individual to take up new interests.

Personal Development	✪✪✪
Leadership	✪✪✪✪
Motivation	✪✪✪✪
Coaching	✪
Interviewing	✪
Fun	✪

16.3 Exercise: The earnest objector

Preparation None.
Running time Five minutes.
Resources None.
Frequency Occasional.

The earnest objector is not uncommon when working with a group. He or she generally has an intellectual outlook and picks up on a point of concern that is genuine, but that most attendees are happy to gloss over. For the objector, however, it causes real discomfort.

A couple of practical examples. Attending a course on presentation skills, the attendees are told that it is better to cancel a presentation than give it when the conditions are poor. Later in the course, each attendee has to give a presentation. The objector refuses to do so, as there are no window blinds and the graphics projector is too weak to be seen properly. In another example, a conference involves a role-play. The objector argues correctly that the role-play is unrealistic because under the circumstances described, those involved would take a totally different course of action. She refuses to take part.

It is tempting to brush over the objection to keep to time but the objector will be quietly fuming about the situation. Equally ineffective is arguing out the matter in front of the group, which can generate a hostile reaction. Instead, have a five-minute comfort break (don't wait for one) and take the objector to one side to discuss the problem. If his or her view is reasonable, make a concession. If this is not practical in the timescale, explain why and undertake to change in the future. If the view isn't reasonable, explain and if possible give the objector the option to sit out that section.

An earnest objector is entirely different from a habitual troublemaker. The troublemaker sees little good in anything. The objector is positive, but finds the particular point difficult or simply wrong.

Demotivation is contagious. Although it may seem overkill to stop a session to sort out an individual, it will be worth it. You may also actually improve your session – and groups benefit from more frequent breaks than they are usually allowed.

Personal Development	✪✪
Leadership	✪✪✪
Motivation	✪✪✪✪
Coaching	✪✪
Interviewing	✪
Fun	✪

16.4 *Exercise: Playing favourites*

Preparation Produce a list of those you motivate.
Running time 10 minutes.
Resources Notepad.
Frequency Once.

Dealing with people is a delicate balance. We're all human and we come equipped with the full range of emotions, likes and dislikes. Of those you work with, there will be some you like more than others. It is inevitable. This assessment exercise will allow you to get a feel for how you deal with this emotional side.

Take a list of those you aim to motivate – people who work for you, your peers, your bosses. Don't worry about groups, this is an exercise about individuals. Being honest with yourself, highlight those you particularly like and particularly dislike.

Now try to highlight those individuals whom you think an observer would pick out as your favourites. How much do the two sets correlate?

Almost everyone who deals with people will be seen to have favourites. If you aren't, the chances are that you are being too impersonal in your interactions. The secret of using this motivationally is to ensure that your favourites are acknowledged as being such because of what they do, what they deliver, not just because you like them.

Often the two will overlap. It's hard not to like someone with whom you work really well. But on the other hand, it is also possible to really like someone who doesn't deliver. These are the relationships to be particularly wary of.

You won't be expected to be inhuman, but you are expected to be fair. This includes lack of favouritism, in the sense of favouring someone just because you like them. By getting the right message across you can influence everyone's motivation.

Personal Development	✪✪✪
Leadership	✪✪✪
Motivation	✪✪✪
Coaching	✪✪
Interviewing	✪
Fun	✪✪

16.5 Technique: Reluctance to improve

Preparation None.
Running time An hour or two.
Resources None.
Frequency Occasionally.

Often the most frustratingly difficult people for a manager to deal with are those who seem determined not to improve themselves. At times it seems almost as though they are happy to be where they are, no matter how much they insist that they are ready for change.

The first and most important thing to say is that this state may seem like wilful ignorance but it rarely is. It is most often the case that people who seem reluctant to improve are actually those who cannot believe in this improvement in themselves. They would happily move to a new them. They would happily improve themselves but they know deep inside themselves that they are where they are meant to be and that they are unable to get any better. They are wrong. Part of your role as a coaching manager is to show them that they are wrong and to help them to lift themselves above the low self-esteem that has caused them to be stuck.

A useful short exercise to use in this situation is to hunt down what it is that is causing them to limit themselves. Get the coachee to think back through their lives and to recall, as clearly as they can, any occasion when they have been told that they are not good or not able. This may even have been given as praise but turned into a limit. For instance, 'You're so bright you'll always be top of the class' becomes a limiting statement as soon as you're not at the top.

Now have them write a list of these statements, then have them choose one that they believe has affected them and have them write a letter (with no intention of ever sending it) to the person that made the comment.

Finally, have them create some positive affirmations that counter the limits that they feel ('I can do X because...'). This may sound worryingly airy-fairy, but a reluctance to improve of this kind is largely about self-image. If the coachee has problems with the self-centred nature of affirmations, look for more subtle ways to help them boost their self-image.

Personal Development	✪✪
Leadership	✪✪✪
Motivation	✪✪
Coaching	✪✪✪✪
Interviewing	✪
Fun	✪✪

Unit 17: Putting on a show

A lot of your role as a leader is rather different from the caricature view of a person standing at the front of an immense gathering and whipping a group of people into a frenzy of action. Your management toolkit will include the whisper of influence and coaching as well as the yell of mass-motivation. But this doesn't mean that there is no requirement to take on the masses. It *is* part of the leader's role, and doesn't sit comfortably with everyone.

This could be a challenge...

Do try out the exercises as you go. Put them off until later and you probably won't ever do them. Read through the techniques. Make notes about how and when you can use them. And make sure you give them a try in the next appropriate forum.

Unit book

There's no obligation to read all, or any, of the unit books, but you will find that they provide excellent support to the course and strengthen your management skills.

'Putting on a show' inevitably brings out the creative in us, and one essential for the good manager is being able to manage for creativity – to get not only 'more of the same' out of your people, but new ideas and new ways of doing things. *Creativity and Innovation for Managers* by Brian Clegg is specifically about setting an organizational agenda for creativity and managing the creative process, but not just when putting on a show – this is the creative process that should be part of all management.

You can find more information on our unit books, or buy them, from our support site www.cul.co.uk/crashcourse.

Web links

Links to sites to help with getting a message across show-biz style can be found at www.cul.co.uk/crashcourse.

17.1 Exercise/Technique: Risk and failure

Preparation Failure.
Running time 10 minutes.
Resources None.
Frequency Regular.

Before rushing out on stage to talk to a large group it's worth thinking about your attitude to risk and failure, because the reason that many of us have real problems with dealing with a large audience is that it feels high risk.

Your attitude to failure will affect both your motivation and your ability to motivate others. Too often in corporate culture, particularly a US-based culture, failure is seen as an ineradicable black mark. Yet all great thinkers sing the praise of failure – fast failure. The desirable approach is to fail fast, learn fast and put the lesson into practice.

The only way to avoid risk is to stick to a totally known procedure in a totally known environment. As all totally known environments are artificial, this has limited application to business. There will be risk; there will be failure. When something goes wrong, take a few minutes with those involved to say 'what went wrong – how can we do better in the future?' This is not a blame-finding exercise, but positive learning.

The Total Quality Management (TQM) movement has many positive attributes, but it gives entirely the wrong impression about failure. The goal of TQM is zero failure – which is fine in a repetitive mechanical process. It's a goal for a production line, not a flexible, evolutionary, constantly changing environment. Keep TQM where it belongs.

The enthusiasm for failure should not blind you to the occasional person who won't learn lessons. Nor does it mean that you should take wild risks because you are generating helpful failures. Risk should be calculated, but once the risk has been taken, look forward not backward.

Fear of being seen to fail is a huge demotivator in many large companies. It results in timid decision taking and minimal innovation. This isn't acceptable in a time of rapid change – if this culture can be modified, and you can do your bit, there will be a huge impact on both motivation and effectiveness.

Now we can come back to your walking out on stage. Large meetings and training sessions are a special case. Because they are in an artificial environment you should generally minimize risk, unless you are involved in a creative exercise or learning about the benefits of failure.

Before the event, look out for opportunities for things to go wrong and have a contingency plan. Imagine you were giving a talk to 200 people at an unknown venue 100 miles away. As an exercise, first jot down your contingency plan. Then test it against these possible risks:

- Due to a motorway blockage you are delayed by an hour on the way.
- The room you were due to use is double booked.
- The projector you were to use fails.
- You leave your notes at home.
- Only three people turn up.

Check your ability to weather these problems before reading on.

Watch out for time problems – always allow too much. Expect technology to fail – have some backup. Ideally you should be able to do your presentation without notes if necessary, and to be flexible enough to change format to a more intimate one if numbers change drastically. If things have gone wrong and they can't be covered up, admit the situation and announce a coffee break (or some other distraction) while you regroup.

Personal Development	✪✪✪✪
Leadership	✪✪
Motivation	✪✪✪
Coaching	✪
Interviewing	✪
Fun	✪✪

17.2 Technique: Energy transfer

Preparation None.
Running time Two minutes.
Resources None.
Frequency Regular.

The attention of your audience is very mood-dependent. However interested you are in a subject, if you are low in energy or depressed you will not be able to put it across well.

To keep large groups motivated, it is essential you examine your own energy levels first. When you talk to them, will you inspire them or put them to sleep? Content is essential, but so is your delivery. Take two minutes just before you start to liven yourself up. Go outside. Jump up and down. Shout. Punch the air. Do anything that increases your energy level and puts a sparkle into your eye. Then deliver while you are still on that high.

It is almost impossible to go over the top with energy. Business guru Tom Peters positively shouts at his audience – and they love it. But beware substituting simulated sincerity for energy. This approach, popular among TV evangelists, is rejected by the traditional 'cold' cultures (UK, Scandinavian, Germanic, Eastern seaboard USA) who find it too calculating.

One of us has come across one negative response to energy. A very effective presenter was waking up a Friday evening audience. One of the audience complained that she found the energy of the presenter (who bounces around a lot) too much after a long day. She is the exception. Others might grumble, but still find benefit; most are positive. In the end, the complainer was implying that what she really wanted to do was curl up and go to sleep. Perhaps that was what she should have been doing, but given that she was present, she was certainly in need of energizing.

Transferring energy to group members is an important motivator – use it, but be aware that it is very draining.

Personal Development	✪✪
Leadership	✪
Motivation	✪✪✪✪
Coaching	✪✪
Interviewing	✪
Fun	✪✪

17.3 Technique: Lasers and dry ice

Preparation Prepare and rehearse.
Running time Five minutes.
Resources Varied.
Frequency Occasional.

Short-term motivation is highly dependent on mood. A powerful combination of imagery and music can dramatically influence feelings. If you are planning a major event, making use of multimedia, technology, dramatic music and practically anything that is an assault on the senses is a valid option to manipulate mood and hence motivation.

You won't do this in five minutes. In fact, since it must be highly professional to be effective, you are unlikely to implement it yourself at all. What is useful at the planning stage, though, is to spend five minutes thinking about the shape of the event – where you want to inject a dose of motivation, and the style of multimedia blitz that will best suit your attendees.

Glitz without any underlying content has a very short shelf life – it will swiftly switch from motivation to demotivation once it appears that there is nothing behind the smoke and mirrors. There has to be appropriate content too.

If you are concerned about manipulation – don't be. There is no secret about what you are doing, and most people will get a lot of enjoyment out of it. This assumes, though, that it is done well, hence the need for a professional team providing the multimedia, rehearsal to spot any glitches, and plenty of preparation. Beware at all costs half-hearted glitz. If you can't afford to do it properly, don't do it at all.

This sort of cheerleading motivation won't have a long-term impact but it is very valuable as a foundation on which to build content-driven motivation. Without the foundation, the best content can still slip away.

Personal Development	✪
Leadership	✪✪
Motivation	✪✪✪
Coaching	✪
Interviewing	✪
Fun	✪✪✪

17.4 Technique: Quality content

Preparation Plan.
Running time 10 minutes.
Resources None.
Frequency Regular.

When you are planning a group session, put a few minutes aside to consider quality of content. Try to assess what you would really get out of the session as an attendee. What would others get out of it (for example, your employer)? Which bits would you get all excited about – and which would you fall asleep in?

If all else fails, you can insert mood-lifting exercises. In fact these are valuable anyway. But they should not be crutches to support a session that lacks content, or is boring. Take the worst points of your event and find a way to improve them – not by a few per cent, but by an order of magnitude. Nothing has to be boring – find a way to make it exciting. If the problem is a total lack of content, drop that section. Sometimes you will find the entire event lacks content. Either cancel it or start from scratch – otherwise you will end up with seriously demotivated attendees.

This exercise may result in radical surgery. Don't let that put you off – sometimes tuning has to be anything but fine.

It's easy to rebel. Of course your session has content, that's the whole point, isn't it? The trouble is, we often engage in large group activities because we ought to. We might decide, for instance, that we need a company-wide session because customer service is poor. This may be true, but it doesn't say anything about the content you devise, and it's tempting to fill it with froth. Don't assume that a worthy cause implies effective content.

It is essential to take a step back like this, because big events rapidly gain a momentum of their own and good intentions can overlook poor delivery. Not only can lack of content directly reduce motivation, it also irritates people to see a lot of money being spent on a worthless event.

Personal Development	✪
Leadership	✪✪
Motivation	✪✪✪✪
Coaching	✪
Interviewing	✪
Fun	✪✪

17.5 Technique: Spice it up

Preparation None.
Running time Five minutes.
Resources None.
Frequency Regular.

Variety really is the spice of life – and is essential for motivation.

Divide a large group event into several activities during the day – typically no more than one hour per session. If the whole event is focused on a single topic, break up that topic and come at it in different ways. However the session breaks down, use time-outs – 5- or 10-minute episodes of doing something completely different to keep the group fresh. Once you have outlined the session, take a couple of minutes to assess it for variety.

Sometimes variety can be a change of pace or environment. If you can't motivate by changing topic, move the people to different locations.

Enrichment goes far beyond spicing up your performance in a show. It is a natural step as we move from the 20th-century, input-oriented view of organization charts, job slots and evaluation to the 21st-century output-oriented view of people-centred work and flexible response. Some will find it difficult, as it means individuals taking more personal responsibility. The unions and old-fashioned managers may fight it too, as it represents a reduction in their power base. But the move is unstoppable; the question is if you will cope, not whether it will happen.

Job enrichment increases motivation, gives better retention of key staff and better productivity. It's sometimes difficult to see the need for variety, especially under pressure. Like breaks, variety can seem a waste of precious time. But without variety productivity plummets, originality withers and accuracy falls.

Personal Development	✪
Leadership	✪✪
Motivation	✪✪✪✪
Coaching	✪✪
Interviewing	✪
Fun	✪✪✪

Unit 18:
You can't motivate

A lot of the management skills we have been discussing are aimed at motivating others. Now for a bit of a setback. In one sense, at least, it is impossible to motivate others. Think about that statement for a moment.

What the statement means is that motivation largely has to come from within. On the whole, people motivate themselves. You can help them, you can stimulate them to generate that motivation (and that's what we generally think of as motivation), but the essential drive comes from within. In this unit we look at making more of the internal motivations of others.

Do try out the exercises as you go. Put them off until later and you probably won't ever do them. Read through the techniques. Make notes about how and when you can use them. And make sure you give them a try in the next appropriate forum.

Unit book

There's no obligation to read all, or any, of the unit books, but you will find that they provide excellent support to the course and strengthen your management skills.

The idea that you can't motivate someone else is at the heart of David Freemantle's *The Stimulus Factor*. Freemantle argues that we can take steps to stimulate others into motivating themselves, but can't do it directly. It sounds like 'how to use "what's in it for me"' – and inevitably there's an element of this, but there's much more too.

You can find more information on our unit books, or buy them, from our support site: www.cul.co.uk/crashcourse.

18.1 Technique: Contributors

Preparation None.
Running time Five minutes.
Resources None.
Frequency Regular.

Highly motivated people are frequent contributors, coming up with lots of ideas and suggestions. Most people come up with occasional contributions – and how those thoughts are treated will make a lot of difference to motivation. New ideas are like tender green shoots – they're easy to trample on and destroy in the early stages, and they don't necessarily resemble the final, valuable, working idea, just as the shoot doesn't necessarily resemble the full-grown plant.

To enhance motivation through contribution, consider this plan:

1. Make it easy to contribute. One of the elements here might be scrapping your suggestion scheme and replacing it with mechanisms to get ideas quickly to the people who can best do something with them (and to get feedback back).
2. Treat contributions with respect, whoever they're from. Be prepared to give five minutes of your time to discuss them.
3. Act quickly. This doesn't mean always doing what's suggested. But whether the action is implementing the idea or having a good explanation of why you aren't, act.

Bear in mind that contributions aren't always ideas – it might just be doing something helpful without being asked – whatever, the contribution needs to be recognized.

This one's either Catch-22 or a self-fulfilling prophecy. The more you take people's self-generated contributions seriously, the more motivated they will feel, and the more they will contribute. Similarly, the more you ignore contributions, the more they will be demotivated and cease to contribute. The difficulty that we sometimes face is to reverse the spiral, especially when it is being enforced by demotivated middle managers. This action may be trivial, or it may require a major overhaul of staff relations – in either case, it's worthwhile.

Although primarily an individual and team technique, large groups involved in an interactive session will also quickly pick up mood and motivation from the way you handle suggestions and questions. If you feel a contribution isn't helpful, or there just isn't time for it, don't squash it; sideline it for a one-to-one after the group session, so that the whole group isn't demotivated.

Personal Development	✪
Leadership	✪✪✪
Motivation	✪✪✪✪
Coaching	✪✪
Interviewing	✪
Fun	✪✪

18.2 Exercise: Do it themselves

Preparation Individual meeting with staff.
Running time 10 minutes.
Resources None.
Frequency Once.

It is often the case that no one can motivate an individual as well as they can motivate themselves. Why not give their self-motivation a chance? Spend a few minutes with each individual you manage (set this up now). Get them to consider what it is that they really enjoy doing, both in and out of a work context. Help them to use these enjoyment factors to motivate themselves, ideally by directly incorporating them in their work or indirectly by giving themselves a target to reach, after which they can have a 'reward' of something they enjoy.

Although time management sounds to some like a lot of mechanistic rules, good time management is essential for self-motivation. It is almost impossible to manage your time without motivation in what you are doing.

Self-motivation is something that writers are often asked about. 'How do you discipline yourself to sit down and work?' is a frequent question. Self-motivation is a mix of making sure you do plenty of what you like doing, survival (because if I don't do it I won't eat) and routine. Enabling your staff to build up their own routine (perhaps coming into work earlier than most or later than most), and maximizing their ability to make their working space personalized, are both very helpful in self-motivation.

If you can get staff motivating themselves, you can't actually relax and not give it any consideration yourself, but it's certainly one of the most effective bits of delegation you are ever likely to do.

Personal Development	✪
Leadership	✪✪✪
Motivation	✪✪✪✪
Coaching	✪✪✪
Interviewing	✪
Fun	✪✪

18.3 Technique: Perspective shift

Preparation Meeting.
Running time 30 minutes.
Resources None.
Frequency Occasional.

Like many motivational exercises, this is essentially one of communication to help staff with self-motivation. The old and still common worldview was of careers as a steady progression through jobs, based on length of time in service. Most people would stay with a company (or even department) all their working life – and what that company did would not change. Rules and procedures were there to be obeyed, not questioned.

This old view was always a fiction (made clear by the fact that most companies have always tended to have a shorter life than that of a working individual), but never more so than now. Careers are becoming more non-linear and aptitude based, with managers often younger than those they manage. Changes from department to department and company to company are frequent, with more and more people contracting out their skills. Loyalty is first to the individual themselves, then to their workgroup and only then to the company. It is more important to get the task done than to stick to rules and procedures.

It's not enough to know that this is happening. A gentle introduction to the reasons behind it and the personal benefits of the approach is needed, particularly for older hands. Spend half an hour thinking through two types of education you need for your staff – understanding of the different world we work in (and the opportunities it gives), and life skills to cope with change.

In a few areas of business there is actually an increase of dependence on procedures, typically where there is a possibility of legal liability. This can lead to inflexibility and low motivation. There is no clear solution to this dilemma.

Providing a new perspective has to be handled carefully to avoid demotivating older staff members, but it is essential both for the motivation of younger staff and for the continued good of the company.

Personal Development	✪
Leadership	✪✪✪
Motivation	✪✪✪✪
Coaching	✪✪
Interviewing	✪
Fun	✪✪

18.4 Technique: Personal projects

Preparation None.
Running time Five minutes.
Resources None.
Frequency Occasional.

Often the opportunity to undertake a personal project is a great self-motivator. However much someone is a team player, there is something special about a solo achievement. Consider giving your staff the opportunity to undertake a personal project. This should be something that can be undertaken in a relatively small timescale, either a regular couple of hours a week, or the whole project in a concentrated day. It should have potential benefit to the company, but part of the attraction of such a project is that it could have a much higher risk of failure than a conventional exercise.

Have a five-minute session with your staff, describing the concept. You might have a specific project in mind, or want them to come up with something. There might not be a burning issue right now – make it clear that there is no stigma attached to putting the personal project slot on a back-burner until an idea or requirement comes up.

How much structure you then give to the project depends on the individual. Your involvement could be limited to 'give me some feedback when you've achieved something' or a weekly five-minute update on progress.

Don't fall into the trap of considering this time wasting. Make sure that it's a small enough proportion of time that it won't have real effect on the individual's ordinary work. Many personal projects may be failures, but some will deliver spectacularly. Be prepared to support and further a positive outcome.

Note, by the way, that there are people who really don't want to do this sort of thing. But for many, the opportunity to work on something that's really theirs is a superb motivator. It's the sort of thing they put effort into in their own time, because it gives them a buzz. As with all good motivators, it's win–win.

Personal Development	✪
Leadership	✪✪
Motivation	✪✪✪✪
Coaching	✪✪
Interviewing	✪
Fun	✪✪✪

18.5 Exercise/Technique: Overcoming a lifetime of learning

Preparation None.
Running time Half an hour.
Resources None.
Frequency When starting a new coaching relationship.

To help an individual to self-motivate you will often have to overcome a natural reluctance to take the reins, particularly when dealing with the coaching aspects of your role.

It is likely that when they first enter a coaching relationship with you, your coachee will have had no experience of coaching (this will not be true for most sportsmen or sportswomen). They may well be expecting you to teach them. The attitude of people new to coaching is often, 'OK, tell me what I need to learn to do next.'

This is not your role and you will need to avoid being sucked into playing it. Almost everything that the coachee needs to learn will come from them. You may be able to add tools that help them or tips that move them in a certain direction, but the learning is theirs. This is counter to all of their previous experience.

If a coachee has had a lifetime of learning from external sources, they may not be good at listening to the learning that comes from themselves. They are likely to attribute more weight to learning from a significant other than from themselves. You may need regularly to play back to them what you hear them say. If you do this, be sure to stress that this is what they have said. This is not your wisdom, it is theirs.

Give some thought now to tactics that you could bring to bear when faced with a new coachee who is not comfortable with a relationship that is not teacher–pupil based. What would you say to them? What difficulties are you likely to face? How would you deal with these? What difficulties are they likely to face? How can you help them through these?

Undertake this exercise before moving onto the next unit, which is particularly concerned with training and learning.

Personal Development	✪
Leadership	✪✪
Motivation	✪
Coaching	✪✪✪✪
Interviewing	✪
Fun	✪✪

Unit 19: Training and learning

As we have seen through our emphasis on coaching, being a manager is about more than just getting enough work out of the people you are responsible for. It should also be about developing them, both because that should mean you get more out of them, and also because, as a good manager, you care for them as human beings.

Do try out the exercises as you go. Put them off until later and you probably won't ever do them. Read through the techniques. Make notes about how and when you can use them. And make sure you give them a try in the next appropriate forum.

Unit book

There's no obligation to read all, or any, of the unit books, but you will find that they provide excellent support to the course and strengthen your management skills.

As we have become more academic in our approach to training we have tended to reduce the value of the oldest and most powerful training aid, the story. Telling stories has always had immense value, and in her *Tales for Trainers*, Margaret Parkin lucidly argues for a greater use of the story-telling process in training (just as it can sensibly be used in many of the areas covered in this course).

You can find more information on our unit books, or buy them, from our support site: www.cul.co.uk/crashcourse.

Web links

Training and learning links can be found at www.cul.co.uk/crashcourse.

19.1 Technique: Developing others

Preparation None.
Running time A few weeks elapsed, less actual.
Resources None.
Frequency At least annually.

You do what you do as a leader only through others. Yes, you are the one that gives them direction. You are the one that motivates and drives them. But they produce your products, they serve your customers. They do it.

If you don't work on developing your people, you are not enhancing the potential of your greatest resource.

The first thing you must do is to establish the development needs of your people. This is traditionally done by a human resources department establishing job role capabilities and then measuring people against these capabilities. My view is that this is, and always has been, a total waste of effort. It gives comfort because it feels rigorous, but in practice it ends up being precisely wrong rather than roughly right.

A good place to start with development is with the people who are to be developed. What do they feel they need? If you were to offer them money to train themselves in anything they wanted to do, what would it be? If it turned out to be flower arranging, rather than the design of administration systems, is that wrong? It might be, but only you can decide. If you have managed to fire people up with the need and the drive to work towards your vision then my view is that they will ask for appropriate development. For sure there will be a few who try to take you for a ride and will want to develop themselves in preparation for leaving you to work elsewhere, but this may actually be a cost-effective way of moving them out whilst still having them feel positive about you.

Finally, don't think of developing people only in terms of training. The business books you give them, the things you ask people to do and the example that you set will also significantly add to their development.

Personal Development	✪
Leadership	✪✪✪✪
Motivation	✪✪✪
Coaching	✪✪✪
Interviewing	✪
Fun	✪✪

19.2 Technique: Train tracks

Preparation Check assessments and past training.
Running time 10 minutes.
Resources Individual meeting.
Frequency Occasional.

Gross generalization: training doesn't just improve skills, it also motivates. Like all generalizations this is not entirely true, as the wrong sort of training is a turn-off. However, provided the staff member feels that the training is worthwhile, being sent on training courses has a positive effect. This makes it more than advantageous to output or productivity – it's a positive management aid.

The reason is not difficult to understand. Sending someone on a course instead of having them occupied in productive work generates a stronger message than words can convey. It says that we value you as an individual, we see that you have a future with this company and are worth investing in. Not only that, it says that we think you can go further, and we are going to put money into getting you there. Next time you think about training, consider the benefits as well as the costs.

Least effective motivationally is large-scale events that everyone attends. They can provide a lot of motivation on the day, but don't give any message of being especially valued. Next comes technical training. This makes the individual feel valued, but be wary of suggesting that they are incompetent. Also, avoid using such courses with 'naturals' who can (say) pick up a word processor in five minutes and will be intensely bored one hour into a course. Most valuable for motivation is development training, improving interpersonal, creative or management skills. This really says 'you are going places, and we want to help you to grow'.

Focused training is a superb winner, both motivating and increasing skills. Don't waste your training budget on too much mundane technical training if you can get that on the job; look for development instead.

Although not as powerful as training, we need to emphasize again that giving individuals developmental books is also motivational (and much cheaper). It's amazing how companies are willing to spend thousands on courses but rarely spend £10 to £20 on a book.

Personal Development	✪
Leadership	✪✪
Motivation	✪✪✪✪
Coaching	✪
Interviewing	✪
Fun	✪✪

19.3 *Technique: Train strain*

Preparation Staff have training.
Running time Five minutes.
Resources None.
Frequency Regular.

While training itself is usually motivational, there's an archetypal example of the aftermath of training reducing motivation. It's a familiar scenario to most of us. You come back from a course all fired up with enthusiasm, and get dropped back into your working environment (with one or more days of work to catch up with). There's no time to put all those great ideas into use now, so you put the training notes aside to get back to when the rush is over. And they continue gathering dust until you throw them away.

Most of us recognize how valuable training is, but ought to add the rider 'provided it gets put into practice'. If you can help your staff to make use of their training, you will bring the motivational effect of that training into fruition. Firstly, bear practicality in mind when you book a course. Does it have clear, usable outcomes? If you can find a course that gives away real books rather than handouts, go for it. Books are more likely to be read after the event, and sit visibly on the shelf while handouts moulder in a pile. When the participant comes back, have a couple of minutes chatting about what they got out of it, and how it might be integrated into the working environment. Try to give them the time and space to work that integration.

The feeling you get in these circumstances is worse than simply having wasted a couple of days – after all, chances are the company were paying for this near-holiday. It's not the wasted time, but the frustration of not being able to put all those great new ideas into practice that grates.

By the end of the course, 90 per cent of the cost has been expended. Don't waste it (and all the associated motivation) by not allowing the participant to bring their learning back into the workplace.

Personal Development	✪
Leadership	✪✪
Motivation	✪✪✪✪
Coaching	✪
Interviewing	✪
Fun	✪✪

19.4 Technique: Knowing what you know

Preparation None.
Running time An hour.
Resources Pen and paper.
Frequency Occasionally.

There's a mystery at the heart of one of the most significant development roles you have. When you are developing one of your staff in a coaching role you will sometimes have to bring on someone who's actually better at a particular task than you are.

It's fascinating that in sports some of the very best coaches never made the top of their sport. Olympic coaches are not necessarily ex-Olympic athletes. A coach can coach a number of events even where they have only competed in one. Some of the best coaches are not athletes at all. So how can they be so smart that they can pass on this knowledge without apparently possessing it?

The answer should be no surprise. They are not passing on knowledge, they are uncovering it. They are not being smart about the event; they are being smart about coaching. Having said that, it is obvious that the coach does need to know a great deal about the discipline they are coaching; they just don't need to know more than the coachee does. What they need to know is how to draw the best out of the coachee.

On your own, sit down and list for yourself the areas that apply to a particular coaching relationship where your knowledge excels that of the coachee. Now write down the areas where their knowledge excels yours. Having done this, think through the future relationship and think through what aspects of your knowledge it is necessary to pass on for them to succeed. Now think through what aspects of their knowledge it is necessary to bring to the fore. Are there likely to be obstacles in the way of this? If so, list them and decide now what approaches you'll make to overcome them.

If you have found that you have a long list of things that you need to pass on to them for them to succeed, and if this list is made up of items of knowledge specific to their goals, then you need to think hard about whether you are truly going to be coaching. Might a straight teaching relationship work better? If on the other hand you have very little knowledge to contribute then you need to think through how you will talk to them about the coaching relationship. They will need to know what you are offering and what you are not.

Personal Development	✪✪✪
Leadership	✪✪
Motivation	✪
Coaching	✪✪✪✪
Interviewing	✪
Fun	✪✪

19.5 Technique: Learning and learning styles

Preparation None.
Running time An hour, sometimes longer.
Resources Pen and paper.
Frequency Annually.

Different people have different ways of absorbing information from the world around them. Understanding how your staff learn and what differences there may between their style and your own could be of crucial importance to establishing your relationship.

Sit down with your staff individually and work through the following questions (if you are coaching a team this exercise may be less applicable or else you may decide to treat them as a collection of individuals). Remember that the answers may not be absolutely either/or. Some people are able to cope with a range of styles:

- What is their action bias? If they are action oriented then they will be better at absorbing information by doing rather than studying or being told. If they are less action oriented then studying would be a better approach.
- How visual or verbal are they? Some people need to see images associated with their learning whilst others need words. What is their bias? Do they prefer to read about something or watch a video?
- What times of day do they best absorb information? Some people's brains perform best in the morning, others in the afternoon, others in the evening. There may well be combinations of best times. Mine, for instance, are morning and evening. The afternoons are relatively poor times for me to be doing anything that requires a brain.

Once you have jointly established how your staff learn, you might want to turn the tables and do this for yourself. Now, between you, look at any differences there may be and discuss what impact these are likely to have on the way you work together. Having done that, you could start to plan your approach on the basis of this. Remember that this information is merely a guide. If there are other factors that affect, for instance, the times of day that you work on something, don't allow this material to dominate.

Personal Development	✪
Leadership	✪✪
Motivation	✪✪
Coaching	✪✪✪✪
Interviewing	✪
Fun	✪✪

Unit 20: The F word

There's a nasty little word that has to creep in if you are to do your job at the top of the management scale – it's fun. Traditionally we've been very wary about fun at work. If you are enjoying yourself, it looks as if you are not taking your role seriously. But this is a terrible misapprehension. Those who are really performing superbly well *will* be enjoying themselves, or will burn themselves out very quickly under the strain.

In the past, putting fun alongside serious concerns didn't seem to be a problem. Note how US citizens claim a right to life, liberty and *the pursuit of happiness* – not misery. Yet this total misapprehension about work is so strong that we need to take a positive stance for fun if anything is to change.

Do try out the exercises as you go. Put them off until later and you probably won't ever do them. Read through the techniques. Make notes about how and when you can use them. And make sure you give them a try in the next appropriate forum.

Unit book

There's no obligation to read all, or any, of the unit books, but you will find that they provide excellent support to the course and strengthen your management skills.

Fun Works by Leslie Yerkes explores the underrated world of fun in the workplace, and how it can be used as one of the most powerful management and motivational techniques.

You can find more information on our unit books, or buy them, from our support site: www.cul.co.uk/crashcourse.

Web links

Links for fun can be found at work at www.cul.co.uk/crashcourse.

20.1 Exercise/Technique: Portfolio matching

Preparation None.
Running time 10 minutes.
Resources None.
Frequency Occasional.

This is one of a number of techniques where you are asked to get your staff to look at what they are doing and compare it with some sort of ideal. You won't want to do all of these at once, so most are listed as pure techniques, but this is one that you should try as soon as possible.

Everyone is more likely to have fun in their job if there is a good match to the portfolio of activities they really want to be doing. Spend a few minutes with someone you want to motivate developing a dream portfolio. Ask them to assume they've won the lottery and never need work for money again. Get them to list the activities they currently do they'd keep, and which they'd drop. Then add a third column of new activities they'd like to start.

Next, put that list to one side and get them to think about their skills and talents. What are they really good at, or do they feel they might be with appropriate training? Produce a list of skills and use the skills list to act as a filter for the dream portfolio.

Finally, use this refined portfolio to compare with their job. Are there activities that aren't in the portfolio that could be passed on elsewhere? Is there something they aren't doing, but could be that's a good match to their portfolio? Don't go for major changes initially – look for some quick hits, but plan to make bigger changes later.

Getting a better match to what you really want to be doing is a great motivator. Occasionally this exercise results in someone realizing they want to be working in a different department or a different company. It might seem dangerous in those circumstances, but bear in mind that it's probably better for both of you to have someone leave highly motivated than totally fed up.

This is a fun exercise, and if you can make something happen as a result of it, it will be very motivational. Beware, though, alerting someone to the differences between their portfolio and reality, then doing nothing to help them bridge the gap.

If you haven't already, do try this exercise for yourself, as well as those who work for you. The fun isn't supposed to stop, just because you are a manager.

Personal Development	✪✪✪
Leadership	✪✪✪
Motivation	✪✪✪✪
Coaching	✪✪
Interviewing	✪
Fun	✪✪✪✪

20.2 Technique: The tea bag

Preparation Collect small items.
Running time One minute.
Resources Small items.
Frequency Regular.

Whether you are motivating a dog or a human being, it's hard to beat the impact of a small, instant reward. Such a reward should be in the 'pocket money' range and should bring a smile to the face – it's pure fun. When you spot someone doing something really well – it can be one of your reports, a peer or your boss – lay your hands on a reward and get it to them straight away. Speed is of the essence with this technique.

You might find it helpful to stock a drawer with suitable goodies. We have used badges, company give-aways, pens, calculators and more in the past.

This is one to do by gut feel. Don't feel that you have to schedule rewards ('it's Fred's turn because he hasn't had one yet'). Simply use it to reinforce saying 'that's really good' or 'thank you'. A good example happened to one of us a few years ago. The person responsible for allocating accommodation helped me out of a crisis. This was a job that was fraught with confrontation, making the person who did it unpopular. When I was given the news, I dashed to the nearest vending machine, bought a walnut whip and plonked it on the accommodation person's desk. It might be a coincidence, but from that time on, this person (who previously had tended to the bureaucratic) was intensely helpful.

Why 'tea bag'? One of my managers once felt the urge to give me a reward for staying late. He looked around frantically – all he could see was a tea bag, so he gave me that. Despite the fact that I don't drink tea, I was really pleased – demonstrating just how low the value of the reward has to be if the sentiment is right.

A treasure trove of low-value goodies is a great way to reinforce the motivational value of a thank-you. It costs very little time or money.

Personal Development	✪
Leadership	✪✪✪
Motivation	✪✪✪✪
Coaching	✪✪
Interviewing	✪
Fun	✪✪✪✪

20.3 Technique: Celebration time

Preparation Choose venue.
Running time An evening.
Resources Cost of celebration.
Frequency Occasional.

Every now and then there is a need to celebrate. We need fun rites of passage to mark major events. Perhaps your team has delivered 150 per cent effort to get a project completed on time. Perhaps they have got you a promotion through superb effort. Such events should not happen often – twice a year at most – and they should not become routine or they lose impact.

With a small group, the best approach is probably a celebration dinner. It may seem trite, but it works (as long as the company pays). It is a win–win for motivation, because the team gets the message that the company has noticed their efforts, and they also grow closer through social interaction. With larger gatherings, all the way up to a whole department or company, you will need to be more imaginative, but the concept is the same.

Beware, however, the annual sales awards or Christmas bash syndrome. Motivational celebrations should be one-offs. Anything predictable and expected every year loses motivational value. You may still need to do it, but don't expect a lot of benefit.

Try to make team celebrations exclusive. The whole focus is on the team. The team leader should be there – because he or she is part of the team – but not a more senior manager or director, even if he or she is paying. Exclude spouses and partners too. Like it or not, they will dilute the feeling of 'we did this together'. I've never been to one of these events where having spouses along hasn't weakened the impact.

As well as the benefits already described, such celebrations act as a wake. Although it is impossible to keep up indefinitely the high-pressure drive that is needed for the sort of success that is being celebrated, the pressure will be missed when it is over. The event helps the team say 'that's over, now we're doing something different' – and gives an opportunity to review and fix in the memory the highlights and disasters of the shared experience.

Don't miss this opportunity if the company is too tight to pay – if necessary the managers should pay for it themselves. This will make the event even more motivational, but may encourage you to be a little more selective about what you are celebrating.

Personal Development	✪
Leadership	✪✪✪
Motivation	✪✪✪✪
Coaching	✪✪✪
Interviewing	✪
Fun	✪✪✪✪

20.4 Exercise/Technique: The F word

Preparation None.
Running time Five minutes.
Resources None.
Frequency Regular.

To manage effectively we need to motivate, and motivation and fun go together like... two things that go together very well indeed. In everything we do, fun bubbles through as a reflection of motivation, and the fact of enjoying ourselves feeds back into the motivational loop. It is, therefore, particularly sad that the Victorian values underlying most businesses preclude fun in the workplace. Gradually this is ceasing to be the case. It's certainly very different in start-ups and some hi-tech companies (not all though), where working incredibly hard is balanced with plenty of fun.

Make a regular date to think about how to bring a bit of fun into the working lives of those you motivate. How you do this will depend on the individuals. Some might react very well to a come-to-work-in-silly-clothes day, or a topical limerick competition on the company intranet. Others prefer their fun to be a little more sophisticated (though don't allow them to shut things down for the rest of us). Anything you can do to make work more fun that doesn't actually get in the way will be enhancing. As an exercise, plan to bring some element of fun to at least one team you work with during the next week.

Fun is something we all deserve and is one of the greatest natural motivators. Why should it be excluded from work?

Personal Development ✪
Leadership ✪✪✪
Motivation ✪✪✪✪
Coaching ✪✪✪
Interviewing ✪
Fun ✪✪✪✪

20.5 Exercise: Building relationships

Preparation None.
Running time 10 minutes.
Resources Pen and paper.
Frequency Infrequently.

As human beings, much of our fun comes from good relationships with other human beings. A manager is in a position of trust and potential power. If they are performing their role properly then they may have a large influence on an individual or a team. In some instances this influence extends well beyond the area being managed.

This power and influence cannot be taken. Those being managed give it. They will not do this unless you have a strong relationship with them. Building relationships is not something that you will truly learn from an exercise like this. If you can't do this easily then the management role is not for you. This exercise is intended more as a memory jog and checklist. Write down for yourself answers to the following questions:

- How much do you know about your staff?
- What do you know of their likes, dislikes, hopes, dreams and desires?
- What do you know of their family and private lives?
- Where do they live?
- When is their birthday?
- Would they appreciate a card from you?
- Have you socialized outside work?
- What do they think of you?
- What would they think of you in an ideal world?

There is no problem in being unable to answer any of these questions. Some management roles call for a closer relationship than others. If you do have problems answering them and you feel that you should not, then work on rectifying the situation. Remember also that it is not necessary to be loved to be a manager. But it is necessary to have respect and trust.

It still holds true that if you do not build relationships easily then no checklist will solve this for you. You must question whether you should be in a high-pressure leadership-style management role. If you feel that you should, then limit yourself to those conventional management roles that do not need close relationships.

There is a particular problem when trying to take this approach with a large number of people. If you are expected to lead 10,000 (say), it is not very practical to expect you to know their birthdays. In part, this process can be delegated – make sure your reports know that it is not an optional 'nice to have'. In part, though, you can exceed expectations. Learn just the name of each of those 10,000 people (quite practical with memory techniques) and each time you meet someone you can boost your rating by recognizing them.

Personal Development	✪✪✪
Leadership	✪✪✪✪
Motivation	✪✪✪
Coaching	✪✪✪✪
Interviewing	✪
Fun	✪✪✪

Unit 21: Pitching it right

When marrying up people and tasks it is important that you get the balance right. You don't want to scare people off with constant failure and pressure. Nor do you want to bore them silly. Achieving such a balance is one of the most difficult challenges a manager faces.

Do try out the exercises as you go. Put them off until later and you probably won't ever do them. Read through the techniques. Make notes about how and when you can use them. And make sure you give them a try in the next appropriate forum.

Unit book

There's no obligation to read all, or any, of the unit books, but you will find that they provide excellent support to the course and strengthen your management skills.

As we have seen before, one of the best ways of learning how to do something right is to hear about someone else getting it wrong. In David Ricks' *Blunders in International Business* we see one company after another pitching it wrong, to great effect. Watch out for Ricks' own minor blunder over the matter of napkins in the UK, illustrating the importance of having up-to-date information.

You can find more information on our unit books, or buy them, from our support site: www.cul.co.uk/crashcourse.

21.1 Technique: Stretch but don't stress

Preparation None.
Running time Five minutes.
Resources None.
Frequency Regular.

Very few people with an interest in their job want to be doing nothing, or performing tasks that they can complete in their sleep. There is something very valuable about being stretched. When thinking about the tasks people are doing, the messages they are being given – any activity – ensure that as much as possible there is stretch incorporated in the content.

Have a regular stretch assessment for your staff (don't call it this; it sounds silly). Make sure that what they are doing is challenging – but possible. An element of stretch is essential – too much challenge becomes dangerous stress. Don't be afraid to ask people, but be aware that most people don't like to define their limitations publicly and may well be uncomfortable saying what is stretching until they are sure that the context isn't threatening. Stretching isn't necessarily about more volume – it is better if it's more responsibility, decision making and depth of content rather than pure quantity.

Stretch is just as important when dealing with a large group as an individual. If what you are talking about or what they are undertaking doesn't stretch them, they are going to lose interest and switch off (or even go to sleep). The problem with dealing with a large group is defining what will stretch them but not go over their head. It is harder to assess than with an individual. Ideally you should have some profile of those involved to be able to match to that reasonably well. If in doubt, though, get on-the-spot feedback (you may need to be quite assertive to get this out of a large group), and don't fall into the trap of underestimating them.

Stretch is another of the motivation all-round winners. Not only will you enhance motivation, but you are actually getting more out of your staff or out of the session that the people involved are attending.

Personal Development	✪
Leadership	✪✪✪
Motivation	✪✪✪✪
Coaching	✪✪✪
Interviewing	✪
Fun	✪✪✪

21.2 Technique: Being realistic

Preparation None.
Running time Half an hour.
Resources None.
Frequency When starting a new coaching period.

The previous technique recommended stretch without too much strain, but doesn't give too many hints on achieving it. This technique is about setting the level of stretch. There is nothing more demotivating than an unachievable target. Making sure that the targets you agree are realistic is fundamental.

Targets are, by their nature, future based. How far in the future will depend upon the type of target being set and the area within which you are managing. It is advisable to start by thinking as far ahead as you and your staff can envisage. Ideally, try to think of an end state. Where do you want to get to? Then break the time between now and this end state into a few (say five) time periods. In order to achieve the target in period five, what would you need to have achieved in period four? In order to achieve the target in period four, what would you need to have achieved in period three? And so on.

Now look at the first period. If your end state is a long way away you might need to break period one into a few sub-periods. Then look at the first of these. Is what you are agreeing as a target for this period or sub-period realistic? Is it possible that this will be achieved? If not, is it possible to push harder on any of the other targets?

Be aware at this stage that it is very easy to set yourself relaxed targets at the start and end-load the effort in a way that makes the targets for the later periods impossible. This is why it is advisable to work backwards in time rather than forwards. If you cannot realistically push the later targets then the solution to making this realistic is to reduce the final target.

Personal Development	✪
Leadership	✪✪✪
Motivation	✪✪✪
Coaching	✪✪✪✪
Interviewing	✪
Fun	✪✪

21.3 Technique: Being unrealistic

Preparation Get magazines.
Running time Two hours.
Resources Pile of illustrated magazines.
Frequency When starting a new coaching period.

In the previous technique we looked at setting realistic levels of stretch. But as a great manager you don't just want to get your staff to achieve, you want to coach them towards something better, and coaching is about making dreams come true. There is nothing realistic about this. The previous exercise was very much done with feet on the ground and with realism in mind. This one is about dreaming.

Give the staff member(s) you wish to coach a pile of magazines – a wide range with lots of images. Ask them to forget about the area you are coaching and to go through the magazines looking for and tearing out any images that appeal to them. Once they have a pile of these, ask them to make a collage of their dream. What would they really love to achieve? Use only the torn-out images. Having done this, ask them to write a short summary of their dream.

Now work with them to set a target that would achieve this dream. The next stage of this exercise is to go through the previous one about being realistic. Break the whole target down into time periods and say what would need to be achieved in each period. Is this possible?

If you are being unrealistic in your dreams then it is likely that you have what appears to be an impossible target. The solution to this is to agree realistic targets and dream targets. If you are being realistic you will achieve this in this time period. If you are working towards your dreams you will achieve this. If you have two sets of targets for every period it is likely that the person or team being coached will achieve more than a realistic target and they may or may not achieve the dream target. Whether they do or not, you are now able to demonstrate how much better they are doing than realistic targets would allow.

Personal Development	✪✪✪
Leadership	✪✪✪✪
Motivation	✪✪✪
Coaching	✪✪✪✪
Interviewing	✪
Fun	✪✪✪

21.4 Technique: Establishing pace

Preparation None.
Running time As long as it takes.
Resources None.
Frequency Regularly.

When you are developing your staff, the pace at which an individual does things can well determine progress. You will work with people who want everything to happen now and so will smash obstacles like a bull in a china shop. You will work with people who will be happy to wait for the tomorrow that never comes.

Sometimes you will want to slow people down. It might be that they are not learning lessons they need to learn because they are pushing too fast. It might be that they are cutting corners and achieving their targets at the expense of some level of quality that you haven't been monitoring.

Sometimes you will want to speed people up. It might be that they are doing themselves a disservice by taking longer than they need over everything. It might be that they are being painstakingly meticulous about things that need not be focused on.

In general, the way to change their pace is to establish the root cause of the issue and to focus on that. It is rare that you will be able to say that they are going too fast or too slow and that this will be enough. If they are cutting corners then discuss other quality measures with them. If they are focusing on unnecessary detail then discuss the bigger picture.

Very often they will understand for themselves where the root cause of their pace issue lies. If they do not then you will need to probe to help them to uncover it. Generally it is a bad idea for you to form an opinion about this and offer it as a solution. Try to uncover a solution jointly.

As a last point, be prepared to accept that the issue with their pace might be your problem. If they are happy with the results they are producing and the rate they are moving then you might choose to back off.

Personal Development	✪
Leadership	✪✪
Motivation	✪✪✪
Coaching	✪✪✪✪
Interviewing	✪
Fun	✪✪

21.5 Technique: 'I can't do it'

Preparation None.
Running time At least an hour, probably much more.
Resources None.
Frequency When coachee hits a block in progress.

You will sometimes get to a stage in the relationship with a staff member you are coaching where you are convinced that they can achieve a goal that they are convinced they cannot. You need to turn around their thinking. It is as Henry Ford used to say, 'Whether you believe you can or whether you believe you can't you're absolutely right.' So, how do you turn around thinking when someone has convinced himself or herself that they cannot do something?

The first step is probably to explore with the staff member you are coaching the source of their limiting belief. How do they know that they can't? Is this limit the result of something that has been said to them, something they know about themselves, something that they know about the world or simply something they know to be true?

Having explored this, you might want to look at the fear that lies beneath the assumption they are making. Any limit that we place upon ourselves stems from an underlying fear. Uncovering this can be a useful trigger to progress. Are they scared of failing? Are they scared of succeeding? Are they scared of letting someone down (including themselves or maybe even you)? What is it that drives the limit?

Often when you feel you have uncovered such a fear it is useful to probe deeper, because the first fear that springs to mind may not be the one that lies the deepest. Once you are satisfied that you have reached an underlying fear that is driving their limit, you need to work on it to overcome its effect.

Look then for rational arguments that can help the individual quell that fear. Give them the tools to do something about it (you can never do it for them). Help them to make positive affirmations about their abilities ('I can X, because'), to repeat these as a personal mantra to help take the steps towards making it happen.

Personal Development	✪
Leadership	✪✪✪
Motivation	✪✪
Coaching	✪✪✪✪
Interviewing	✪
Fun	✪

Unit 22: Coaching in all directions

Coaching is one of our prime themes for the developing manager, and the natural inclination is to think of yourself primarily as coaching the staff who work for you. In this unit we examine the ways that coaching can benefit the manager working in many different directions.

Do try out the exercises as you go. Put them off until later and you probably won't ever do them. Read through the techniques. Make notes about how and when you can use them. And make sure you give them a try in the next appropriate forum.

Unit books

There's no obligation to read all, or any, of the unit books, but you will find that they provide excellent support to the course and strengthen your management skills.

There are two unit books on coaching. The first, *The Coaching Pocketbook* by Ian Fleming and Allan J D Taylor, uses keywords and cartoons to get the key messages across in a very small book, ideal for filling in short gaps of input time. The second, *Life Coaching* by Eileen Mulligan, is one of those books aimed at 'changing your life in 7 days', but despite this it is lively and readable and contains a lot that is transferable to the wider world of business coaching.

You can find more information on our unit books, or buy them, from our support site: www.cul.co.uk/crashcourse.

Web links

Coaching links can be found at www.cul.co.uk/crashcourse.

22.1 Exercise: Coaching outside work

Preparation None.
Running time 10 minutes.
Resources Pen and paper.
Frequency Once.

The bulk of this course is written from a business perspective. It is written for use by those in business who want to improve their management performance. But the opportunities to coach do not end at the end of the working day. There are many more situations where the skills of coaching are applicable, and can repay with gained experience that can be of benefit in the workplace.

Should you want to develop your coaching skills outside work, it would be useful for you to have in mind those situations where coaching might be a useful skill. This short exercise allows you to think that through and then take this a step further.

Ask yourself on which of your current pastimes or activities you could bring coaching skills to bear. Would those with whom you are involved welcome this or reject it? On which pastimes or activities that you are not currently involved in, but might become involved in, could you bring coaching skills to bear?

For instance, could you get involved with the local tiddlywinks team? Do you have any friends (close friends!) that you could offer some informal coaching to help them to achieve a dream? Are there any members of your family that you could offer some coaching to help them achieve a dream? Finally, can you think of any other situation that might present opportunities for coaching?

Once you have drawn up this list, go through it and think about where you would enjoy getting involved and where you would not. Then go through again and think about where others would enjoy you getting involved and where they would not. Finally, think through how you would offer yourself as a coach in whichever area or areas you decide to progress.

Remember, the coaching relationship is explicit and open. It is not one that you slip into while others are not looking or that you do in an undercover or hidden way. Whichever of these areas you decide to progress, you must get the agreement and cooperation of those to be coached.

Personal Development	✪✪✪✪
Leadership	✪✪
Motivation	✪
Coaching	✪✪✪✪
Interviewing	✪
Fun	✪✪

22.2 Technique: Coaching with others

Preparation None.
Running time An hour for the first meeting and regular bits thereafter.
Resources None.
Frequency When coaching alongside someone else.

More often than not you will act as a sole coach. This is the most common and the easiest way of working. There are circumstances, though, where you may need or want to work in conjunction with someone else. This can have advantages in terms of two heads being better than one, in terms of support and in terms of companionship. It has disadvantages, and the biggest of these is communication.

When you are coaching with someone else you need to ensure that they know everything you know about the coaching situation and that they are thinking in the same way as you about the future development of those being coached. This is pretty much impossible to do fully, so your objective must be to share as much as you can.

The two of you need an initial meeting. Sit down with the person you are going to be coaching with and agree a few ground rules. Are you going to share responsibility or does one person lead and the other act as support? Is your role the same for everyone being coached or does one of you take the lead with some and the other with others? How will you develop and share progress on targets? How will you develop and share progress on methods used to improve?

You then need to share information regularly. You will have agreed the what and some of the how on this. You have to make sure that you schedule time to make this possible and then stick to it. Updating one another is vital to your success as a team. Give it the time it needs.

Personal Development	✪✪✪
Leadership	✪
Motivation	✪
Coaching	✪✪✪✪
Interviewing	✪
Fun	✪✪

22.3 Exercise/Technique: Coaching your boss

Preparation None.
Running time Half an hour to prepare for a meeting.
Resources None.
Frequency Occasionally.

Usually you either have the explicit role of coach in a particular situation or you are a leader of others who is acting as a coach to them to improve their performance. If you are coaching your boss, this assumption does not hold.

You will want to get involved in coaching your boss when his or her performance in a particular area falls down and this affects you in some way. You might also want to get involved in this out of a sense of altruism where their shortfall in performance does not affect you.

There are two ways of approaching this. The best (in our opinion) is to be open and honest with them and to offer your services as a coach. The other is to be less explicit and to take on the role of coach without agreeing that openly. The second of these is risky.

Whichever you decide, you need to agree targets in some way and then to question, probe and monitor performance against targets on a regular basis. This is where the risk of trying to do this less explicitly comes in. Can you imagine how it will feel to your boss, having regular meetings with you at which you question them about their performance if you haven't agreed the role?

As a quick exercise to prepare for this role, write down for yourself the area in which you wish to coach your boss. What is their area of performance shortfall? How does this affect you? How could you sell to them the idea of you coaching them? Anticipate their reaction and think through counters to any problems you might come across. Then go meet them!

Personal Development	✪
Leadership	✪✪✪
Motivation	✪✪✪
Coaching	✪✪✪✪
Interviewing	✪
Fun	✪✪

22.4 Technique: Coaching your peers

Preparation None.
Running time Half an hour to prepare for a meeting.
Resources None.
Frequency Occasionally.

If they understand the coaching role, your peers are much easier to coach than your boss. If they don't understand the role and yet you feel you could be useful to them, the first thing that you need to do is to educate them about the role and its advantages.

However you decide to approach this, the exercise that you start with will be much the same as the one for the boss. There will, however, be a greater likelihood that you are doing this solely for their benefit and not because an aspect of their behaviour impinges on your role.

This may not be true, but if you are coaching them solely for your own benefit then you need to be absolutely explicit with them about your motivation. The coach's role is based on trust, not manipulation.

So, write down for yourself the level of understanding that you feel your peers have of coaching. If it's low then how will you educate them? Now what area would they be most likely to want to develop? What is their area of performance shortfall? How does this affect the business? How could you sell to them the idea of your coaching them?

Anticipate their reaction and think through counters to any problems you might come across. Then go meet them! Yup, I told you it was similar.

Personal Development	✪✪
Leadership	✪✪✪
Motivation	✪✪✪
Coaching	✪✪✪✪
Interviewing	✪
Fun	✪✪

22.5 Technique: Coaching yourself

Preparation None.
Running time Two hours.
Resources Pen and paper.
Frequency Occasionally.

It is possible to act as coach to yourself. Taking on this role requires a great deal of self-exposure and honesty and some of us are not ready to be this candid with ourselves. If you feel that you are, then read on. You need also to be prepared to do a lot of writing down – when you have only yourself as a sounding board you need a written record.

Decide on a specific area in which you wish to coach yourself. Write this down at the head of a sheet of paper. Now write down for yourself all of the ways that you have really succeeded in this area over the past year. Don't be shy about this and don't try to rush it. This is an exercise that is worth spending time on.

Next write down all of the ways that you have not done so well in the last year. In what ways have you fallen short of your goals or your expectations? In what ways have you let yourself down?

Now think about how you would like to do in the year ahead. What would be different? What would you not do? What would you do more of or do for the first time? Write this down.

Finally, you need to think through your goals. What goals would you set yourself over a long time period? Now break this down into a few (say five) smaller time periods. What would need to be in place in the penultimate time period in order to achieve your goal? Now work back through each one, answering that question.

If your first period is more than a couple of months then break that one down again. If your subsidiary goals feel unrealistic then you can either decide to change them or to work miracles. Don't just dismiss this last comment as flippancy. You may find that you can work miracles if you want to enough.

Personal Development	✪✪✪✪
Leadership	✪
Motivation	✪
Coaching	✪✪✪✪
Interviewing	✪
Fun	✪✪✪

Unit 23: Modelling the role

Picture a leader. Spend a moment or two envisaging what a leader is like. Now imagine someone who spends a lot of time locked away in a room, issuing orders by e-mail. Does this second image match up to the leader picture? Hardly. A leader can't simply issue instructions. A vast proportion of leadership skills is tied up in the seemingly simple phrase 'do as I do, not as I say'. As they say, a leader can't just talk the talk, he or she has to walk the walk – to model the role to perfection.

Do try out the exercises as you go. Put them off until later and you probably won't ever do them. Read through the techniques. Make notes about how and when you can use them. And make sure you give them a try in the next appropriate forum.

Unit book

There's no obligation to read all, or any, of the unit books, but you will find that they provide excellent support to the course and strengthen your management skills.

Sometimes a great leader will be a media character like Virgin's Richard Branson. Other great role models are hidden to some degree behind their organizations, but would not have been able to achieve what they have without leading from the front. Perhaps the supreme example of walking the walk instead of just talking the talk came from the management of Scandinavian engineering giant ABB, which split up into many near-autonomous units, a process that was only possible by the centre letting go and all but disappearing. This ultimate role modelling is described in Kevin Barham and Claudia Heimer's book *ABB, The Dancing Giant*. This could have been a more exciting book than it is, but bear with it – the subject is well worth the effort.

You can find more information on our unit books, or buy them, from our support site: www.cul.co.uk/crashcourse.

23.1 Exercise/Technique: Watch my feet, not my lips

Preparation Buy a selection of *Dilbert* cartoon books (see section 11 unit books).
Running time Half an hour.
Resources *Dilbert* books.
Frequency Occasionally.

We have stressed and will continue to stress that what you do is far more important than what you say. It doesn't matter how many pragmatic justifications you can generate for every action that you take in conflict with your stated beliefs, it is the actions that will endure, not the words. It takes only one slip to undo a huge amount of work so the first piece of advice here is don't slip. You can't afford to.

As a leader you are human. You will make mistakes. In many instances you will be less aware of those mistakes than others around you. If you are able to, it is useful to have a confidant, someone who will let you know how your actions are seen by others. Ideally this should be a person with a great future behind them. In other words, someone who has a track record of success, so that you can trust them, but has no ambition to move further, so that you can *still* trust them.

Whether or not you can establish a confidant it is also necessary to get feedback directly from your people. We have already looked at 360 degree feedback. This is something that is essential if you are to get a real picture of your actions. Making it truly anonymous and fairly widespread is also essential.

As an exercise, start by reading a selection of Scott Adams' *Dilbert* cartoons. If you haven't already got the Adams book recommended in unit 11, rush out and buy a collection now – it doesn't matter which one. Read them not from the Dilbert perspective (as most of us do) but accepting that you are the pointy-haired boss. Some, perhaps many, of your actions will be seen in this light. If you find these cartoons amusing it is probably because you have, or have had, a boss that you can identify in this role. Don't you find it scary that your people find these cartoons amusing?

Personal Development	✪✪✪✪
Leadership	✪✪✪✪
Motivation	✪✪✪
Coaching	✪
Interviewing	✪
Fun	✪✪✪✪

23.2 Technique: Honesty is the best policy

Preparation None.
Running time A few minutes.
Resources A conscience.
Frequency Regularly.

Honesty is the best policy – a great aphorism and one that we choose to ignore much of the time. But we ignore it at our peril when role modelling.

Business ethics is becoming big business. Teaching people how to be ethical, or in some cases, teaching people how to appear to be ethical, is a growth industry. How can this be? How can you need to be taught basic values?

The answer appears to be that fudging issues, half-truths and avoidance have become so commonplace that we accept them as normal business practice. Quite recently one of us found ourselves defending someone's actions in what appeared morally indefensible circumstances using the phrase, 'But that sort of behaviour has become normal business practice'. I stopped myself and took a step back, admitted what I really felt and apologized for the slip but even so, I surprised myself. I have always had a very strong personal moral code. It often gets in my way but I stick by it. Yet in business, it seems, I am more willing to compromise. It's almost as though because it's business these aren't real people.

It seems to be similar in politics. People will indulge in activities that they would find unacceptable in their private lives but seem to use the notion of the end justifying the means or some notion of a greater good. In my view this is just so much bull. The means are part of the end. If what you do requires you to act in a way that you regard as wrong then what you do is wrong. If you still want to do it that's your choice but don't pretend to yourself that the ethical basis is sound.

Our advice on this, for what it is worth, is always tell the truth. Communicate to your people and your customers more than you are comfortable communicating. Any half-truth that you hide behind will come back to bite you later. You will become known as untrustworthy and that is no basis at all for good leadership.

Personal Development	✪✪✪
Leadership	✪✪✪✪
Motivation	✪✪
Coaching	✪✪
Interviewing	✪
Fun	✪✪

23.3 Exercise/Technique: Going the extra mile

Preparation None.
Running time Half an hour or less.
Resources Pen and paper.
Frequency As required.

Role modelling is important in all aspects of leadership, but never more so than when coaching. At times, as a coach, you will need to push the coachee quite hard. At times they will push themselves quite hard. Guard against falling into the trap that poor sports coaches sometimes do of shouting at and berating their coachees. People perform from fear very poorly and only for a short time. They respond far better to love. This sounds horribly soft and fluffy but often this is what coaching is about.

Because you are role modelling, going the extra mile applies to you every bit as much as it does to the coachee. One of the huge drawbacks of adopting a coaching role is that it is demanding of your time, it is demanding of your attention and it is demanding of your emotional commitment.

Giving your all to the coachee(s) can be extremely draining and so you need to establish some limits for yourself.

Sit down with a pad of paper and a pen and answer the following questions:

1. Are there any times that you are not prepared to deal with a coachee? Some people set aside specific coaching sessions, some do not. Whatever you do, where are your limits?
2. Are there specific places that you are not prepared to deal with the coachee?
3. If you set specific session times with them, are you prepared to overrun?
4. Are you prepared to help them with issues that fall outside the area you are coaching?

If your answers to these questions are universally expansive – you are prepared to give hugely of yourself – you need to question what protection you have to guard against coaching taking over your life. If your answers are extremely restrictive – you give of yourself only at prescribed times and in prescribed places – you might need to question whether you are really going the extra mile on behalf of the coachee.

Personal Development	✪✪✪✪
Leadership	✪✪
Motivation	✪✪
Coaching	✪✪✪
Interviewing	✪
Fun	✪✪

23.4 Technique: Love

Preparation None.
Running time Half an hour to an hour.
Resources None.
Frequency As required.

The trouble with love is that it is a word that carries a huge amount of emotional baggage for most people. The difficulty with using any other word is that nothing else conveys the passion that sits behind the word.

So, what's love got to do with it? Well, what's love got to do with anything? It seems to be a fundamental driving force of human nature. Most of what we do seems to stem from a basis of love or fear. The philosophy behind this would take too long to go into here, but do take a look at the questions in this exercise, if only to establish in your own mind what is driving you.

How well do you love yourself? This is a really tricky one to be honest about. Human beings are experts at lying to themselves about how they feel about themselves. If you find this a tough question then let's break it down. Firstly, how much do you love your body? Is it the body of your dreams? Does it do for you what you want it to? How much would you choose to change it if you could? Secondly, how much do you love your mind? What aspects of your thinking processes would you change if you could? Would you want a better memory? Would you want to be wittier? Would you want to think faster and respond quicker? Finally, how much do others love you? Are you inherently loveable? Every one of the changes you wish to make in yourself is an indicator of not loving yourself. True love is unconditional.

Having looked at how much you love yourself the next thing to ask is how much do you love what you do? If you won the lottery tomorrow and no longer had to work, would you stop? Would you change what you do? What aspects of your life would remain unchanged and what aspects would you choose to alter?

The final question is how much do you love those you coach? This is very tricky territory because love has so many sexual connotations. It is possible to truly love others without there being a sexual relationship. Think about the coaching relationship and ask how much you base it on love.

Once you have been through this soul searching, and it can be pretty tough to do if you don't treat it glibly, you could ask yourself what would you like to change about yourself, what you do and your relationship with your coachees.

Personal Development	✪✪✪✪
Leadership	✪✪
Motivation	✪✪
Coaching	✪✪
Interviewing	✪
Fun	✪✪

23.5 Technique: Role models

Preparation None.
Running time Half an hour to an hour.
Resources Sources (books, videos etc).
Frequency Occasionally.

We've already looked at role modelling – now let's see how looking outside for role model examples can be equally valuable, particularly when coaching. The role models that are used need not be people that your staff know or that they can interact with, but they do need to be observable. That is, the coachee must be able to see and analyse their performance in order to learn from it.

Where the discipline that you are coaching is in the public domain, such as sports, theatre, or any public performance, then observation of the performance is easy. More than this, finding role models is easy. Where the discipline that you are coaching is more private, such as most business, then you are relying more on your network. In this instance you will either need to get the coachee together with the role model in some way or pass on observations to them.

Coachees themselves may know of someone that they admire who is ahead of them in performance. If this is the case then they should use them as a role model and you will need to find ways of observing their performance in order to challenge and draw out the coachee.

Books can be a useful source of business role models. Since the 1980s there has been an increase in the business autobiographies, biographies and case studies being written. They provide useful insights into the performance of others. They should also be taken with a pinch of salt. Whoever wrote them, there is likely to be an angle. There is likely to be a bias in the perspective in one way or another. Still, they are useful for all that.

Sit down with your coachee and discuss the area of role models. Check with them whether they have any that they could suggest. In turn you can suggest any ideas that you have. If you happen to find a role model that appeals to the coachee and works for you then you need to discuss ways that the coachee can get closer to them, find out more about them and generally learn from them.

Personal Development	✪✪✪
Leadership	✪✪
Motivation	✪✪
Coaching	✪✪✪✪
Interviewing	✪
Fun	✪✪✪

Unit 24: Preparation for interviews

Just as unit 22 concentrated on some of the specifics of coaching, this section homes in on the interview as one of the essential management roles. We are rarely given enough time to deal with interviews, yet they can benefit hugely from the right kind of preparation. And such preparation need not take up a huge amount of time; in fact, overall it could save you some.

Do try out the exercises as you go. Put them off until later and you probably won't ever do them. Read through the techniques. Make notes about how and when you can use them. And make sure you give them a try in the next appropriate forum.

Unit book

There's no obligation to read all, or any, of the unit books, but you will find that they provide excellent support to the course and strengthen your management skills.

This unit's book is a straightforward guide to interviewing, but as this skill is vastly underrated (and undertaught) it needs just such a guide. Even if interviewing doesn't seem to be a regular part of your job it's worth reading Margaret Dale's *How to be a better Interviewer*, as every manager will need to interview formally or informally to extract information from others.

You can find more information on our unit books, or buy them, from our support site: www.cul.co.uk/crashcourse.

Web links

General interviewing links can be found at www.cul.co.uk/crashcourse.

24.1 Exercise/Technique: Understanding the job

Preparation None.
Running time 10 minutes.
Resources Job description.
Frequency Once.

It may seem a self-evident truth that you, as interviewer, need to know the details of the job you are interviewing for, but it is surprising how difficult it can be on the spot to translate a job description into the requirements for a successful candidate. Get hold of one of your company's job descriptions for a job you don't know too much about. If this isn't possible, ask a friend to write one for you. Take a couple of minutes to read it through, then try to jot down a description of a successful applicant. Don't do this in job description language – make it as if you were writing a personal letter, describing an acquaintance. What would they be like? What sort of questions would you need to ask to establish whether a particular applicant was like this? If an interviewee asked you to summarize what the job entailed and how it benefited the company, in a few sentences, what would you say?

Getting practice at absorbing a job description before an interview is very valuable. Each time you interview for a job you haven't interviewed for before, you should undertake this exercise. A job description may be very valuable, but it does not usually translate directly into the foundations of an interview. By spending a few minutes really getting into the nature of the job beforehand, you can leave your concentration free to listen to what the interviewee has to say. In some circumstances there will be no job description. Still undertake this process, but base it on your understanding of the job. When this is the case it is important that you test your understanding with the job's stakeholders, specifically the new boss (if it's not you) peers and customers (in the broadest sense).

Personal Development	✪✪
Leadership	✪
Motivation	✪
Coaching	✪
Interviewing	✪✪✪✪
Fun	✪✪

24.2 Exercise/Technique: Sifting applications

Preparation None.
Running time 10 minutes.
Resources Application forms (if available).
Frequency Once.

It is often the case that you will have more letters, CVs and application forms than you can deal with. Getting practice at sifting these quickly to cut them down to a manageable quantity is an important pre-interviewing skill. For the purposes of this exercise you need either a set of applications, or some equivalent pile of documents that you can work through quickly. If you haven't anything else, get hold of a heavyweight newspaper, and use the articles as if they were applications. You can't use these as effectively, but can approximate to the process.

Before undertaking the exercise, you will need to be clear just what it is that you are looking for in an application, and particularly what are the exclusion criteria. Do you have any minimum academic or experience criteria? To get some further criteria, look through the first couple of applications in detail. Are there aspects of the application that you can quickly pick up that you might use to include someone in or out? Look at the presentation. While you aren't looking for professional styling (at least for most jobs), you ought to have an easy visual exclusion criterion if an application looks terrible. Look out for similar, easy-to-spot exclusion criteria that fit your particular requirements. (If you have to do the exercise with a newspaper, you will have to use quite different criteria. Exclude anything about sport, or with obvious grammatical errors. Keep in anything with a scientific topic, or whatever. Use your imagination.) Now run through all the rest of the applications as quickly as you can. Don't spend more than 20 seconds on each. Finally, revisit your exclusion pile, giving each a little longer. Be prepared to reinstate a few that have redeeming features you didn't spot on the first pass.

This approach can seem highly arbitrary, but the fact is, you need to sort out a workable subset of the applications, and you need to be able to do this quickly. Sad though it is for the individuals who are rejected, it doesn't honestly matter if you do exclude some good applicants as long as you are left with other equally good candidates to choose from. The visual exclusion criterion is particularly easy to apply quickly, so worth having. If you feel any concern that these individuals are being excluded on an arbitrary measure, bear in mind the message that a candidate who produces an application that is messy or illegible seems to be giving: 'I don't care much about the job, and can't be bothered to put much effort into this.' Does this sound a desirable interviewee? Arbitrary though this is, I suspect it will usually be more effective than the widely used criterion of a certain level of academic achievement.

You may also have other small details that trigger suspicion. I have always worried about the personalities of applicants who either write only in upper case, or have clearly written each line of text along a ruler – but perhaps I am being arbitrary. Certainly I would not recommend going into pseudo-science like handwriting analysis. If you need to be that arbitrary, you might as well select the first *n* applications to arrive, or everyone whose surname begins with C.

As a second exercise, take your existing CV (résumé), or whatever equivalent information you have about yourself, and transform it as much as possible into the ideal CV. Here are a few tips, but make sure the result matches your own requirements:

1. Avoid being too technical; the CV may be filtered out by the HR department if they don't understand it.
2. Keep it short – one page if possible, two at most.
3. Include a brief summary, a reverse chronological experience guide (with more weight on recent and impressive roles), details of education and any special skills and characteristics.
4. Don't go mad with layout. Use one font (or at most two, the second for headings). Keep the layout simple and straightforward.
5. Unless requested, don't include a photograph of yourself.
6. Accompany the CV with a covering letter emphasizing the key reasons why *you* are ideal for the post.

There is no other CV that you know more about than your own. By using this as a model for your appreciation of what makes a great CV, you can make it easier to assess and consider other CVs.

Personal Development	✪✪✪
Leadership	✪
Motivation	✪
Coaching	✪
Interviewing	✪✪✪✪
Fun	✪✪

24.3 Technique: Information checklist

Preparation Find information.
Running time 10 minutes to an hour.
Resources Internet, internal sources of information.
Frequency As required.

An interview is a conversation with a purpose. That purpose is to extract the appropriate information from the interviewee to match the interviewer's requirement. In job-related interviews, this is normally the information necessary to understand how the individual would perform in a particular job, though it will often involve the background information that answers 'What kind of person is this?'

However, the candidate is not the only source of information, and to go into an interview unprepared is to risk the session being unstructured and uninformative. There's nothing worse than completing an interview and realizing that you are no more able to make a decision based on the information you have elicited than you were before the exercise. Getting access to appropriate information up-front and either absorbing it or having it readily available during the interview is an essential precursor, enabling you to ask the right questions and to get a full picture.

This technique involves building an information checklist – a short list of information that you can check off before undertaking an interview – and some detail on each of the items listed. The checklist is divided into three sections:

- All – information that will be valuable in any interview.
- External recruitment – information that is particularly relevant when interviewing an outside job applicant.
- Internal interview – whether considering an internal job applicant or a career review.

All

- Goals – what is the point of the interview?
- Key questions – have you prepared 10 to 20 questions that open up the heart of the issues?
- Interview plan – do you have a broad structure for the flow of the interview?
- Interviewee's CV – have you read through the CV?
- Application form – … and the application form?
- Test results – do you understand any test results available?
- Job description – what are the essential requirements, and what criteria will you use to measure up the candidates against them?
- Letter of invitation – is the letter to the candidate telling them what to expect clear?

External recruitment

- Details of interviewee's last company – do you know some context for their experience?
- Information on your own company – will you be able to answer questions put to you about your company?

Internal interview

- Interviewee's performance appraisals – are there any known strengths and weaknesses to probe?
- Conversations with boss, peers and customers – real people will always tell you more than forms and references.

Personal Development	✪✪
Leadership	✪
Motivation	✪
Coaching	✪
Interviewing	✪✪✪✪
Fun	✪✪

24.4 Technique: Environment checklist

Preparation Check environment.
Running time 10 minutes to an hour.
Resources None.
Frequency As required.

Like the information available to you, the environment in which the interview takes place is a factor that you can influence before the interview in order to maximize the effectiveness of the time spent with the candidate. If you do nothing about the interview environment, perhaps thinking that it is none of your business, the interview might take place in an uncomfortable setting that does not bring out the best in the interviewee.

There is another important reason for considering the environment too. There are elements that can be prepared in the environment that can make the experience of running the interview easier for you. This will help you to concentrate on your questions and the answers, rather than having your thoughts constantly flitting around environmental issues. Getting the environment right beforehand so you can relax and get on with the interview proper is an essential preparation:

- Appropriate office booked – don't try to undertake a serious interview in the corner of a cupboard.
- Other locations considered – sometimes off-site can provide a better environment (but the candidates don't get to see the workplace).
- E-mail queries considered – look at the use of e-mail to gather background information, reducing the simple, factual content of the interview.
- Telephone interview considered – telephone interviews are not ideal but may be the best available. If so, make sure they're at an arranged time.
- Mobile phone/pager switched off – it's a horrible distraction. If you forget and it does ring, just turn it off, don't even look to see who is calling.
- No phone or phone disconnected – mobiles aren't the only possible distraction. If the phone will ring (even if voicemail answers), unplug it.
- *Keep out* signs – there are few more embarrassing moments than when someone wanders in in the middle of an interview. Don't let it happen.
- Chairs in position – make it clear where the interviewee should sit. Try not to be too confrontational.
- Coffee table – interviewing across a desk is over-distancing, but no barrier at all is intimidating. Go for a coffee table as separator.
- Notepad – you can't keep it all in your head, and a keyboard is too distracting. Stick to a good old-fashioned notepad.

- At least two pens – yes, they can run out and you don't want the distraction.
- Clock in sight – to keep the interview on schedule without seeming to pressure the interviewee, have a clock that you can look at without this being obvious.
- Personal preparation – remember your own needs in a series of interviews. Give yourself comfort breaks.
- Dress – specify the expected dress, so the interviewee doesn't have to agonize about what to wear. Try to dress in a similar way yourself.
- Hospitality – keep on a level. If you are drinking coffee during an interview, offer one to the interviewee – but not part way through the interview.

Personal Development	✪
Leadership	✪
Motivation	✪
Coaching	✪
Interviewing	✪✪✪✪
Fun	✪✪

24.5 Technique: Selling checklist

Preparation Find information.
Running time 10 minutes to an hour.
Resources Internet, internal sources of information.
Frequency As required.

It's very rare that an interview doesn't involve a degree of selling. Unless your company and your job are simply the best possible options on the market and nothing else comes close, you will be in the position that your most favoured applicants have a choice. Not only will you want them, so will other companies. So part of the role of the interview will be to sell your company and your job to the applicant: to explain why he or she should want this job over and above any other (though avoid getting into this literal position if possible), and to emphasize all the advantages and opportunities that arise from coming to work for you. Inevitably there is a balance here. You can't offer so much that it ceases to be cost effective to make a job offer – but you need to offer something.

At first sight this might seem to imply that you have to be soft. That you are going to roll over and let the applicants walk all over you. But it's not like that. Your interview can be as intense and probing as you like. Towards the end, though, you need to change tack a little. Ask the interviewee if there's anything they would like to ask about the company and the job. And whether or not they do, give the applicant a short sales pitch. Send him or her out on a high, inspired by the thought of coming to work for your company. This won't be the case for every single interview. With some candidates you know all too well by the end that there isn't the slightest hope that this applicant will get a job offer, in which case limit yourself to asking if they have any questions. But otherwise, if there's a chance of making an offer, sell.

In an internal interview it will obviously be unnecessary to sell many of the features of working in this company, but there will still be opportunities for stressing some of the selling points – anything from flexibility of working to career opportunities. Even in a performance review interview (at least for a good candidate) you will want to sell, to keep the individual in the company, and ideally in your part of the company:

- Company brochures – do give these, but only at the end, so it doesn't become a distraction.
- Details of the package – make sure you know them and they are pitched right against the market.
- Flexible working options – offering flexible working can still be very attractive as many organizations haven't got it right.
- Dress – chances are you will have more appeal with a 'back office' policy of no dress code. This is the 21st century, for goodness sake.

- Support options – the most distinctive places to work look for opportunities to differentiate, and a big one is still how well you support your staff at exceptional times – bereavement, childbirth, moving, and more.
- The office space – most people spend a lot of time in the office. Anything you can do to show that it is an attractive place to be can't fail to help.
- Food and drink.
- Car parking and public transport.
- Details of social facilities – you might not run to your own social club, but why not look at ways to get special deals from existing facilities?
- Tools for the job – a surprisingly easy one to fall over on. All too often we don't give people the right tools to get their job done. So demonstrate you're different.
- Opportunities for advancement.
- Career flexibility.
- Training.
- Travel.
- Perks.
- Migration support – will you help them get from where they are now to where they need to be to work for you?
- A visit – why not arrange one? It's a variant on the old salesman's trick of showing you the goods and saying 'you can have this right now'.

Personal Development	✪
Leadership	✪
Motivation	✪✪
Coaching	✪
Interviewing	✪✪✪✪
Fun	✪✪

Unit 25: Notes and listening

As a manager you should be listening as much as you are talking. More so, in fact. Yet listening is a skill that rarely comes naturally. It needs working at. And if you are to retain what you hear, you will need some form of note taking to reinforce your memory. This is particularly true in a formal environment like an interview, where there is simply too much pressure to rely on memory to get the detail right.

Do try out the exercises as you go. Put them off until later and you probably won't ever do them. Read through the techniques. Make notes about how and when you can use them. And make sure you give them a try in the next appropriate forum.

Unit book

There's no obligation to read all, or any, of the unit books, but you will find that they provide excellent support to the course and strengthen your management skills.

Conventional note-taking methods can be difficult to use in an interview. Much more effective is some form of graphical note taking, and this unit's recommended book takes you to the foot of the master. Tony Buzan, inventor of the mind map, and his brother Barry make an excellent case for doing notes differently in *The Mind Map Book*.

You can find more information on our unit books, or buy them, from our support site: www.cul.co.uk/crashcourse.

25.1 Technique: Ask them

Preparation Opportunity to chat.
Running time 10 minutes.
Resources None.
Frequency Once.

Listening doesn't have to be a passive activity. For example, when trying to work out what motivates a group, you don't always have to devise cunning tests to assess motivation: often you can get away with asking people what works for them. This technique is simple in theory, harder to do.

Fit the subject into a general developmental meeting or informal chat, as it will feel artificial if you arrange a meeting specifically for the purpose. Ask your subject what motivates him or her and (as a separate question) what demotivates. Get an immediate reaction, then probe that response. The response may be a knee-jerk element like money. Take this on board, but look beyond it. Stress that you aren't looking for a specific answer – you genuinely want to know what will help them get on. A valuable question to cover is 'what could I do better?' The fact that you value their opinion enough to ask this (provided you pay some attention to the answer) can be highly motivating.

Although it seems most natural to apply this technique to your staff, it is equally useful for your peers and your bosses. In such circumstances, you may approach the subject by talking about the motivation of someone else, then turn it round to them.

Even if you have a bad memory, this is one circumstance where it's not a good idea to take notes; it looks manipulative. Note taking should be done alone, as soon as possible after the event.

This won't produce a definitive set of drivers. Few people are honest enough (even with themselves) to open up entirely. There may be some suspicion of your motives, and you will probably get an unnatural stress on demotivating tranquilizers (pay, conditions etc). Even so, bearing in mind that motivation is very individual, this is a valuable exercise.

This exercise can be undertaken with a team. If doing so, emphasize that you want to look at those factors that influence the team *as a team*, not as individuals.

Personal Development	✪✪
Leadership	✪✪✪
Motivation	✪✪✪✪
Coaching	✪✪✪
Interviewing	✪
Fun	✪✪

25.2 Technique: What did I say?

Preparation None.
Running time One minute.
Resources None.
Frequency Regular.

Sometimes what you are listening for is an echo. You can deliver a stirring message, seeing only the positive aspects, and those listening can hear something quite different, with disastrous consequences. Take the opportunity when you are communicating to check back on what was heard. Make sure that your key motivational messages were heard at all, and that they put across the feeling that you intended them to. Don't assume – check.

This shouldn't feel like a test, or an attempt to make sure that your audience was paying attention. Ask the recipients to give a summary or to pull it together. You can encourage people to do this without being prompted by testing understanding yourself when people communicate to you.

This is just as necessary with teams as with individuals. Sometimes there will be reluctance to feed back the message actually within the team meeting. You may well find that a particular individual in the team is good at feeding back the message to you as the team heard it. If this is the case, make use of that individual but bear in mind that their view will be filtered through their own perceptions, and that if you are seen to listen only to that individual it will suggest demotivating favouritism.

No matter how clear you think your message is, it has the potential for misunderstanding, transforming it to a force for demotivation. Checking what was heard is an essential.

Personal Development	✪✪✪
Leadership	✪✪
Motivation	✪✪✪✪
Coaching	✪✪
Interviewing	✪
Fun	✪✪

25.3 Technique: Checking for understanding

Preparation None.
Running time A few minutes.
Resources None.
Frequency As required.

Having checked that they heard what you said, there's still a further stage to go. Did they understand what you meant (not necessarily the same thing at all)? If you are misunderstood or if you misunderstand, you can undermine huge amounts of good work or even misdirect effort into the wrong areas. It is essential that you check regularly for understanding.

One useful tip is to get your staff to summarize, in writing, their own understanding of long-term and short-term targets and immediate work under way to achieve them. This will allow you to see that these areas have not been misunderstood.

Where you feel that there is a breakdown in communication, this short exercise may prove useful. It may feel somewhat false to both you and the staff members, but do try it out anyhow. It has been most useful to me.

Say what you are trying to have understood. Ask the other person to play back to you their understanding of what you have said. If what they have said does not tally exactly with what you want them to have heard then reiterate in different words and ask for a playback. Only when you are completely satisfied with their repetition can you move on.

This can of course be a two-way process. If you are not sure that you are understanding what they are saying then you can play back to them what they have said and ask them to confirm that you have an exact understanding.

Sometimes misunderstanding occurs because of associations that someone makes to an initial idea. If you feel that this might be causing a problem then ask for a playback but also ask for them to spell out the consequences of what you are saying. This can often uncover some interesting misconceptions about intention or motivation. Again, this form of playback can be two-way.

Personal Development	✪✪✪
Leadership	✪✪✪
Motivation	✪✪✪
Coaching	✪✪✪
Interviewing	✪✪
Fun	✪✪

25.4 Exercise/Technique: Great note taking

Preparation None.
Running time 20 minutes.
Resources Pen and paper.
Frequency Several times.

Note taking is an essential in interviewing and other aspects of management, but you don't want to take your concentration off what is being said. There are two skills that need to be practised here – making notes as you interact with another person without losing the thread of your conversation, and making notes without looking at the paper.

The next time you are involved in a business conversation or meeting, try taking notes in this way. Try to let the notes flow without taking your attention off what is being said.

You may well find, to start with, that your notes are virtually unreadable, hence the need for practice. Equally, you will find that the words come faster than your ability to keep up. Keep at it, though – this is a skill that improves with practice.

Once you are reasonably happy with this stage you can move on to graphical notes, which will need a little more of your concentration to construct (you will have to look at them sometimes), but which are much easier to revisit. For this exercise, take about 20 minutes to make graphical notes of the main points you know about management.

Start at the centre of a page and draw a circle containing the core of the issue. From this, radiate out branches that represent the major themes of the issue. From each of these draw progressively lower and lower level themes each on its own twig off the main branch, the result being a tree of information.

On each of the branches write one or two keywords above the line to say what that issue is. For instance, one branch might be management styles, splitting into leadership and traditional management, then each of these broken down into its prime features.

In general, try to make the image organic. Start with larger and fatter branches at the centre, moving to smaller and smaller ones and eventually twigs at the extremities. If you are already familiar with graphical techniques like mind mapping, don't go overboard. This isn't the right environment to be using different colours and fancy graphics; speed of capture is more important than memory retention.

Note taking while keeping focus improves with practice. This exercise is one-off in terms of learning the basics of visual note taking, but should be repeated by putting the technique into use. Every time you go to a meeting, for instance, try taking notes this way (whether or not you need any) as practice. It is also possible to get practice at this sort of technique away from the pressures of meetings and interviews by using it to summarize knowledge. Try drawing a visual map of the *Crash Course in Managing People* as you proceed through it.

Better note taking will result in staying on top of a meeting or interview, giving you the ability to really listen to what is being said, but also to be able to jump back to your key points at a moment's notice. It's a must.

Personal Development	✪✪✪✪
Leadership	✪
Motivation	✪
Coaching	✪
Interviewing	✪✪✪✪
Fun	✪✪

25.5 Exercise/Technique: Using silence

Preparation None.
Running time Five minutes.
Resources Someone to talk to.
Frequency Regularly.

One of the most effective tools of the interview, whether it's a job interview or any other structured conversation, is silence. Forcing yourself not to say anything can be quite difficult. You might have something you are just dying to bring up – but the point of the interview isn't for you to get going on your favourite topics. Or it may be that the interviewee seems to be struggling. You want to help him or her out, and so plunge in. Or maybe you can't cope with the silence. If so, you are a victim of this technique yourself, whether applied consciously or unconsciously.

Using silence is a technique that needs practice. Try it out in social conversations during the next week. Don't always plunge in with your opinion, or the story you desperately want to tell. Give the other person a chance to develop their argument.

A silence, except between people who know each other very well, is usually regarded as a social irritation. If nothing is being said, you start to feel that you are not contributing enough. You cast around, looking for something, anything, to say. Often what comes out will be rubbish. Yet silence is a great technique for the interviewer. It may be that your interviewee is taking a moment to collect his or her thoughts. That's a good sign, not a bad one – don't ruin the moment by starting to waffle. Or it may be that the interviewee is feeling the pressure. It's cruel and unnecessary to actually attack them at this point, but to leave a silence is a neutral way to allow the pressure to build until the interviewee is ready to take action.

Silence has to be used constructively. After an interviewee has made a full and effective answer, there is little point in allowing them some silence. But if the answer is short, or is yet to appear at all, give silence a chance to work for you. If you can overcome your natural tendency to fill in silence, you will have a great technique to encourage an interviewee to say more.

Personal Development	✪✪
Leadership	✪
Motivation	✪
Coaching	✪✪
Interviewing	✪✪✪✪
Fun	✪✪

Unit 26: Decisions and choices

A great manager is never in danger of being pushed out of a job, because they don't just work to a set of rules. They act on a huge knowledge base, and from that produce ideas and directions that are most likely to achieve a desired outcome. However, this doesn't mean that managers aren't regularly faced with processes that can be helped immensely by taking a structured approach, and one of these is decision making. Whenever you are faced with a decision or making a choice, your management skills are being put to the test.

Do try out the exercises as you go. Put them off until later and you probably won't ever do them. Read through the techniques. Make notes about how and when you can use them. And make sure you give them a try in the next appropriate forum.

Unit book

There's no obligation to read all, or any, of the unit books, but you will find that they provide excellent support to the course and strengthen your management skills.

Decision making and many other aspects of management fall under the experienced eye of Robert Townsend in his Up the Organization books. It doesn't really matter whether you get our recommendation *Further Up the Organization* or one of the others, Townsend's books are crammed with short, humorous articles showing just how things have been done badly in organizations in the past – and how they could be done better in the future.

You can find more information on our unit books, or buy them, from our support site: www.cul.co.uk/crashcourse.

Web links

An Excel spreadsheet to help evaluate options and Web sites on decision making can be found at www.cul.co.uk.crashcourse.

26.1 Exercise: Decisions, decisions, decisions

Preparation None.
Running time A small amount over a week and then ongoing.
Resources Decision diary.
Frequency Once.

Many years ago, when one of us first became a manager, I took a Diploma in Management Studies. One of the exercises I clearly remember was an activity where all those on the course measured the time they spent doing various activities. The discussion of this activity, once we'd done the measurement, centred around the notion that a manager's role was about making decisions. When we looked at our results we were extremely embarrassed. None of us had taken any time making decisions during the week that we had measured. Indeed, I had spent a measurable (not significant but still measurable) amount of time fixing a printer. My role could more honestly be described as printer repairer than decision maker.

We argued about this and said that the actual process of making decisions was embedded in the role and took no time. So we were then asked to list all of the decisions we'd made during that week. This became even more embarrassing because they all fell into the trivial and not worth mentioning area. Hardly the stuff of major business titans. Years later, at a very senior level within an organization, with hundreds of staff spread around the world, I still found that my role wasn't about minute-to-minute, day-to-day decisions. It was about driving forward major decisions that I'd already made and then keeping out of the way.

In order to understand your decision-making profile, try monitoring yourself for a week and keep a note of every decision you make. At the end of this process, remove the trivial and then note how much of your time is genuinely spent making decisions. Experience shows that this is not at the heart of the leadership role, whatever thought we may have cherished for years. Decisions are necessary to make things happen and you will be relied upon to make the decisions sometimes. The more you can force the decision back to those working for you, the more you will develop them and fulfil your true leadership role.

Personal Development	✪✪✪
Leadership	✪✪✪
Motivation	✪
Coaching	✪
Interviewing	✪
Fun	✪✪

26.2 Exercise/Technique: Setting criteria

Preparation None.
Running time Five minutes.
Resources Job description, notes.
Frequency Once.

Whenever you are making a decision involving selection from a number of options, you need to establish the criteria by which you are going to make a choice – this is equally true when selecting candidates for a job or destinations for a holiday. The criteria are the measures that describe how well the option comes up to your requirement.

Imagine for this exercise that you are looking for a new candidate for *your* job. Come up with at least three and no more than seven measures against which each candidate can be rated, which represent the most important factors for being successful in the job.

Having these measures will allow you to do an objective comparison of the candidates. Note that they cannot make the decision for you. They can only provide guidance. Sometimes other factors will push you in a different direction. Sometimes, for instance, the objective criteria are overruled by gut feel – in such circumstances there are one or more hidden criteria that are influencing the decision. One of the valuable outputs of this exercise is that if you disagree with the objective assessment you can try to establish just what those hidden measures are.

Note also that each of the criteria may not be equally important. When we come to the *Sophisticated option evaluation* exercise, this will be taken into account.

With a clear set of criteria it will be much easier to compare candidates.

Personal Development	✪✪✪
Leadership	✪✪✪
Motivation	✪
Coaching	✪✪
Interviewing	✪✪✪✪
Fun	✪✪

26.3 Exercise/Technique: Simple option evaluation

Preparation *Setting criteria* (26.2).
Running time 15 minutes.
Resources Notepad, pen.
Frequency Once.

This exercise follows on from the previous one.

List a number of candidates for your job on a piece of paper. Make them real people, either ones you know or famous people. Start with seven or eight, but then try to eliminate some immediately as totally unacceptable.

Now list the criteria by which you will decide between candidates (you should have these from the previous exercise). Again, if there are more than a handful, try to trim it down to the absolutely crucial criteria.

Finally score each candidate against each criterion. Either use a 1 to 10 scale or a High/Medium/Low scale. Combine the results: with a 1 to 10 scale this means simply adding the scores together. For High/Medium/Low add how many H, M and L scores each has.

This should give you a ranking of the candidates according to these logical criteria. With High/Medium/Low scoring this ranking could be on high scores first, then medium, then low, or by giving each a weighting. However, the ranking shouldn't be used as a fixed decision, but rather a guide to put alongside your intuition. If your gut feel differs from the logical assessment, try to see why. Are there criteria you are ignoring? Are some criteria much more important than others?

Using a simple mechanical comparison like this will give you a first cut at how the candidates stack up, but more importantly, it will also help you understand just how you are coming to a decision if you disagree with the assessment.

In practice it is usually the case that not all criteria are equally important to the job, so before using this technique in anger, move on to the next exercise, *Sophisticated option evaluation*.

The systematic approach will both help to make the decision more rational and help you to understand how you are making your decision.

Personal Development	✪✪✪
Leadership	✪
Motivation	✪
Coaching	✪
Interviewing	✪✪✪✪
Fun	✪✪

26.4 Exercise/Technique: Sophisticated option evaluation

Preparation *Simple option evaluation* (26.3).
Running time 20 minutes.
Resources Notepad, pen.
Frequency Once.

Like the previous exercise, this technique can be used when deciding between any type of option – in this case candidates for a job. Sometimes criteria aren't enough to decide between candidates. You need to be able to give different weightings in order to say that, for example, experience is twice as important as qualifications. The process used is much the same as in *Simple option evaluation*, but will take a little longer.

List the candidates on a piece of paper. Even more so than with a simple evaluation, it is important that you restrict the list to perhaps three or four. Then list the criteria by which you will decide between candidates. What will you use to distinguish them? Again, keep to a handful of the most important criteria. You can pick the information from the previous exercise at this point to avoid repetition.

Before going any further, weight the criteria. Give the first criterion the value 1 and give each other criterion a value that reflects its relative importance compared with that key criterion – for example, if it's half as important, give it a value 0.5. If it is twice as important, make it 2.

Finally, score each candidate against each criterion using a 1 to 10 scale. When you have done this, multiply each score by the criterion weightings before adding up the results.

This should give you a ranking of the candidates according to these logical criteria.

Using this more sophisticated approach, you should in theory be able to read off just who is going to get the job. However, the ranking should only be a guide to put alongside intuition. If your gut feel differs from the logical assessment, try to see why. Are there criteria you are ignoring? Are your weightings incorrect? There could be a number of reasons for diverging from the 'logical' criteria. It might be experience overruling theory, or simply that you are taking in a complex mix of signals that you can't quantify as criteria. Either way, this process provides a simple guide, a starting point for discussion and an understanding of how and if you are diverging from your stated criteria.

A systematic approach ensures that you have considered all the options, and that you are picking one with a conscious awareness of the criteria by which you will make the choice – the outcome is a more rational, thought-through decision.

If the numbers are getting a bit of a strain, you may find it helpful to use a spreadsheet like the sample provided on the Web via www.cul.co.uk/crashcourse.

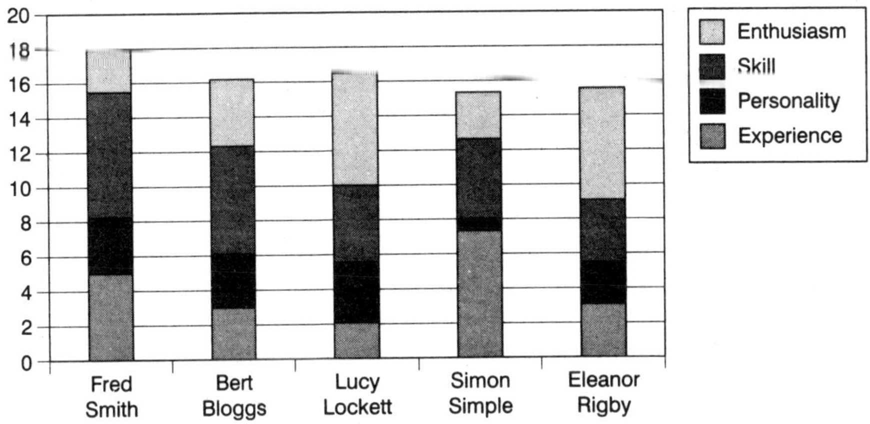

Personal Development	✪✪✪
Leadership	✪
Motivation	✪
Coaching	✪
Interviewing	✪✪✪✪
Fun	✪✪

26.5 Technique: Comparing apples and oranges

Preparation None.
Running time Two minutes.
Resources None.
Frequency Once.

It's convenient to think of a decision involving selection from a number of options, such as a series of interviews for the same job, as a production line, matching up a series of near-identical products against the packaging and choosing the best. In practice, it's rarely that simple. Specifically, you are liable to have the unenviable task of comparing metaphorical apples and oranges.

Imagine you had two equally excellent candidates for a job. One has lots of experience and is very laid back, quietly confident about his abilities. The other has significantly less experience, but is better qualified and has incredible drive; she will clearly give 150 per cent to the job and will enjoy every minute. Spend a couple of minutes thinking about how you would make a decision between the two.

It would be possible to perform an option evaluation on the candidates. In fact, this would prove very useful to help understand more about the different criteria that you are using. But you would still end up having to make a direct comparison of experience and qualifications, confidence and drive.

In the end it will be necessary to have relative weightings for some very different properties of the individual. For instance, you might decide that experience is more important than academic qualifications, but that enough experience to prove competence combined with enthusiasm was better than lots of experience combined with a lack of drive.

The essentials to dealing with apples and oranges are to be very sure of your criteria, how they combine and what your weightings are. Performing an option evaluation won't necessarily give you the answer of whom to recruit, but it certainly can help with this understanding.

Human beings don't come out of a mould; you will have to compare very different people with very different abilities, each of which may be more or less valuable to this particular job.

Personal Development	✪✪✪
Leadership	✪✪
Motivation	✪
Coaching	✪
Interviewing	✪✪✪✪
Fun	✪✪

Unit 27: Coping with time

Time is a limiting factor for all of us. We can no more manage time than we can manage the progress of life towards its inevitable conclusion – it will proceed along a steady progress, second by second. But we can manage how we use time, and this is an essential skill for the good manager. Be very careful to listen out for key lies like 'I haven't got the time' – and translate them to their real meaning – 'It's not important enough to me.' Particularly watch yourself for this habit.

Do try out the exercises as you go. Put them off until later and you probably won't ever do them. Read through the techniques. Make notes about how and when you can use them. And make sure you give them a try in the next appropriate forum.

Unit book

There's no obligation to read all, or any, of the unit books, but you will find that they provide excellent support to the course and strengthen your management skills.

The Mythical Man Month by Frederick P Brooks has been a classic in the IT development world for years, but it deserves a wider audience. Pointing out why big IT projects so often go wrong, Brooks shows the differences between our imagined idea of time, and how we can add it up across multiple staff members, to the realities of how bigger and bigger groups produce less and less productive time.

You can find more information on our unit books, or buy them, from our support site: www.cul.co.uk/crashcourse.

Web links

Time management Web sites can be found at www.cul.co.uk/crashcourse.

27.1 Exercise/Technique: Diaries

Preparation None.
Running time A few minutes.
Resources Diary.
Frequency Daily.

Every manager knows how to manage their diary. So, read no further. Then again, maybe you could pick up a tip or two.

The diary (in the most general sense – it could be a small book in the pocket, an electronic organizer or a package like Outlook on the computer) is the most useful tool most of us have and we tend to take it for granted – at least until things go wrong or it gets lost. Most of us have developed ways of working with the diary that are successful for us. Changing some of these could improve your effectiveness.

There is a close relationship between managing your diary and managing meetings. When you book a meeting in your diary, always ask how long it will take. If the organizer can't say, ask them to give it some thought and come back with an estimate. It is unreasonable to expect you to commit your time if you don't know how much you are committing. When a meeting overruns its planned time it must be your decision whether you stay or leave. You will need to have words with the chairman or organizer of the meeting.

You should also book slots in your diary other than meetings. Time for thinking, time for creative ideas, time for your staff to drop in on you. This last one is important. We have both known managers who claim to have an open door policy, except when in meetings, who seem to spend 25 hours a day in meetings and are unavailable. Since your people are your primary resource for achieving your objectives, there can be very few meetings more important than giving time to them.

As an exercise, go through your diary for the next few weeks. Take out the useless meetings. Add in meetings with yourself and informal drop-in times (for you to go to others and have others come to you). Also add in additional, non-meeting-based information that might be useful as reminders.

Personal Development	✪✪✪✪
Leadership	✪✪✪
Motivation	✪
Coaching	✪
Interviewing	✪
Fun	✪✪

27.2 Exercise/Technique: Mastering time

Preparation Knowledge of what you do with your time.
Running time Minutes, to save a lifetime.
Resources Diary, to-do list, pen and paper.
Frequency Regularly.

The first thing to note about time is that it is remarkably elastic. Generally speaking, it is your management of priorities that will let you down, rather than the amount of time available. Plan to achieve in impossible timescales – but make sure if you do so that you are only working on a very small number of ultra-high priorities.

The next essential is that you do the things you want to do. Sometimes we have a perverse streak that means that there is a whole load of things that we 'should' do that we allow to take priority, but in general you will make time for what you want. Write a list of things you are not managing to do. For each item, question why it is low on your list. Certainly question why you are allowing other things to be higher. Why be busy if it is not delivering what you want?

Get rid of the 'should do' things. There are things you want to do and there are things you have to do in order to do the things you want. There are no 'should do' things. When you examine them you find that the things in this category are being done to meet the expectations of others. You cannot do this and be a leader. Meet your own expectations.

Go through your to-do lists and diary now and allocate less time to the 'have to' things and more time to the 'want to' things. Identifying which is which is an important exercise in itself.

Personal Development	✪✪✪✪
Leadership	✪✪✪
Motivation	✪
Coaching	✪
Interviewing	✪
Fun	✪✪

27.3 Technique: Marking time

Preparation None.
Running time Under an hour.
Resources Your goals.
Frequency As required.

Time is one of the key dimensions that you have to deal with as a manager. It is also a key tool in your toolkit. Never underestimate the power of timescales in terms of targets.

Firstly, you have to have them. Without a timescale a target is not a target. Secondly, you can work with the form that they take. A very long-term goal becomes much more likely to be achieved when it is broken down into a series of very short-term goals.

The long and the short of this is that whenever you hit a snag that looks like it will get in the way of achievement of a goal, one of the first things you should think about is how to manipulate time.

Assuming you have hit a snag, here are some questions that might well prove useful for you and your staff to think through:

- How important is the original deadline? If we change it, what knock-on effects might it have?
- How much are we using time between now and the deadline? Could we fit more periods of activity into this time?
- How are resources being used? Could we bring in more resources and crash the timescales?
- What time are we misusing currently? Are there things that are being done that we could bypass or do without altogether?

Having considered these questions you are in a strong position to change things for your team's advantage.

Personal Development	✪✪✪
Leadership	✪✪✪✪
Motivation	✪✪
Coaching	✪✪✪
Interviewing	✪
Fun	✪✪

27.4 Exercise: Now is all you can do

Preparation None.
Running time An hour.
Resources Pen and large sheet of paper.
Frequency Once.

Think about yesterday. What did you do? Where were you? What were you feeling? Having done this for a few moments, ask yourself where yesterday exists. The answer is that it exists in your head as a memory.

Now think about tomorrow. What plans do you have? Who are you seeing? What pressures will you have on you? Having thought about this, ask yourself where tomorrow is. It also exists only in your head. Even now, this very instant, you are receiving the world as sensory inputs and these are being interpreted inside your head.

The present also is merely thought. The thing that makes now different from the past or the future is that you can act now. You can have an impact now. You can do things now. You cannot do anything in the past. It is gone. You cannot do anything in the future. You can plan for it but by the time you can act, that future must be the present. The present is the only time you can do anything.

When you are involved in all forms of management, this is by its very nature a future-oriented task. Take coaching. You plan with the coachee for an improvement in the future. The only way that you can make this real is by acting now. This is an important concept for your coachee to grasp. If they are perpetually future focused they will miss the levers that they have right now. If they are stuck in looking at past performance they will miss the changes they can make to the future by the choices they can make now.

As a quick exercise, sit down with your coachee and ask them to draw a chart of the time between when you started working together and the achievement of their goal. Ask them now to draw a line on this chart that represents the level of effort they need to make. Now ask them to draw another line that represents the significance of this effort in the achievement of their goal. This should give an indication of where they feel their leverage is. Now is the time to have a discussion about the nature of time and the fact that the only point they can put in effort is now. The only point of any significance is now. They can plan for their effort and they can plan for significant events but these plans are only conceptual. Reality is now. It is where effort needs to be.

One final look at the nature of time when coaching. You and your coachee should both have a sheet of paper and then draw three circles that represent past, present and future. You should not be able to see each other's sheets. The circles can be any size; the relative size expresses the relative importance of each of these periods of time in your mind. They can be anywhere on the paper; the relative position indicates the relationship between each of these periods of time. They can be in any order or any position.

Once you have done this, compare the results. What similarities are there in the relative size, position and relationship of the circles? What differences are there? Do these similarities and differences tell you anything about your relative notions of time? Does what they tell you give you any insights into your relationship? There are no right and wrong answers to this. Whatever you come up with is right for you. Similarly, there is no notion of you trying to change your coachee's view of time or vice versa. This exercise is about understanding, not convergence.

Personal Development	✪✪✪
Leadership	✪✪✪
Motivation	✪✪
Coaching	✪✪✪✪
Interviewing	✪
Fun	✪✪

27.5 Technique: Quick results

Preparation None.
Running time An hour or two.
Resources None.
Frequency As required.

Sometimes, in management in general and in coaching in particular, the people you are working with will have very different ideas about time to you. If you have undertaken the previous exercise, you may have already discovered this. You will meet coachees who accept everything that the two of you talk through about their needs and the time that it will take to make these happen but who still want results now. There are often things that you can do to offer quick results. There are also, more importantly, things that you can do to focus them into a more realistic time frame.

If you are OK about rushing their development and looking for quick results then you jointly need to look at their time. In general, the way to move faster in most fields that you will coach in is to spend a greater proportion of your time on developing the skill in the coachee. If the coachee is willing and able to do this then you could plan accordingly. Another important factor to consider here is that this plan is likely to commit a greater proportion of your time because the targets will be coming around sooner.

If you feel that rushing their development is not appropriate then you need to work with them on the reasons why they need the results now. It might be that they have set themselves a particular deadline and cannot move to change it. Why is the deadline important? How much is the attachment to it real and how much in their heads? Exploring the pressure they are putting on themselves could help to relieve it. Do not push too hard one way or the other – to accept the deadline or to refuse it. Remember that they are the people you are helping, not you. Remember that these are their goals, not yours. Explore them, develop them and be honest with them if you feel that they are unrealistic, but ultimately this is their life.

Personal Development	✪
Leadership	✪✪
Motivation	✪✪
Coaching	✪✪✪✪
Interviewing	✪
Fun	✪✪

Unit 28: Questions, questions

In another unit focusing purely on interviews we consider the currency of the interview – the question itself. The aim of this section is to help you understand how different questions work and can be used. Most people enjoy talking about themselves – if you make them comfortable in an interview, your questions become simple pointers to the right direction and the information comes out.

In this unit there are 50 sample questions. There is no suggestion that you limit yourself to these – they are just examples of effective questions and the sort of response each question might elicit. Feel free to use actual questions from the list, but in many cases it will be more effective to use them as guides and develop your own questions that fit best with your personal style. You should never seem to be reading questions – at that point an interview ceases to be a conversation. Make sure that a number of your questions flow from what has already been said, and that the questions you prepare are written down in keyword form, so the phrasing you use is natural and spur of the moment, rather than stilted reading from a script.

Unit book

There's no obligation to read all, or any, of the unit books, but you will find that they provide excellent support to the course and strengthen your management skills.

This unit's recommended book turns the topic on its head. *Great Answers to Tough Interview Questions* by Martin John Yate is designed to help applicants make it through the tough questions they may face in an interview. But to the interviewer it can both provide a great source of questions, and give some idea of how the more thoughtful candidates may have prepared themselves.

You can find more information on our unit books, or buy them, from our support site: www.cul.co.uk/crashcourse.

Web links

The Crash Course Web site holds another 50 useful questions for interviews at www.cul.co.uk/crashcourse.

28.1 Personality and skills

1. **What do you think you will bring to the job?** – A double question as it asks the interviewee both what they think the job requires, and what they can do to satisfy that requirement. The interviewee has to tread the fine line between modesty and boastfulness, which can provide useful insights into his or her interpersonal skills.
2. **What is your greatest strength...?** – Another testing question for the individual. Look out for (and if necessary probe for) a specific example of this strength being applied, rather than a general assertion. Obviously the strength should be aligned to the job requirements.
3. **And your greatest weakness?** – It's always worth throwing this one in as well. Despite any preparation they may have had, this is always a tricky one for the interviewee. Be wary of a candidate who can't identify any weaknesses – or has too many. Look for a weakness that has positive attributes as far as your job is concerned.
4. **Describe a difficult situation you have had to handle.** – Look for the way the candidate assessed the situation, making sure that he or she understood just what it was, developed one or more solutions, selected an appropriate approach (if there were several solutions) and planned and executed the implementation. Also look for an understanding of why the situation was difficult.
5. **Why have you chosen to apply to this company?** – An element of business awareness here, but a lot of it is about the candidate themselves. Look for good preparation, and be prepared to go into a bit more depth if you get general remarks like 'It is a large, well-respected company.' Why is it well respected? Why does that make it worth applying to? Why does that appeal to this individual?
6. **Have you any questions?** – A useful closing question, which makes it feel as if the interview is over, but it isn't. If the candidate has no questions, they are poorly prepared or indifferent. Look for questions with a degree of insight and openness. Don't be put off because a question is hard for you to answer – and that includes questions about you, the interviewer, as an employee.
7. **Which aspects of this job do you think are most important?** – It's all very well to have nominal skills for the job, but any post will have different priorities and an understanding of these is crucial to being able to do the job properly.
8. **Which areas of the job do you consider you are most skilled at?** – Looks into the candidate's perception of their skills, and how they apply. Correlate the response to both the job description and the other information you have about the candidate, and be prepared to reflect what you discover back to the candidate.
9. **What basis do you have for this assertion?** – Be prepared to ask for a justification of the interviewee's claims, even if it feels a little cruel. If he or she has already given examples and justification, there is no need for this question, but don't take a straight statement without some corroboration.
10. **What would your first steps be in training someone else for this job?** – A rather different and often valuable way of getting a feel for the candidate's understanding of the job. It also takes the pressure off slightly, as it feels like the candidate is 'one of us'.

28.2 Business awareness and teamwork

1. **Why do you think you would like this job?** – A deceptively simple question that probes the interviewee's preparation for the interview. You are not only asking for their match to the job, but also what they know about the role.
2. **What business do you think this company is in?** – Encouraging the interviewee to think a little about the realities of business. The more perceptive candidates may see beyond the simple label ('it's an airline', 'it's a publisher') and bring out the realities of the business ('we're about getting people where they want to go', 'we fulfil dreams', 'we package expertise'). Don't worry, though, if there isn't a neat phrase like this, as long as the candidate sees beyond the basics.
3. **Who are our main competitors likely to be in five years' time, and why?** –This question expects the candidate to really think about the world in which the business operates. It doesn't matter if the answer is the one your strategists would give – the important thing is that the candidate thinks outside the predictable competitors of today in new and innovative directions.
4. **What do you think are our top three costs?** – A nitty-gritty examination of the candidate's gut feel for one of the prime business drivers. It doesn't matter whether or not the answer is 100 per cent right, as long as it is logical and well thought out.
5. **Give me a picture of our most important customers.** – This could either be literal (ie who the most important customers are) or a more general description of the type of customer that is liable to be important to the company. Part of the value of the question is seeing how the candidate deals with the key word 'important'.
6. **Can you describe circumstances when you work best alone, and when you work best in a team?** – Expand on this if necessary to explore the individual's understanding of teamwork. If they are simply trying to follow the party line that 'team is best', they will have difficulty coming up with both examples – if they understand the reality better they will realize that some tasks need solo concentration while others benefit hugely from being part of a team.
7. **What role do you tend to take in a team?** – Check out the candidate's understanding of teams and his or her preferred role. Practically everyone has a preferred role, so if the interviewee says they don't, you ought to be suspicious. It may be, though, that he or she doesn't understand the concept of roles in a team. If necessary, probe by discussing different team roles.
8. **What makes a good team?** – Again looking at an understanding of teams. Look for something more than 'the members work well together'. Concepts like synergy, the complementary nature of differing roles and so on should be present.
9. **Give an example of when you were involved in a great team, and describe why it was great.** – A useful expansion on the previous question if you suspect the answer was based more on book theory than on practical experience. Almost everyone should

have *some* example of good teamwork, even if it was in an unimportant context. Make sure you get the 'why' as well as the 'what'.

10. **Why do some teams fail?** – Again, looking for a good understanding of the way people work together. This is an interesting question, because you can understand how things ought to be without knowing the realities of how things fall apart. Ask for specific examples (whether or not the candidate was part of the team in question).

28.3 Leadership and manageability

1. **If you are in a room full of people with a group task to do and no one in charge, what is your response?** – Be wary of the person who wades in and tries to take charge immediately. A good leader is more likely to try to bring everyone in, assess their potential contributions and encourage them into action – to take charge of the process rather than the people. Look for this in the response.
2. **Are you a natural leader?** – Look for someone who understands the personality traits that makes a good leader, and says that they feel they are well endowed with these, but that there's always more to develop – anyone who is prepared to say outright that they are a great natural leader should be treated with suspicion. This is an intentionally closed question. It can be answered 'yes' or 'no' – but anyone who does so is not very good at communication. Use silence to get a response.
3. **How would you influence people over whom you have no authority?** – You are looking here for an understanding of the common necessity in business to set a lead where there is no formal structure of power.
4. **Describe the time you acted best as a leader, in work or outside.** – This question might not be necessary as a result of developments from questions 2 or 3 (if used), but if the candidate hasn't come up with a good example, it's worth pushing for it to help clarify his or her understanding of leadership.
5. **Where do you want to be in five years' time?** – A lot of potential value in this one. Does the interviewee have realistic aspirations (and self-valuation)? Does he or she understand what the sort of job that might be mentioned for the future implies? Is the current post seen as a stepping-stone, or an end in itself? Is the increasing move to flatter organizations, with more opportunities for variety but less for promotion, a good fit with his or her profile? If you get a blanket answer like 'in management', explore the candidate's understanding of what management is and why he or she wants to be involved in it – a particularly testing consideration.
6. **How do you feel about being told you are doing something wrong?** – Look for human understanding, rather than just parroting that he or she is always willing to take advice. A better reply would be something along the lines of 'I think, like everyone, that I find it difficult sometimes when I'm criticized, but I have found that I can take helpful comments and feel good about doing things better. Occasionally I won't agree and then I'll say so and discuss the matter rather than hiding it away.' Worry about anyone who says 'I can't ever remember being wrong' (and it does happen).
7. **How long do you want to stay with this company?** – Be suspicious of both those who expect a job for life, and those who see it as a year or two's stepping-stone. The former will lack drive, while the latter will be concentrating more on job applications than on the task. The best answer is likely to be conditional on the company offering enough challenges, but with the expectation that it will be a long-term relationship

(because it's a great company). Expect the more astute interviewees to turn this one round and ask what you think, or how long you've been with the company.

8. **How many hours a week do you think you should work?** – This verges on a shock question, as it puts the interviewee under considerable pressure. Most companies like to present an image of being caring, and considerate to employees' needs, but is yours a company that expects everyone to work overly long hours? Be suspicious of anyone who is categorical about working the contracted hours. Probably the ideal answer is someone who will put in extra hours when there is a special requirement, but does expect a reasonable time away from work – you want balanced employees with fully rounded lives.
9. **Could you do your current boss's job?** – A good test of the balance between confidence and hubris. Be suspicious of both those who could never do the job, and those who could do it better today. A good balance is for the individual to feel that they could, with the appropriate experience and training, aspire to the job should the occasion arise. However, don't be entirely dismissive of either extreme. It's a poor assumption that everyone should have the aspiration of achieving management. Some of the best workers love their job and want to remain productive rather than become administrative (doctors, for example).
10. **If you think a co-worker could do his or her job better, what would you do about it?** – There's a fine line between being helpful and being a pain. We've all come across people who are constantly moaning about the way things are – and the way they should be. Look out for someone who is likely to be too free with his or her opinions, or constantly carping and complaining. A much better answer would be that the interviewee would discuss the situation with the other person, encouraging them to explore the problem, but never actually point out a fault or criticize (or complain to the boss).

28.4 Self-starter and creativity

1. **What's the best example of your showing initiative?** – Every candidate should have some good examples, though frighteningly a fair number are fazed by this question. Look for understanding of what initiative is required for, and the difference between showing initiative and being a pest by constantly challenging authority. Questions like this will often result in a longish pause while the interviewee collects his or her thoughts. This isn't a bad thing – it shows that the question is being taken seriously.
2. **How do you feel about your career so far?** – You are probably looking for someone who will stick with the job, but you don't want a candidate without ambition, so the ideal reply should suggest that the individual has made good progress, and is happy to take things at the right pace, but expects more still. If yours is a relatively flat organization, look for appreciation of variety and personal growth rather than simply looking for promotions.
3. **Do you prefer to be absolutely clear about what is expected of you, or to work within broad principles?** – Be careful to phrase this one so that the two options are equally weighted. You aren't going to get a lot of information by asking 'Do you prefer to be lead by the nose, or to act with initiative?' There isn't a right answer here, it really does depend on the job, though an increasing number of positions do depend on individuals being able to act flexibly and with initiative.
4. **What makes for an effective meeting?** – All too often a lot of time is wasted in meetings with no clear agenda, where conversations are allowed to stray all over the place and no actions are generated. Look out for an understanding of these prime points (clear agenda, meeting well chaired to follow the agenda, action points produced and followed up) from the candidate.
5. **Your boss is due to attend an important meeting, but does not arrive at work that morning. What do you do?** – Again this question is looking for the self-starter's ability to assess need and take action. He or she should probably try to contact the boss (mobile phone, home), but if it's impossible, to get whatever information they can together and either attend the meeting on the boss's behalf or discuss the possibility with the other attendees (being sure not to drop the boss in it). Look for both initiative and social understanding here.
6. **If you had to come up with a new product or service for our company, what would it be?** – A good opportunity for thinking out of the box, which also probes the candidate's understanding of what your company is all about. Look for something original that would mean a significant step forward for the company.
7. **Why is it important for a company like ours to be innovative?** – Although the specifics of the answer will vary, any company these days has reasons for needing creativity. Much will focus around differentiation (making the company better than the competition) and cost saving, but in the end it comes down to survival.

8. **Do you like taking risks?** – This is a closed question, but it should be very easy to move on from a yes or no answer. The ideal reply is probably to say that the candidate doesn't like taking just any risk (showing they're not irresponsible) but recognizes that some calculated risk taking is necessary if the company is to progress.
9. **How do you think the failure of a new idea should be treated?** Another one digging into the understanding of the nature and value of calculated risk taking. It is almost impossible to be creative without taking risks – and this implies failing sometimes. The reaction to failure should be to learn from the outcome, and move straight on. Failure, used right, is a positive tool for advancement. This one could be turned round on you, by the candidate asking if yours is the sort of company where it is safe to fail in the name of progress. Be prepared to answer.
10. **What would you say is the most creative thing you do?** – Look for a creative answer. It might be a traditional creative task (painting or writing or whatever), but it might just as easily be selling a company's products. If there's no explanation included, ask why the particular activity was chosen. If a hobby is chosen, ask for an example in the work context.

28.5 Shocks and analytical thinking

1. **What makes you *the* right person for this job?** – This really shouldn't be a shock question, but a surprising number of applicants are not prepared for it and get flustered. The difficulty for the interviewees is partly that they are being asked to compare themselves against an unknown (the rest of the applicants) and also because they are being asked to sing their own praises, which few like to do.
2. **How will you add value to the company?** – This is an alternative to 'what do you think you will bring to the job' that has a much harder edge. It is asking the candidate to justify his or her existence. Most interviewees will respond with generalisms. If you want to be even tougher, follow it up by saying something like 'you are going to cost us X a year – how much financial benefit can we expect to get from you to offset this, and how will you contribute to that benefit?'
3. **What other jobs have you applied for? What would you do if they all offered you a position?** – It may be that this is the candidate's only application: if so, ask why. Is it really the only suitable job on the market? Is he or she wildly over-confident or just testing the water? It's the follow-up if there are other jobs that makes this a below-the-belt question, as it asks the interviewee to rank your job against the competition. Look for good reasoning, and an answer that gives some good points to your competitors (otherwise it would be fair to ask why he or she is applying to these competitors at all).
4. **Sell me one of our company's products or services.** – It's only fair to give the interviewee a little thinking time here with this double nasty. You are expecting them to know something about one of your products, and to sell it to you. It's reasonable for the interviewee to say 'While I've got a good broad picture, can you tell me a little about a specific product you'd like me to sell?' This one tests communications skills and thinking on his or her feet. It's nasty but effective.
5. **I'm not really sure this is the job for you.** – A particularly nasty one this, expecting the candidate to be prepared to argue that, in fact, things are very different from this apparent perception. Be prepared to answer a response like 'what makes you think that?' from the more astute interviewees.
6. **Why are US manhole covers round?** – This is a classic analytical thinking question, the answer being that, unlike square or rectangular covers, round ones can't fall down the hole. US companies sometimes ask the variant 'Why are manhole covers round?', which suffers from implied cultural imperialism – in many countries this simply isn't true, and 'they aren't' is a perfectly valid answer if you ask that form of the question.
7. **If you fill two buckets with water and take one to 20 degrees Celsius and the other to 20 degrees Fahrenheit, then simultaneously drop a coin into each, which will reach the bottom first?** – The 20 degrees Celsius bucket. The other will never reach the bottom: the water is frozen. This question tests the candidate's ability to really listen to the requirement, otherwise they may rush off into all manner of complex consideration that is irrelevant.

8. **You put a single amoeba into a box and seal it up. Each minute the number of amoebae doubles. If the box is full an hour after starting the experiment, how long did it take to get half-full?** – Again we're looking out for attention to what has been said. The number doubles in a minute, so the box goes from half-full to full in a minute, so it was half-full after 59 minutes (or one minute before it was full). Everyone should get there, but it's a matter of how quickly and logically.
9. **A man goes into a bar, sits down and orders a double brandy, three pints of beer and ten glasses of water. 'Ah,' says the barmaid, 'you must be a fireman.' How does she know?** – Because he was wearing his uniform. This sort of distraction puzzle is useful at seeing how well the candidate, under pressure, can see around the sort of irrelevancies that are often flung up when trying to understand a real-life problem.
10. **A farmer has two large fields. One is two square kilometres, the other two kilometres square. Which, if either, is bigger?** – Some people will simply know this, but others will exhibit good logical deduction in working out that two kilometres square (ie 2 kilometres each side of a square) is 4 square kilometres, and hence bigger. It's a very simple question, but not every job requires the same level of analytical skills.

Unit 29: Removing demotivators

Most of the actions we take in good management are active – but sometimes it's more about getting things out of the way so that your staff can get on with their jobs effectively. We've already seen this when dealing with the system – this unit provides more mechanisms for removing factors that will demotivate your people.

Do try out the exercises as you go. Put them off until later and you probably won't ever do them. Read through the techniques. Make notes about how and when you can use them. And make sure you give them a try in the next appropriate forum.

Unit book

There's no obligation to read all, or any, of the unit books, but you will find that they provide excellent support to the course and strengthen your management skills.

Understanding different cultures is critical if you are not going to demotivate an international workforce (or an international customer base). The essential book on the subject is Fons Trompenaars' *Riding the Waves of Culture*.

You can find more information on our unit books, or buy them, from our support site: www.cul.co.uk/crashcourse.

29.1 Exercise: Money, money, money

Preparation None.
Running time 10 minutes.
Resources None.
Frequency Once.

We've already considered the pure management aspects of reward, but the purpose of this exercise is to consider how you use money as a motivator. Remember first of all that giving someone extra money generally only has short-term motivational benefits – though not paying enough certainly demotivates in a big way.

Think about your staff and the elements of pay. How is the money divided into basic salary and other elements like overtime and performance pay (in different forms)? What do you actually pay people for – what do they have to do to get the money? What influences any extra payments? What influences an increase in salary?

Having done this analysis (it may seem obvious, but too many assumptions are made about this sort of detail), think if you got the balance right, or whether there are some items that would be better done differently. The next paragraph has some points for stimulus.

Are you paying for attendance? Is time all that meaningful, apart from being easy to measure? There's nothing really motivational about payment for time spent 'at work'. Do you have special payment for skills? If so, is there any positive recognition of the use of those skills, or are you really paying for a (potentially worthless) certificate? Do you consider how an individual meets objectives? Does the quality and timeliness of output come into the equation? If not, why not – that's the whole point, isn't it? Do you reward creativity and sensible risk taking? This implies occasional failure, but without it you will have a workforce that never goes beyond the mundane.

We take money for granted. This exercise gives you an opportunity to think about how and why we use money to make sure the maximum motivational power is gained from it. You may not have direct influence over how money is used in your company – if this is the case, having thought about it, discuss it with your boss and encourage him or her to do the same. Eventually it may reach someone who can make a difference.

Personal Development	✪✪
Leadership	✪✪✪
Motivation	✪✪✪✪
Coaching	✪
Interviewing	✪
Fun	✪✪

29.2 Technique: Promises, promises

Preparation None.
Running time One minute.
Resources Diary.
Frequency Regular.

If ever they bring out a management phrase book, 'leave it with me' will be translated as 'I'm not going to do anything.' Sadly, a manager's promises often aren't worth the paper they aren't printed on. If you don't fulfil your promises, you are guaranteed to demotivate, whether on a one-off, extreme basis or as a drip-feed of small disappointments.

The first requirement to solving this problem is being aware when you make a promise. Sometimes a casual remark will be interpreted as a promise – if that is likely, consider it to be one. You might mean 'I'll consider it', but if the most likely interpretation is 'I promise to deal with it', you had better do something. Once you are aware of your promises, keep track of them, hence the requirement for a diary. Capture what you have promised, by when. If there is any possibility of not delivering, let the people concerned know as soon as possible and re-negotiate. Promise keeping applies equally to individuals, teams and groups.

We're all good at making promises, sometimes unconsciously. It might take you a while to spot when you make one. When problems arise because you didn't do something you said you would, work out when and how the promise was made so you can trap similar promises in the future. Note that failing on promises is equally bad for those who work for you, your peers and your boss. Each will find a different way of responding to the reduction of motivation, but you will find them all painful.

Delivering on promises builds trust and avoids a powerful demotivator. Don't worry if you can't deliver occasionally – provided someone is kept well informed and is sure that best efforts are being made they will feel that the promise is being fulfilled.

Personal Development	✪✪✪
Leadership	✪✪✪✪
Motivation	✪✪✪✪
Coaching	✪✪
Interviewing	✪
Fun	✪✪

29.3 Technique: The rumour mill

Preparation None.
Running time 10 minutes.
Resources Team meeting.
Frequency Once.

There are few things with the same power to crush motivation as a rumour. The frightening thing about rumours is that they seem airy and insubstantial, but they can create wholesale damage. They're very easy to start, and much harder to stop.

Hold a 10-minute rumour dumping session with your team. Find out as much as possible about the sort of rumours that are common. If they're about the company – its future, what it is doing – look at ways that you can get company information spread more effectively. Could you use an intranet or other computer systems? Is there any reason why employees shouldn't have free access to most company information? If they're about individuals, it might be worth talking with those individuals or their managers to take action to change things. Your aim should be to kill rumours by spreading more accurate if less salacious information.

Favourite topics for rumours are redundancies, relocations, staff leaving the company, salaries and emotional entanglements. You won't be able to eradicate every rumour, but it should be possible to minimize the threat of demoralizing business-oriented rumour by ensuring that your staff have appropriate information.

The truth might not be particularly pleasant – but it's almost always better than drawn-out uncertainty. In the case of a lot of rumours, it's also a lot better than the rumour. There's a big motivational opportunity here as long as you are prepared to be more open about company information.

It's useful to repeat this technique occasionally, trying it with different groups of people to see what the state of the rumour mill is. Note that the quick part here is identifying rumours – putting in place the appropriate information flows may take much longer.

Personal Development	✪
Leadership	✪✪✪
Motivation	✪✪✪✪
Coaching	✪
Interviewing	✪
Fun	✪✪

29.4 Technique: No secrets

Preparation None.
Running time 10 minutes.
Resources None.
Frequency Once.

To put this technique into practice you need to be quite senior in the company, or be able to get an idea reasonably high up the tree.

Secrets are demotivating; being open and honest is a real positive asset. But you knew that. So why do you keep so many things secret? Consider this course of action. Put all your personnel details, including pay, in open filing cabinets that anyone can access – or publish them on the intranet. Make sure you do it properly. No exceptions. And full disclosure – all your rewards, please, directors.

The first reaction to this proposal is shock. You *can't* do this. It will result in anarchy and confusion. Yet it's exactly what computer consultancy CMG and engineering firm Semco do. And the result is positive motivation. It takes a little while to get used to, but it eliminates the rumours and suppositions and petty concerns over parity with other staff.

Of course it also implies implementing your reward system extremely fairly, but you are doing that anyway, aren't you? It will temporarily demotivate some people, who find they are doing less well than others they think they're better than. Discuss this with them. Make sure they understand why they aren't so highly rated, and what they can do about it. Turn it into an opportunity for motivation.

Any disbenefits from personal irritation will be far outweighed by the benefits of trust and openness. This is a bold step, but has great potential to make a difference.

Look also at other 'confidential' information and make sure that it really will endanger the company if it is more widely known. The more information about the company you get to the staff, the more motivated they will be to give their best, and the better chance they'll have of delivering on it.

Personal Development	✪
Leadership	✪✪✪✪
Motivation	✪✪✪✪
Coaching	✪✪
Interviewing	✪
Fun	✪✪

29.5 Exercise/Technique: Positive visualization

Preparation None.
Running time An hour.
Resources Imagination.
Frequency Occasionally.

Some of the demotivators and blockages you have to deal with are external. This is a technique that can help overcome mental blocks. This exercise is only one type of visualization exercise. There are many, many more that you could learn and usefully employ.

Your subconscious mind deals with the world in symbols. This fact can be a very useful tool for talking to the subconscious and affecting the way that it sees the world and, thus, the limitations it places upon you.

Think of something that limits you and the qualities you'd have in your life without the limit. Many people will think of money, some will think of other things. Now sit yourself down and relax. To do this, breathe slowly and with each breath out imagine that you are breathing out tension. As you breathe out the tension, feel a different group of muscles in your body relaxing. Spend some time doing this.

Now create in your mind the picture of a wooded glade. At one side of this glade is a cliff with a cave in it. On your back is a knapsack with your limit inside it. Leave this at the entrance to the cave and enter the cave. As you walk in, you notice that the interior of the cave is warm and comfortable and surprisingly light. Ahead of you, you can hear the sound of running water. As you approach this sound you see a golden goblet that is overflowing with a crystal-clear liquid. This liquid is the qualities you wish to bring into your life. It is flowing from this goblet and spilling onto the floor.

You drink from the goblet. As you drink, you feel the qualities suffusing your being. Miraculously, as you drink, the goblet continues to fill and to overflow. It will never empty. There is an abundance of what you desire and this abundance will always be there for you. When you have drunk your fill, replace the goblet, knowing that you can return at any time. Make your way out of the cave into the dappled sunshine and slowly bring yourself back to wakefulness.

This sort of imagery and visualization can be extremely powerful when working on your own blocks, and also when coaching others and working with them to remove their own.

Personal Development	✪✪✪✪
Leadership	✪✪
Motivation	✪✪
Coaching	✪✪✪
Interviewing	✪
Fun	✪✪

Unit 30: Subtle inspiration

The final unit looks at some further ways to inspire others. This isn't about razzmatazz, but rather a subtle influence. This is management using the same sort of forces that produced the Grand Canyon – small, but constant and unavoidable.

Do try out the exercises as you go. Put them off until later and you probably won't ever do them. Read through the techniques. Make notes about how and when you can use them. And make sure you give them a try in the next appropriate forum.

Unit book

There's no obligation to read all, or any, of the unit books, but you will find that they provide excellent support to the course and strengthen your management skills.

The final recommendation is some light relief, although it provides some excellent management lessons (both good and bad). In *Accidental Empires*, Robert X Cringeley documents the rise and rise of the high-tech companies. As the subtitle *How the boys of Silicon Valley make their millions, battle foreign competition, and still can't get a date* suggests, it's as much about people as businesses, as every good management text should be.

You can find more information on our unit books, or buy them, from our support site: www.cul.co.uk/crashcourse.

30.1 Technique: Own pocket

Preparation Buy something.
Running time Five minutes.
Resources Small amount of cash.
Frequency Occasional.

This technique can be used in association with any other involving giving something to the people you manage, but it stands alone as a technique. We have seen how a gift can be much more effective as a motivating reward than cash. You can, in some circumstances, emphasize this motivational value by buying the gift from your own pocket, rather than on company expenses.

Obviously you don't want to put yourself hugely out of pocket, but it's arguable that the good manager (or presenter) will be prepared to suffer a small outgoing to gain the return.

You will have to be a little subtle about this. Loudly announcing that you are out of pocket in the process isn't going to make anyone motivated. It should either be simply the sort of gift that you are very unlikely to buy on expenses (for instance, a chocolate bar) or phrased in such a way that it seems likely that you bought it.

This is a technique to be used with some care. The gift should be of low value, and you should make sure that it is given in such a way that it is clearly a thank-you for something done in the work context, so there is no danger of it being taken as a sexual overture. It is also an approach that will devalue with over-use. Just as swearing has more impact if used infrequently, this sort of gift is particularly special if kept sparing. Even with birthdays or Christmas it is probably more effective to be an occasional giver than regularly, as it is then seen as something special. (This is with respect to work contacts; your family may expect more regularity!) As always, be careful to avoid the appearance of favouritism.

Personal Development	✪
Leadership	✪✪✪
Motivation	✪✪✪✪
Coaching	✪
Interviewing	✪
Fun	✪✪

30.2 Technique: Taskforce opportunities

Preparation None.
Running time 10 minutes.
Resources None.
Frequency Regular.

We all grow stale in the same job. Sometimes there is enough variety from career progression – in fact, some would appreciate the opportunity to sit in the same seat for six months at a time, but for many a lack of variety and challenge results in gradual dulling of motivation. A good way to return to sharpness is making use of taskforces. Typically these bring together a cross-functional team to tackle a specific task. Taskforces might be full time, with secondment from the existing job, or part time.

On a regular basis, and when you are aware of an initiative in the company, consider the staff you are responsible for and the opportunities for taskforce work. The motivational factors are significant and varied. A new role, working with different people, a more exciting atmosphere than normal office life, a specific challenge (for many administrators, a real demotivating factor is the lack of specific objectives, there's just more of the same) and clear arrival.

It's often the case when on a part-time taskforce that the staff member is expected to do everything they did before as well. If you are to have someone involved, they should be able to offload some of their responsibilities in the interim. A full-time secondment always has a degree of uncertainty about there still being a job to come back to. It may well be that they won't return to the same job (in fact, it's a good idea not to, as it may seem very stale), but there should be a clear path for getting one when the taskforce ends.

Taskforce places aren't in everyone's gift, but if you can get some of your staff involved in them, you will find a real boost to their motivation. Even if you can't get someone into a taskforce you may be able to find other special, short-term tasks with specific endings for them.

Personal Development	✪✪
Leadership	✪✪✪
Motivation	✪✪✪✪
Coaching	✪
Interviewing	✪
Fun	✪✪✪✪

30.2 Exercise/Technique: What's in it for me?

Preparation None.
Running time Five minutes.
Resources None.
Frequency Regular.

Underlying an understanding of motivation is the ability to put yourself into someone else's shoes and ask 'What's in it for me?' Of course this isn't the sole driver of the human spirit – in fact time and again under pressure other factors win out over personal gain – but taking this viewpoint can be a valuable check on your motivational input, especially when dealing with a large group.

If you are planning a group session, think yourself into the mind of Isobel, a typical attendee. Perform a crude cost/benefit analysis. What would she have been doing if she wasn't attending? What is it costing her to attend? What will she get out of it personally or in status? What would she enjoy anyway and what is she merely attending out of loyalty?

Surprisingly often when undertaking such exercises, the benefits come at a remarkably high price. If you want to maximize motivation, look for opportunities to reduce costs and improve personal benefits for Isobel. You can also increase benefits for the company or the country or the world, but they will generally have significantly less impact on motivation.

As an exercise, imagine you were setting up a press conference for a new product launched by your company. You decide to put on a big event in the Lake District. Now put yourself in the mind of a journalist and do the 'What's in it for me' exercise. Remember to include both costs and benefits.

The cost aspect isn't entirely straightforward. Bear in mind the opportunity cost – the cost of missing what could have been done. This can be particularly strong if attendees are self-employed, where attending a day's session means a day without earnings.

You're never going to get entirely into someone else's mindset, and you will often be dealing with a group of very different people, so the concept of a 'typical' person may be difficult to pin down. This does not make the exercise less valuable, though.

This approach is essential with group sessions. It is less so with individuals and teams where you will normally have more information and a longer relationship – but it is always valuable to see a force like motivation from the viewpoint of the recipient.

Personal Development	✪
Leadership	✪✪✪
Motivation	✪✪✪✪
Coaching	✪✪
Interviewing	✪
Fun	✪✪

30.4 Exercise/Technique: Ambience chasers

Preparation None.
Running time Five minutes.
Resources None.
Frequency Once.

Spend a few minutes on an ambience review. Look at the environment of the person or people you are trying to motivate. Is it pleasant? Is it comfortable? Is it personal? When you consider ambience from the viewpoint of a participant, you often come across distressing truths. For example, let's say you were a supermarket, trying to motivate shoppers. Consider the checkout. There's nowhere to sit, there's nothing to read but the covers of glossy magazines, nothing to entertain you and not so much as a pot plant. You might make similar observations about a person sitting on a hard seat in an auditorium, or the hapless Dilbert in Scott Adams' masterful cartoons, stuck in his demotivating cubicle.

Ambience problems aren't necessarily easy to fix. You can't put seating at a supermarket checkout because there isn't room and it would get in the way of the trolleys. There have to be hard seats in that particular auditorium because they can't afford to replace them. Dilbert has to have his cubicle to fit with company policies. Yet these are all excuses, and the creative manager can overcome them.

As an exercise, do an ambience review for someone who works for you.

If beauty is in the eye of the beholder, ambience is in the senses of the experiencer (it just doesn't sound as good). While there are some reasonably universal requirements – a comfortable temperature, for example, that doesn't freeze you or put you to sleep – many aspects of ambience are personal. What may be intolerable mess to one person could be cosy surroundings to another. When working at a group level you have to work at a generic level, though.

Ambience can have a startlingly strong effect on motivation. Generally it does so when other motivational factors are weak – if you are really interested in what you are doing, you won't care where you do it. Even so, ambience should be ignored at your peril, especially if you are in a competitive area like supermarket checkouts.

Personal Development	✪
Leadership	✪✪
Motivation	✪✪✪✪
Coaching	✪✪
Interviewing	✪
Fun	✪✪

30.5 Technique: On the up

Preparation None.
Running time Half an hour.
Resources None.
Frequency Occasionally.

This final technique is particularly useful when undertaking the coaching role. We cannot stress enough the importance of improvements in performance being obvious to the coachee. If they can't see progress they may well lose heart. They will certainly not move forward as well or as fast as they would if they can see progress. This is one reason why I always recommend breaking long-term goals down into a series of short-term ones. Progress becomes more obvious and the individual steps are smaller.

A corollary to this is that measurement is important. Having a goal that is measurable is necessary if you are to measure improvement. Even if the measure is subjective it is better than nothing. Do, however, avoid subjective measures that depend on how the coachee feels. This will cause the measure of their performance to be a reflection of their mood and that can lead to a downward spiral when things start to go wrong.

As a quick exercise to see how successful your goals are on this scale, go through all of the goals you have for all of your coachees and ask yourself these questions:

- How objective is the measure of performance? How much does opinion come into it and if it does, whose opinion are we talking about?
- How directly is the measure related to success? Remember, there may be some measures that are indicators of something that you would like to measure but cannot. For instance, you might not be able to measure staff morale but you could measure absence through sickness.
- When will the coachee next have an indication of increase in performance? This is a tricky area to get right because the intervals need to be far enough apart to allow a real increase in performance but close enough together to be motivating.
- How clear are you about what shortfall in performance would indicate something going wrong and what shortfall is acceptable as variation and noise?
- How able are you to see the results (do you work alongside your coachee?) and how much must you rely on them reporting back to you?

Whilst going through this you might want to be asking yourself which goals you would change to make them more successful as motivational measurers of performance. If you decide that something needs changing, you will need to talk this through with your coachee.

Measures are important but alone they are not enough. You also need constant feedback that reinforces any improvement. Whether you see your coachee every day, once a week or even coach by telephone sessions you must always ensure that any improvements are referred to. Any work that has been done to move towards the goal needs to be mentioned. All steps that have been taken must be highlighted.

Have you thought about the structure of your coaching sessions? If not then now might be a good time. There are a number of activities that you need to make sure you have covered, not in the way of a checklist or a clumsy move from one to another but more in the way of a reminder at the back of your head.

Each coaching session needs to have a huge amount of listening. This is not an inactive task; it is very active and may need you to probe and question fairly vigorously. You will then need to structure what you have heard and play it back to the coachee in a way that highlights the moves towards their goal. Between you, you then need to plan activities for the period up until the next coaching session. If your coaching sessions also involve the activities for improvement (most often the case with sports coaching), then these things will be at the start of the session and the actual activities for improvement later.

Plan now the next coaching session you will hold. Think through how much time you need to give to each element of the session and how you will make it happen.

Personal Development	✪✪
Leadership	✪✪
Motivation	✪✪
Coaching	✪✪✪✪
Interviewing	✪
Fun	✪✪

4 Review

PULLING IT TOGETHER

In the 30 units of the course you will have tried out a wide range of exercises and added a whole collection of techniques to your toolbag. Where now?

Begin by re-reading chapter 1. Get the basics well established. Make sure you are familiar with the essential nature of leadership, motivation, coaching and interviewing. Get familiar with the underlying principles of establishing clear goals, providing support, using trust and communicating effectively. In the appendices at the back of the book you will find listings that will enable you to pick out a technique that's particularly appropriate for one of the aspects, but bear in mind that the divisions are arbitrary – it really is all about people management.

Next, move from theory to practice. Make sure that you are using the techniques in your everyday management role. Try to keep an eye on your own performance – see how much you are managing and how much you are leading. Look for opportunities to set clear directions, to communicate, to support and to trust.

What might be useful is to use the checklist in chapter 2 not just as a marker that you have finished a unit of the course, but as a reminder. Revisit the elements of the course several times over the next year to ensure that they are well embedded in your way of doing things.

One final thought – read. Reading is one of the easiest and most pleasurable ways to develop your management skills. Read voraciously and as widely as possible. If you didn't have time to read all the unit books, continue picking them off. But make sure you read.

COLLECTED READING LIST

An overview of the unit books from the course

Abraham, J (2000) *Getting Everything You Can Out Of All You've Got*, Piatkus, London
Adams, S (2000) *The Dilbert Principle*, Boxtree, London
Barham, K and Heimer, C (1998) *ABB, The Dancing Giant*, FT/Pitman, London
Belbin, M (1995) *Team Roles at Work,* Butterworth Heinemann, Oxford
Block, P (1987) *The Empowered Manager,* Jossey Bass, San Francisco, CA
Branson, R (2000) *Losing my Virginity*, Virgin, London
Brooks, F P (1995) *The Mythical Man Month*, Addison-Wesley, Wokingham
Buzan, T and Buzan, B (2000) *The Mind Map Book*, BBC, London
Carroll, P (1993) *Big Blues: The Unmaking of IBM*, Orion, London
Clegg, B (1999) *Instant Time Management*, Kogan Page, London
Clegg, B (1999) *Creativity and Innovation for Managers*, Butterworth Heinemann, Oxford
Clegg, B (2000) *Instant Stress Management*, Kogan Page, London
Clegg, B (2001) *The Professional's Guide to Mining the Internet*, Kogan Page, London
Clegg, B and Birch, P (1998) *Instant Teamwork*, Kogan Page, London
Cooper, C L and Palmer, S (2000) *Conquer your Stress*, CIPD, London
Cringeley, R X (1996) *Accidental Empires*, Penguin, London
Dale, M (1996) *How to Be a Better Interviewer*, Kogan Page, London
Denny, R (1993) *Motivate to Win*, Kogan Page, London
Fleming, I and Taylor, A J D (1998) *The Coaching Pocketbook*, Management Pocketbooks, Alresford
Freemantle, D (2001) *The Stimulus Factor*, FT/Prentice Hall, London
Handy, C (1995) *The Hungry Spirit*, Arrow, London
Handy, C (1995) *The Empty Raincoat*, Arrow, London
Harvey-Jones, J (1994) *Making it Happen*, HarperCollins, London
Klein, N (2001) *No Logo*, Flamingo, London
Larson, G (1996) *Last Chapter and Worse*, Time Warner, London
Morris, D (1978) *Manwatching*, Grafton Books, London
Mulligan, E (1999) *Life Coaching*, Piatkus, London
Parkin, M (1998) *Tales for Trainers*, Kogan Page, London
Pease, A (1997) *Body Language*, Sheldon Press, London
Peters, T (1994) *The Tom Peters Seminar, Crazy Times Call for Crazy Organizations*, Vintage, New York, NY

Ricks, D (1999) *Blunders in International Business*, Blackwell, Oxford
Semler, R (2001) *Maverick!*, Arrow, London
Townsend, R (1984) *Further Up the Organization*, Joseph, London
Trompenaars, F (1997) *Riding the Waves of Culture*, Nicholas Brealey, London
Yate, M J (1998) *Great Answers to Tough Interview Questions*, Kogan Page, London
Yerkes, L (2001) *Fun Works*, Berrett-Koehler, San Francisco, CA

Appendix

TECHNIQUES WITH HIGH PERSONAL DEVELOPMENT RATINGS

Ref.	*Title*
1.4	Becoming a figure-of-eight person
2.1	Charisma
2.2	Being an inspiration
2.3	Getting *your* inspiration
5.1	Using stress
5.2	Learning to relax
5.3	Get fit
5.5	Stop and think
6.1	Conversations
6.2	Networking
6.4	Eye eye
7.4	Knowing yourself
7.5	Keeping abreast
8.4	Saying 'No'
10.1	Energy
10.3	Being obsessive
12.5	Doing yourself out of a job
13.2	The genuine article

13.4	Your body
15.1	360 degree appraisals
15.4	What do they look like?
17.1	Risk and failure
22.1	Coaching outside work
22.5	Coaching yourself
23.1	Watch my feet, not my lips
23.3	Going the extra mile
23.4	Love
25.4	Great note taking
27.1	Diaries
27.2	Mastering time
29.5	Positive visualization

TECHNIQUES WITH HIGH LEADERSHIP RATINGS

Ref.	*Title*
1.1	Understanding your style
1.2	Culture
1.3	Creating a team
2.4	Learning to love your business and staff
3.1	Leadership and management
3.2	Vision and mission
3.3	Strategy
3.4	Setting goals
3.5	Developing a business plan
4.1	Meetings and how to chair them
4.2	Meetings and how to develop them
4.3	Meetings and how to kill them
4.4	Visible improvement
4.5	Break time
7.1	Technical competence
7.2	Knowing your competitors and customers
7.3	Knowing your people
8.1	Taking responsibility
8.2	Teaching responsibility

8.3 How to be an ideal leader
8.4 Saying 'No'
10.2 Leading a team over time
10.3 Being obsessive
10.4 Being ubiquitous
11.1 Creating change
11.5 The hardest cut
12.1 Destroying the system from the inside
14.1 Delegation
14.2 Responsibility
14.3 Recognized authority
15.2 Appropriate appraisal
16.1 Daggers drawn
16.2 Confronting troublemakers
19.1 Developing others
20.5 Building relationships
21.3 Being unrealistic
23.1 Watch my feet, not my lips
23.2 Honesty is the best policy
27.3 Marking time
29.2 Promises, promises
29.4 No secrets

TECHNIQUES WITH HIGH MOTIVATION RATINGS

Ref. *Title*
1.5 It's catching
4.4 Visible improvement
6.3 Publish or be damned
6.4 Eye eye
7.3 Knowing your people
9.1 Arrivals
9.3 Recognition
9.4 Somewhere to go
9.5 Small gifts and big sums
10.2 Leading a team over time

10.5	Warm-ups
11.2	Change control
11.3	Change as motivator
12.1	Destroying the system from the inside
12.3	Bureaucracy and how to kill it
12.4	Making it sane
13.1	E-motivation
14.2	Responsibility
14.3	Recognized authority
14.4	Managing George
15.3	Catch them doing it right
16.2	Confronting troublemakers
16.3	The earnest objector
17.2	Energy transfer
17.4	Quality content
17.5	Spice it up
18.1	Contributors
18.2	Do it themselves
18.3	Perspective shift
18.4	Personal projects
19.2	Train tracks
19.3	Train strain
20.1	Portfolio matching
20.2	The tea bag
20.3	Celebration time
20.4	The F word
21.1	Stretch but don't stress
25.1	Ask them
25.2	What did I say?
29.1	Money, money, money
29.2	Promises, promises
29.3	The rumour mill
29.4	No secrets
30.1	Own pocket
30.2	Taskforce opportunities
30.3	What's in it for me?
30.4	Ambience chasers

TECHNIQUES WITH HIGH COACHING RATINGS

Ref.	*Title*
5.4	Getting beneath anxiety
9.1	Arrivals
9.4	Somewhere to go
13.3	Giving feedback
14.1	Delegation
14.5	Backing off
15.3	Catch them doing it right
16.5	Reluctance to improve
18.5	Overcoming a lifetime of learning
19.4	Knowing what you know
19.5	Learning and learning styles
20.5	Building relationships
21.2	Being realistic
21.3	Being unrealistic
21.4	Establishing pace
21.5	'I can't do it'
22.1	Coaching outside work
22.2	Coaching with others
22.3	Coaching your boss
22.4	Coaching your peers
22.5	Coaching yourself
23.5	Role models
27.4	Now is all you can do
27.5	Quick results
30.5	On the up

TECHNIQUES WITH HIGH INTERVIEWING RATINGS

Ref.	*Title*
6.5	Open questions
13.4	Your body
13.5	Non-verbal replies

15.4	What do they look like?
15.5	Assessing test results
24.1	Understanding the job
24.2	Sifting applications
24.3	Information checklist
24.4	Environment checklist
24.5	Selling checklist
25.4	Great note taking
25.5	Using silence
26.2	Setting criteria
26.3	Simple option evaluation
26.4	Sophisticated option evaluation
26.5	Comparing apples and oranges
28.1	Personality and skills questions
28.2	Business awareness and teamwork questions
28.3	Leadership and manageability questions
28.4	Self-starter and creativity questions
28.5	Shock and analytical thinking questions

TECHNIQUES WITH HIGH FUN RATINGS

Ref.	*Title*
10.5	Warm-ups
20.1	Portfolio matching
20.2	The tea bag
20.3	Celebration time
20.4	The F word
23.1	Watch my feet, not my lips